DORNFORD YATES

A. J. Smithers

DORNFORD YATES

A Biography

HODDER AND STOUGHTON
LONDON SYDNEY AUCKLAND TORONTO

British Library Cataloguing in Publication Data

Smithers, A. J.
   Dornford Yates.
   1. Yates, Dornford
   2. Authors, English – 20th century – Biography
   I. Title
   823'.912   PR6025.E56

   ISBN 0 340 38473 5

Hodder and Stoughton Editorial Office: 47 Bedford Square, London WC1B 3DP.

Ah, but a man's reach should exceed his grasp,
Or what's a heaven for?

Robert Browning
'Andrea del Sarto'

The strawberry grows underneath the nettle,
And wholesome Berries thrive and ripen best,
Neighbour'd by fruits of baser quality.

William Shakespeare
King Henry V

ACKNOWLEDGEMENTS

Far more help has come my way over writing this book than I had any reason or right to expect. Were William Mercer still living he would be within four years of his hundredth birthday and it is remarkable how many people still remember him vividly. Lieutenant-Colonel F. H. Farebrother, of Letchworth, has kindly told me of his activities as a boy at Harrow nearly eighty years ago. Major G. St G. Stedall, of Folkestone, well remembers him as a brother cornet of Yeomanry, introduced him to his first wife, became best man at his wedding in 1919 and was a regular house guest at Pau. Mrs Diana Barnato Walker, MBE, of Horne in Surrey, knew in her childhood William and Bettine Mercer as a young married couple soon after the Kaiser's War. Mr Arthur Kennard was Mercer's bank manager there throughout the Pau years, and no man is a hero to his bank manager. Mrs Marjorie Hare and Mrs Joan Lauchlan have most kindly made me free of their memories of life in Pau and at Eaux Bonnes between the wars.

I am deeply indebted to Mrs R. E. Croall, of Edinburgh, for permitting me to use parts of a long account written by her friend Mrs Elizabeth Mercer of all that happened between leaving Pau in 1940 until her husband's death twenty years later. Mrs Juniper Bryan, of Belfast, has been generous with information about her family, especially over the connection with Mercer's cousin, 'Saki'—H.H. Munro—and allows me to quote from her letters.

In the matter of the South African and Rhodesian years I have had much help from Mrs Lucy Day, Mr Donald Clark, Mr Dick Hobson, Mr Chris Windows, Mr B. Faktor, Mrs Maitland-Stuart, Mrs Phyllis Beeching, Major C. H. MacIlwaine, DSO, MC, Lieutenant-Colonel R. A. Wyrley-Birch, DSO, MC, Mrs E. D. Semple, Major T. C. D. Leaver of the Rhodesian African Rifles, Mrs D. M. Mountain of Cape Town, and the Rev. Mark Wells, now of Stoke-by-Nayland in Suffolk. Mr Gary Rymer of Croxley Green and Mr W. J. A. Boyle of Walberswick have been good enough to tell me of Mercer's period at Durban.

ACKNOWLEDGEMENTS

Miss Yvonne Coen, Archivist to the Oxford University Dramatic Society, and Mr George Ovenstone, Secretary to University College, have put themselves to much trouble in answering my questions. The late the Hon. Sir Gerald Thesiger furnished me with valuable information about Mercer's contemporaries on the Bench at the Bar and the more celebrated criminal trials of his day. Mr Simon Trusler, of TQ Publications, London, has been good enough to excavate details of the musical comedy *Eastward Ho*. Amongst those sufficiently generous to have trusted me with letters and photographs are Lieutenant-Colonel A. G. S. Alexander of Lighthorne, Mr Michael Bailey of Hassocks, Mr Robert Aplin of Barford St Michael, Mr John Williams of Malmesbury, and Mrs B. E. Hughes, late of Johannesburg. Mr D. R. Ruscoe of Balsall Common near Coventry has added to my fund of knowledge and I am grateful to him. Mr Michael Horniman of A. P. Watt Ltd, agents for the copyright owners, has been most helpful.

Tom Sharpe, the well-known author and authority on Dornford Yates, demands a paragraph to himself. When, at an early stage, he was kind enough to invite me to his home it soon became apparent that we did not see eye to eye about many aspects of Cecil William Mercer (Dornford Yates). This makes it all the more magnanimous of him to have put so much of his hard-won material at my disposal. Had it not been for his ungrudging help—help for which I had not the slightest claim upon him—I doubt whether this book would ever have been finished. The best I can hope for is that he will not disapprove it too strongly.

To all the ladies and gentlemen named above I offer my thanks. Honesty compels a less sensible feeling towards official sources. Fortified though I was by the good wishes of the Chancellor of the Duchy of Lancaster, I was unable to persuade the Ministry of Defence to endanger the realm by telling me the exact nature of Captain Mercer's duties at the Ministry of Labour in 1918; nor would the Divorce Registry divulge what was said by whom during the divorce proceedings in 1933, even in the course of a public hearing. My economy of warmth is, of course, for the rules and not for those who obey them.

Lastly, to the hundred or more kind people who have written to say that although they have nothing to contribute they wish the book well, I can only return one possible answer. May you not be disappointed.

A Note for the Second Edition

After this book first appeared a number of kind people wrote to fill in gaps in my information. I had long been puzzled by the plural used by the *Punch* reviewer of *The Brother of Daphne* in August 1914: 'Dornford Yates, a name I seem to recall as a contributor to the magazines.' His stories in the *Windsor* were well known, but all my searches in the other probables ended in failure. I now know that in 1910 and 1912 he wrote two stories for *Pearsons*, a magazine that was to the *Windsor* as Blackpool is to Frinton. The first, 'The Babe In The Wood', is a Boy-Daphne-pretty-girl-and-lost-shoe tale; the second, 'Rex v Blogg', is a jokey Old Bailey yarn. Neither represents his best work.

The second piece of information came by accident. In the course of a letter about something else Mrs Barbara Cripps, Mercer's secretary in Rhodesia, mentioned that she had a copy of Charles Stamper's book *What I Know* with an inscription implying that Mercer had, for all practical purposes, written it. Mr Stamper, King Edward's chauffeur, was quite a famous man in his day and the book was widely read. It seems fair to assume that he had made an agreement with Mercer that it should appear to have been all his own work for nowhere does Mercer even hint at having had any hand in it. It goes some way towards explaining his close knowledge of both his Sovereign and the Rolls-Royce motor-car.

The last chance discovery came from Ward Lock, for many years Mercer's publishers. In the course of moving office they discovered six box-files of correspondence covering the years after Hitler's war. They make very entertaining reading. Mercer, of course, was then living in Rhodesia and quite out of touch with an austere England. Publishers, starved of paper, were having to make agonising decisions about what they could and could not bring out and were compelled to turn down their thumbs to many authors they would have liked to take on.

The whole tenor of Mercer's letters is to demand that they use most of their meagre allocation to keep his works in print and he was not above a good deal of self-praise. An internal note from one director to another speaks of his 'stupendous conceit'. On the face of it this is fair comment but Mercer's point of view deserves consideration. He was, as he points out in more than one Introduction, a tradesman with wares to sell. Had he employed an agent to puff him at second hand nobody would have complained, but he preferred to act as his own publicity man.

There are bitter complaints about dust-jackets. Colette, in *Cost Price*, was a slip of a girl. Of the draft picture he says that 'she looks like a Rugby scrum-half, a small squat man with bulging calves'. The appearance of Richard Usborne's *Clubland Heroes* angered him greatly and he wrote a furious letter complaining that his publishers had actually lent Usborne some of his books. Quite unaccountably he had got it into his head that Usborne was an enemy, 'out to do me as much damage as he can. You wait and see'. It was useless to tell him that Usborne was an admirer.

My own book contains one factual error. The balusters of old Westminster Bridge never reached Cockade. They were stored in England during the war and then sent direct to Umtali.

Though I have found more to praise in Mercer than did many critics I am not looking forward to meeting him in the Hereafter. I fear he may have found some of my writing disrespectful and this he was always slow to forgive.

A. J. Smithers

April 1985

To Robert Atherton, Esq., of Beckley in the county of Sussex.

My dear Robert,

One reads in so many books an Acknowledgement saying that without the help of some kind friend they would never have been written. This, I had always assumed, was not meant to be taken literally. Just for once, however, it means exactly what it says. Deprived of your thirst for information, your persistence in disinterring it, often from unlikely places, and your lawyer's insistence on accuracy, I doubt whether I should have been able to put together a story worth the telling. Every birth, marriage and death of every Dornford, every Yates, every Mercer, Wall, Dimsdale, Munro and others denied space was run to earth by you. Nor was that all. When I came near to abandoning the struggle you, without fail, came up with the missing piece. Let one sample serve for all. Being innocent, I insisted that Captain Samuel Mercer had never attained Flag rank because Navy Lists must be Gospel. You harried the Admiralty into producing unpublished Lists of promotions of retired Officers and prevented me from doing Admiral Sam grave injustice.

This all sounds an agreeable, almost a restful, pastime for a gentleman of leisure. It does not suggest the hours and days spent on journeys, in the queues at Government Offices, in Churches and Town Halls, amongst census returns, voters' lists and even postal directories; at the Law Society's Hall, in almost unexplored parts of the City of London, at the Beaney Institute in Canterbury amongst files of old newspapers, and closeted with the County Archives at Maidstone. Add to these an encyclopaedic knowledge of the works of William Mercer, possibly greater than that possessed by any other man, and the whole of your knowledge placed enthusiastically at my disposal without any expectation of return save only the certainty that we have our facts as nearly right as human diligence can make them.

It is sober truth that without your powerful help I could never have written this book. To say that you have my gratitude would be meiosis of high degree. The best I can do by way of requital is to make it plain to any into whose hands this book may come that much of what they are reading is your work.

Yours ever,

JACK SMITHERS

The Family Tree of Dornford Yates and 'Saki' pruned to a few espaliers

William Wall = Ann Brett
(of Ashford, Kent; (m. 1773)
1735~1809)

John Yates = Mary Curtis
(of London;
1756~1807)

John Mercer = Sarah Noakes
(of Deal, Kent;
1781~1844)

Josiah Dornford = Elizabeth Macnab
(Lt. R.N.
1783~1855)

John Wall = Harriet Mary Wells
(1779~1839)

Charles Yates = Jane Collins Yates
(1778~1849)

Samuel Mercer =
Rear Admiral, R.N.
(1809~1878)

Eliza Mary Dornford
(b. Heligoland, 1813)

William Henry Wall
(1816~1872)

Harriet Yates
(1815~1890)

Helen Wall
(b. Pembury, Kent;
1858~1918)

Cecil John Mercer
(1850~1921)

Mary Frances = Charles Augustus Munro

CECIL WILLIAM MERCER
(DORNFORD YATES)
(1885~1960)

HECTOR HUGH MUNRO
('SAKI')
(1870~1916)

INTRODUCTION

Dornford Yates, the pen name of Cecil William Mercer, was not one man but a combination of several men in one body. His forefathers, with two colourful exceptions, were lawyers, men trained in the precise use of language but, as they would have readily admitted, without any claim to literary style. The common ancestors of both Mercer and his cousin Hector Hugh Munro, 'Saki', were Lieutenant Josiah Dornford, RN, and Elizabeth his wife, formerly Miss Macnab of Dumfries. Little is known of the Macnab side but the Dornfords had been landed gentry and had produced considerable scholars. One of their number had been distinguished as a philosopher at the University of Göttingen towards the end of the eighteenth century and it seems reasonable to suppose that it was from Dornfords that most of the brains came.

At Harrow School William Mercer became pupil to Norman Kenneth Stephen, the man who had taught Winston Churchill to understand and to use English. In 1956 Mercer acknowledged his debt. 'It was he who showed me how I could teach myself to master the English tongue . . . He showed forth the spirit and meaning of polite letters.' Such as this one.

DEAR BROTHER—As one to whom the contemplation of vice in any shape or form has always been repellent, I have no desire to learn the nature of the filthy and corrupt procedure to which you doubtless resorted to procure your release. This is a matter which I prefer to leave—not, however, without grave misgivings—to your 'conscience'. If you do not recognize the word, Jonah will explain what I mean.

Harrow and Oxford (particularly the OUDS) soaked him in Shakespeare and thus fixed his manner of writing. Anthony

1

Hope and Robert Louis Stevenson furnished the raw material for the plots of his thrillers, a circumstance Mercer made no effort to conceal. The Berry books, however, were his own creation and owe nothing to any other writer.

Equally interesting is Mercer's general theme. At the time he began his writing the belief amongst authors, according to Compton Mackenzie, was that nothing mattered apart from the plot. Characters were transients and of little importance. Conan Doyle, bitterly though he came to regret saddling himself with Holmes, was the pioneer. Make your people interesting and congenial, let your readers become well acquainted with them, and they will be less critical of any weakness in the story. To Mercer this became something like an article of faith.

Throughout his life Mercer was always on the edge of things, never in their centre. In August 1914 he was among the first to go for a soldier; after not much more than a couple of years, during which he endured much hardship, but saw little that could have been called action, he was invalided home. This must have been a bitter thing for him. Ever afterwards his heroes ran to a type, the demobilized officer of the 1914 rather than the 1918 model. Their names sound like an Elizabethan muster-roll: Bohun—there are three of these—Boleyn, Scrope, Bagot, Willoughby and the rest, with Christian names to match. For most other proper names he had the habit of promoting common nouns—Brooch, Vigil, Bladder, etc.—a trick that some people have found irritating though one soon becomes used to it.

I suspect him always to have regretted the ill-luck that denied him the chance of showing his mettle in war, for Henry V is never far below the surface, and he loved England. To his mind the country had reached something like perfection under King Edward VII and in telling of how he came to write *Lower Than Vermin* he makes this plain. '[The young] are taught by fellow-travellers—for they can be nothing else—that the old days were wicked days, when the rich oppressed the poor, when no one who was not well-born had a chance of making good, when Great Britain did robbery with violence on nations weaker than she . . . We know that such things are lies, and the fellow-travellers who tell them know they are lies. We know that the England of our youth was a happy, prosperous land, where most men, high and low, were well content with their lot,' he wrote to his contemporary Mr Carter of Pau. Many people who can draw on their own memories still think the same.

To a greater extent than most writers, Mercer merged himself into his creations. Though he speaks with the voice of Boy Pleydell, he was more than that. In letters to admirers (in answering which he was punctilious) he concedes that he was also Berry; probably he was Mansel, Chandos and the rest when the mood took him, for he had the ability to withdraw into his study, shut the door and live in a dream-world that was as real to him as the one outside. It became so impossible to disentangle the two that his quasi-autobiographies (*As Berry and I Were Saying* and *B-Berry and I Look Back*) need to be read with care. Part of his philosophy is entrusted to the character Florence in *Wife Apparent*. 'For a fool she has no use: to the wicked she shows no mercy,' reads the back of the dust-jacket.

Throughout his life Mercer remained the observer rather than the observed. In company with John Buchan and 'Sapper' he dominated the market for adventure stories between the wars, and that in addition to continuing the light romances with which he had begun his writing career. Buchan also achieved fame for other reasons, and 'Sapper' died before his time. Dornford Yates, whoever he might have been, continued for another twenty years, a mere photograph on a cover of a rather forbidding-looking man whose aspect did not suggest a refined wit. His 'fans' are still legion, though few could pass the most elementary examination about him. The old hands read his books over and over again and still find themselves laughing aloud: those stumbling upon him for the first time are introduced into a world as fresh as it was half a century ago. I am told that Dornford Yates Clubs still exist in the most unlikely places.

During the last few years Mercer has become the subject of newspaper articles, not all of them using facts, which not only deny him the ordinary human virtues but insist that he was a humbug and a hypocrite. I have the misfortune to differ from the writers on many matters, and venture to show another and a more agreeable picture. Any possible reader of this book who may persevere to the end will, I hope, be able to join with the consensus of opinion expressed to me by many people who knew its subject at various stages in his life. To adopt the words of Major Geoffrey Stedall, who knew him better and for longer than most, 'Bill Mercer was kind to me, and I liked him.'

As to his literary merit, there stands the opinion of Cyril Connolly, no bad judge of form in these matters. Speaking of the wide appeal made by the writings of Dornford Yates to those whose habitat was 'great garden parties, literary luncheons or the quiet of an exclusive gunroom'—the last sporting rather than naval—he observes that they 'appreciate fine writing when we come across it, and a wit that is ageless united to a courtesy that is extinct'. This is true, but the adjective exclusive is too restrictive. The scraps of conversation, spreading over more than half a century, that I have had with all manner of people have long persuaded me that his books appealed with equal force to working folk as much as to the leisured. In particular they have always attracted the younger readers, many of whom appreciate fine writing more greatly than their elders realize.

The quality of literature between the wars was not outstanding. Too many authors, especially authors of thrillers, set more store by making money than by craftsmanship and rushed out book after book, sloppily written, as if they used a rubber stamp. There were, of course, honourable exceptions. Mercer was insistent that the best novel of the period was James Hilton's *Lost Horizon*, a book that closely resembles in plot William Archer's 1920 play *The Green Goddess*, though there was nothing much wrong with Hilton's syntax. His own books were meticulously cut and polished before the public was permitted to put down its money for them. Mercer, like a good tradesman, valued the goodwill of his customers and was at pains to see that they got their money's worth. Undoubtedly he raised the tone of the between-wars novel by careful craftsmanship, well thought-out plots and some of the funniest dialogue ever written. Nor do his books carry any suggestion of being tied to a period, except upon the odd occasion when a word like 'Nazi' puts a date upon them. If the wit is ageless, so the stories are timeless. Come fresh to them now—they are still not too hard to come by, though getting scarcer—and you may well believe them to have been written only a few years ago.

As he lived abroad for so many years it is possible that he drew out the long sunset of the well-to-do Englishman of good family beyond its real limits. Like Robert Browning he wrote of an England that he no longer knew, but he had no wish to be in it. All the same, his books still give pleasure to those who know of the country as it once was only from the tales of their grandparents; and should Macaulay's New Zealander chance upon a copy of *Berry & Co.* he will be able to go home with a very decent idea of what the land of his ancestors once was. It could even be that he will like it better than his own surroundings.

The common criticism is that he wrote only of the rich and idle. This is perfectly true. Only rich men, free from the brute necessity of earning a living, could possibly have carried out the plans he made for them. When life is punctuated by butchers' bills, the washing of nappies and the necessity of being at the office every day by nine o'clock there can be little enjoyment in reading of the activities of others similarly placed. Stars are less tangible than mud, but they give more pleasure to the beholder, and it was of stars that Dornford Yates told his tales. If they are unfamiliar to you then you may count yourself fortunate, for thirty-four books should keep the most dedicated reader in play for quite a long time.

1

Environment & Heredity

The promontory of East Kent, with a stubby finger called Thanet pointing towards Europe like an old-fashioned direction sign, has always been the outpost zone of England. An occasional invader has varied the monotony by landing at Pevensey or Harwich, but it is on the beaches between Ramsgate to the north and Dungeness to the south that most of our enemies have found it expedient to seek to disembark themselves. From the day when the aquilifer of the Seventh Legion screwed up his courage and cast himself into the surf that grinds against the shingle of Walmer beach, until the day when Dover's keep was arabesqued by vapour trails and newspapers called it Hell Fire Corner, this has been the place where the men of Kent, arms in hand, have waited to take the first shock of battle. After Rome had gone the time came when, as every properly read schoolboy knows, Hengist and Horsa, covered in brine, landed at Pegwell in 449. A stone's throw away stands Ebbsfleet, where, a century and a half later, Augustine's monks of Rome landed to a different welcome and bearing a different message. Looting Saxon and bloody Dane came and went, the complex of caves under Eastry village remaining to tell posterity of the endurance of its ancestors. Sandwich was burnt by the French with a regularity that became almost tedious, and under the dunes of Sandwich Bay lie the dead of Rupert's long sea-fight with the Dutch. On a clear day you can see the Goodwins, where, amongst the bones of many a strong ship there may still be discerned the upper works of *Montrose* which carried Dr Crippen to Canada. The men and ships of the Five Ports for centuries kept the Channel, their memorial being a largely unravaged countryside, and public houses miles inland still abound with names such as

The Ship and The Anchor. Memories are long in these parts and it is only within the present generation that there disappeared the last of the old men and women who, as children, were told by those who had lived through it of Boney's flat-bottomed boats poised to invade. It is a country of castles; not the great inland fortresses such as Windsor and Nottingham, but ancient defence works laboriously built with their feet in the sea for a single purpose. The mighty ruins of Richborough, though long stripped of the last piece of marble facing, tell of a Roman province in all its power. Deal, Walmer, Sandgate and Sandown—the last only a memory—speak to the work of Henry VIII, and Martello towers from Folkestone to New Romney remember the Grande Armée and Trafalgar. Proudest of all rears up the great keep of Dover, neighboured by its Roman lighthouse, a symbol of invincibility and a sight of great comfort not so many years ago.

Naturally enough East Kent has always attracted sea officers as a place for retirement, a place where a view and a telescope could still keep some sort of touch with times past. Hornblower, we are told, was born in the village of Worth, near Sandwich, and it is possible that his model was a real man, or a combination of two real men, who form part of this story.

One of them, to become the great-grandfather of the man who is the subject of this book, was Josiah Dornford, born in 1785, the son of a family then settled in Deptford and prominent in the world of shipping, especially with the East India trade. A Dornford had commanded one of John Company's ships and, early in the war with revolutionary France, Josiah decided that the Royal Navy was the place; before his tenth birthday he was mustered as midshipman aboard HMS *Active*. At an age when most boys were struggling with *mensa* and vulgar fractions Josiah received his first wound. Off Newfoundland, *Active* became engaged with a Frenchman and two blocks falling from the mizen-top struck the boy down. His head seems to have been tougher than most and he was soon back at duty. Josiah's career was eventful enough. As Directory gave way to Consulate and Consulate to Empire, he moved slowly up the ladder. In 1802 he was captured by the privateer *Le Brave*, but was released under the terms of the Treaty of Amiens. By 1809 he was commanding the *Thrasher*, brig, in the attack on the Boulogne flotilla; he served at sea during the Walcheren expedition and in 1820, the war over, transferred to the

Coastguard, still no more than lieutenant. Ten years earlier he had married Elizabeth Macnab of Dumfries who bore him six children; among them a younger Josiah who followed his father into the Navy and a daughter, christened Eliza Mary but never called other than Fanny.

On the other side, John Mercer of Ramsgate, was a solicitor whose name first appears on the Roll in 1809. Of his two sons, one, George, followed him into the profession but the other, Samuel, had no appetite for an occupation so dispiriting. In 1822 he reported on board HMS *Leven*, 26, as midshipman under Captain William Fitzmaurice Owen. It is not necessary to leave East Kent in order to find a memorial to Sam Mercer's first captain. Owen was as much scientist as sailor, a man with a rare talent for charting waters so far unexamined, and in due time he became Hydrographer to the Navy. By Sandwich toll-bridge stands the sign of The Admiral Owen, a public house that keeps his memory fresh. Owen obviously thought well of his new young gentleman for, after they had spent four years together in taking soundings along the coasts of both East and West Africa, he signed him on for a second voyage, this time in HMS *Eden*, correcting and adding to the charts they were making.

It was not all deep-sea lead and sounding-pole work. In August 1826 *Leven* landed a small naval brigade at Cape Coast Castle to help out Colonel Purdon's small force, at grips with the Ashantis at the battle of Dodowah. Sam made one of the party. Later, Owen and his subordinate became engaged in the setting up of a short-lived colony at Fernando Po, an island so charmless that it was with as much astonishment as gratitude that the Colonial Office agreed to hand it over to Spain.

Samuel Mercer was promoted to Lieutenant in 1829, to Commander in 1834 and, after service in other ships, he was given command of HMS *Charybdis*, being made Post in 1837. In *Charybdis* he returned to the Guinea coast, for this was the time when slavery had been finally abolished throughout the King's dominions and it was to the Royal Navy, almost unaided, that the task of putting down the trade was given. *Charybdis*, under Sam Mercer, had a good record; before her commission ended in September 1837, she had chased, taken and brought into port fourteen slaving schooners, Portuguese and American. Sam Mercer could handle a ship as well as any man in the service.

9

On 20 February 1839, in the little church of Worth, by Sandwich, Captain Samuel Mercer, RN, married Fanny Dornford. The certificate shows the places of residence of both of them as being in that village. It is a pity that it is now too late to ask C. S. Forester whether he knew of these things; with both Lieutenant Dornford and Captain Mercer living in the same obscure little place and with such a wealth of adventure behind them both, he would have needed to look no further for material to keep his Hornblower afloat for a professional lifetime. Be that as it may, the wedding of Sam and Fanny was a naval occasion, boat-cloaks, cocked hats, swords and blue jackets heavy with bullion walking alongside fur pelisses over crinolines topped by Kate Greenaway bonnets. The Royal Navy was still thick on the ground, Josiah and Sam were both sea-officers of good repute and the Navy always enjoys rigging a garland. There is no reason to suppose that brother George, soon to be admitted attorney and solicitor, absented himself from the ceremony. Nor, in all probability, was he the only aspirant to his profession amongst the guests. James Edwards, aged twenty-two and nearing the end of his service under articles, was already attracted to Sam's sister; when he was himself admitted, in 1841, they married and in the same year set up the new family firm of Mercer & Edwards. James Edwards was professionally the senior of the two and the sequence of their names suggests that they took over the practice of John Mercer. The business of the firm expanded rapidly, for both George and James were bright young men. Everybody predicted a prosperous future for them. Two years after their marriage Sam and Fanny Mercer moved to Swiss Cottage at Great Mongeham, on the skirts of Walmer, for Sam had been appointed Superintendent of the Packet Service at Dover, a post he held until 1846. In the following year he went on half-pay, but was employed again in 1848, this time under the Treasury, for relief work in Ireland during the potato famine. In 1851 he became King's Harbourmaster at Cardiff, where he served for the next eight years, and in 1864 he became, for a short time, British Vice-Consul at Granville in Normandy. When his tenure expired, Sam bought a house in Upper Deal named The Firs. In 1878, with the rank of Rear Admiral on the Retired List, he died in the home of his youngest daughter, in South Street, Deal.

Of the ten children born to Sam and Fanny Mercer, two are important to this story. Mary Frances, born at Mongeham in 1842, was to marry Major Charles Augustus Munro of the Indian Staff Corps and travel with him to Burma. Their son, born at Akyab on 18 December 1870, was christened Hector Hugh; he is better known by his pen-name, 'Saki'. Cecil John, born on 28 August 1850 at Swiss Cottage, was to become the father of the man known as Dornford Yates.

There is expert evidence that Sam's household was a happy one, for Hector Munro became a great authority on aunts. His mother having died soon after his birth, he was committed to the care of two of them, both sisters to his father. Aunt Tom—nobody ever called her Charlotte—was well enough, but Aunt Augusta has a horrid immortality in 'Sredni Vashtar'. The Mercer Aunts were a very different proposition. 'We went too seldom to visit my mother's people in Kent,' wrote Hector's sister Ethel in her biography of him. 'Rear Admiral Mercer was full of fun, and his daughters were young and lively, and they let us do lots of things we could never do at home. Grandpa was very fond of practical jokes, which fondness his grand-children inherited in full measure.'

So much for the spear side of his ancestry. The distaff was of a more stay-at-home kind. William Henry Wall, yet another solicitor, had learned his mystery in London, operating from 43 Bedford Row before putting up a plate in Brentwood. In 1842, at the age of twenty-five, he moved again, this time to Pembury, near Tunbridge Wells, and started a practice which, under another name, still exists. The firm's archives suggest that he was not an entirely satisfactory partner to the younger man who joined later, for he had many extraneous interests and was bent upon making his fortune. He took to farming and acquired more than two hundred acres of valuable land, somehow combining this with running a successful practice; by various means he made a lot of money, but the making of it shortened his life. In 1842 he had married Harriet, the daughter of Charles Yates, a substantial grocer with his headquarters at Ely Place in the City of London, who became a partner in the firm of Bedwell & Yates in John Street. By her he had two sons and seven daughters, of whom only one need concern us, for the six aunts of William Mercer (Dornford Yates) were not to bulk large in his life. William Henry Wall died in his home at Pembury on 26 May 1872 at the age of fifty-five; the cause

11

of death was gout. His widow and children were provided for handsomely.

Cecil John Mercer, Sam's son, whom we left as a baby, found himself without appetite for a seafaring life and turned to the old family trade of solicitor. There must have been a coolness between Sam and his brother George, possibly because Sam knew George too well, for Cecil John was articled in London and was duly admitted in 1873. He was very much a man who liked to run his own ship, for he neither joined an established firm nor took in a partner. In the beginning he set up a one-man practice in Great James Street, Bedford Row, with a branch office in Ramsgate. For a year, 1876 to 1877, he ran a further branch in Margate, but its elusive charms were wasted on him and he soon let it go.

It was presumably in London that he met and courted Helen Wall, one of the seven sisters, for they were married on 21 October 1884 at Kensington Parish Church. The ceremony was performed by 'George Henry Rigby, Officiating Priest'. *B-Berry and I Look Back* contains a story of how the future Lord Justice Rigby was taken by his clergyman-brother to see the local Squire who paid for him to go to the Bar. This was, almost certainly, the former Vicar of Pembury. Nor is it the only point at which Berry's anecdotes and provable facts touch each other. In *As Berry and I Were Saying* he tells a story of John Dimsdale of 50 Cornhill, 'a banker, for he came of banking stock'. Berry speaks of him as a co-trustee, mentions that he was sent to Eton at the age of nine, and was the best of good fellows. Berry's creator does not say that John Dimsdale was his uncle by marriage, husband to Helen's sister Mary. Both John and his elder brother Joseph justified their description, for Dimsdales had been at the business for at least four generations and John, at the time of his marriage, was a partner in a Bank in Cornhill. Curiously enough both the Yates and the Dimsdales seem to have originated in Crutched Friars as merchants. It may be that a passage in one of the later novels, *Shoal Water*, suggests its author to have had limited regard for the place; the hero, Jeremy Solon, informs his young woman that he is 'trying to be a merchant in Crutched Friars' and is told scornfully that she would rather lie out in the open as a shepherd. Be that as it may, the Dimsdales were rich and became benefactors. Joseph was elected Lord Mayor of London in 1902; as John and Mary were childless their nephew came in for worthwhile legacies on their deaths.

At the time immediately before his marriage Cecil John was living economically over the shop at 108 High Street, Ramsgate, no place in which a gentleman might bring up a family. Unfortunately Cecil John had little money but he had a considerable sense of his own position. The Wall family might be only solicitors like himself but they were undeniably much richer ones. William Henry Wall had owned a 200-acre farm as well as a fine house; Cecil John Mercer had only the tenancies of several depressing little offices. Harriet Wall left Pembury and, after living for a time in Folkestone, bought Wellesley House, one of a row of decent Georgian houses behind the Castle at Walmer, with the object of making a home for the three of them. Wellesley House now bears a plaque asserting that Lieutenant-General A. Wellesley (later Duke of Wellington) lived there before embarking for the Peninsula and fame in 1808. As Arthur was in Dublin at the time and sailed from Cork the claim seems doubtful. Cecil opened an office in nearby Deal.

Thanks to the Duke it was not unmanageable. His long residence at Walmer Castle, as Lord Warden of the Cinque Ports, had brought the railway from London in 1840. As it could hardly stop there, its promoters continued the line to Ramsgate and a man could easily spend an hour or two every day at several offices separated only by a train journey counted in minutes rather than hours. A trip to London took no longer than it does today. At the leisurely pace then demanded it gave time enough to keep many pots boiling at once.

Harriet Wall had ample means, and it was she who paid the greater part of the household expenses. Despite, or because of, this, relations between Cecil John and his mother-in-law seem to have been easy enough. As he must have been out of the house most of the time, between his various offices, it was probably not too difficult. It is quite a big house.

On 7 August 1885 Helen Mercer, aged twenty-six, gave birth to her only child, in the main bedroom at Wellesley House. They christened him Cecil William, names that he soon grew to hate. In *Wife Apparent* he deals with the first: 'I do hope it isn't Cecil'; in many books 'Willie' is the contemptuous name for his betters used by 'Rose' Noble and other bad men. Like it or not, Willie Mercer he became and remained for a long time.

13

Walmer in the 1880s was a pleasant little place, much over-shadowed by memories of the Duke. Every man or woman of middle age could remember the tall, solitary figure taking his regular constitutional along the seafront, punctiliously touching his hat to all who might acknowledge him. Cecil John, as a two-year-old, might very probably have been taken by the Admiral to see the cortège leave the Castle for Deal Station; engravings made at the time suggest that neither is much changed. Willie had one early memory of his own: 'The first wedding I graced was in 1888, and in honour of the occasion I was promoted to breeches. These were too tight and my action was consequently restricted—which was probably just as well.'

His early boyhood was happy enough, with fond parents, a grandmother devoted to him and a pleasant place in which to live. He tells of Helen's habit of reading Dickens aloud to his father and himself, but it kindled no enthusiasm for the author's work. The only mention he makes of it is to describe Tree as Fagin. Oddly enough he had no interest in the sea or those who used it. None of his books have anything much of a maritime setting and no character is a seafaring man.

The late eighties passed pleasantly but the nineties brought trouble. On 26 February 1890, Harriet Wall, born in the year of Waterloo, died and her life interest under her father's trusts died with her. Meanwhile Sam's younger brother George had long been something of a local grandee after half a century in practice as a solicitor. He was Coroner for the borough, Clerk to the Justices both of Deal and the Cinque Ports, Registrar to the Commissioners of Salvage, Town Clerk of Deal for the last fifty years, Clerk to the Walmer Local Board and to numerous charities in addition to his private practice in Deal, Sandwich and Walmer. Not surprisingly, George Mercer in his seventies was a patriarchal figure and Mercer & Edwards were generally reckoned to have the biggest and best practice in the district. The substantial families of Deal and Walmer appointed them to be trustees of their marriage and other settlements without doubting their solidity any more than the solidity of the Bank of England.

It was about the end of the year 1890 that a number of strange rumours were current that all was not well with the old-established firm of Mercer & Edwards. Tongues began to wag when it became known that George, Willie's Great-Uncle, whom he was always to deny he ever met, had asked to be excused from having his portrait painted to the order of the Mayor and Corporation to mark his half-century as Town Clerk. Such an action was quite out of character, for George, in the manner of many Town Clerks, had an elevated view of his own importance. In addition to this strange display of self-effacement, it was noticeable that he had become snappy, bad-tempered and obviously extremely worried about something. Some of the clients took it sufficiently seriously to present themselves at the office and to require the handing over of their money and securities, but all were fobbed off with excuses by an even more worried-looking clerk.

All of a sudden, at the beginning of 1891, George's partner, James Edwards, disappeared; he was a man of a professional seniority even greater than that of George Mercer, for he had been admitted in 1839, and the partnership had begun two years later. Then, on a September day in 1891, George Mercer, plainly very ill, took to his bed in the house at 2 Victoria Road, Deal. On 4 October he announced that he must go to London on business of pressing importance, and he would not be stopped. When he returned, carrying a small brown paper parcel, he went straight back to bed. Early next morning his wife, already sick with worry, heard two shots and rushed into the room. George Mercer lay in his bed dying from two self-inflicted wounds; the first, in his chest, had missed his heart, but the second, through the head, had killed him. The pistol, with its wrapping paper, lay beside him. The deputy Coroner's jury returned a verdict of 'suicide while temporarily insane'. He was not the first Mercer to die with an unbalanced mind. His father John had expired at sixty-three of a 'diseased brain', and his nephew, another John, at the age of fifty-one, had succumbed to 'sanguineous apoplexy and general paralysis of the insane'.

The scandal was enormous, the more so when the truth came out. Mercer & Edwards had been embezzling clients' money for years, and the amount lost turned out to exceed £70,000, most of it the money of local people who had entrusted it to them, and a huge sum by the standards of the time. As soon as the police began their inquiries it became apparent that from the beginning of the partnership the two brothers-in-law had been conducting the financial side of it in a manner all their own. No accounts deserving of the name had ever been kept; all money received, no matter what its purpose, had gone into a single account and it was no more possible to attribute any sum to any given client than to identify grains of rice in a sack. Whenever a partner had needed some cash he had simply drawn himself a cheque, and that with a fine insouciance about whether there was enough of the firm's own money to cover it. Since neither man had stinted himself the money they used to pay their bills had long ago ceased to be their own. The plan, if plan it can be called, was compounded of equal parts of dishonesty and plain dottiness, for once it started it was inevitable that a day of reckoning had to come. The only matter in doubt was the date on which it would arrive.

James Edwards was run to earth, arrested and tried at Maidstone Assize in November 1893 by Coleridge, J. His age—he was seventy-six—did not save him from a sentence of eight years' penal servitude, and he was adjudged bankrupt the following year. It may have been that as George Mercer had held all the public appointments, the running of the private side of the firm's business had been left to Edwards: it may equally well have been that Sam did right not to article his son to his brother's firm.

The trial was of a kind to send a frisson down the backs of many a Kentish solicitor, and probably down those of any number of clients with settlements being administered by them. The first charge related to events as far back as 1880—fraudulent conversion of more than £2,000, the property of Helen Maria Betts and her children—and there were twenty-eight others, including some charging him with conspiring with George Mercer deceased. Mrs Betts, over the years, had been relieved of nearly £13,000. Mr Willis, QC, and Mr Archibald Bodkin appeared for the Crown; Mr Harry Dickens, QC, and Charles Gill for the prisoner. The names of the last three will appear again in this story. Edwards pleaded guilty; the newspaper report tells that he 'leaned forward to a gentleman sitting in front of the dock and asked what was the sentence, as he could not hear'. A note of the proceedings was made by the Clerk of Arraigns, Arthur Denman, whose name will also recur.

Cecil John, though completely innocent of any wrong-doing, was badly hit by the disaster. The Official Receiver asked him to take over his uncles' firm, Mercer & Edwards, in order to clear up the mess, probably a gesture to demonstrate official confidence in his integrity, but there was no escaping the fact that the name of Mercer had become suspect, and his practice, then at West Lea—a more modest address after the sale of Wellesley House—suffered. He was fortunate in finding a partner of about his own age, Thomas Tancred Whitehead, who was willing to join wth him, and the firm of Mercer & Whitehead came into existence. Though Willie was only six when the blow fell, he was old enough to have a fair idea of what it was all about and, as small boys are merciless to each other, he probably soon had all the details. For the remainder of his life he was haunted by memory of the fraud, and swindling solicitors abound in his stories. Berry, at one point, is even made to explain how it was all done. From that time on Deal lost its charm for Willie. His revenge on the place came much later.

Willie Mercer was fortunate in his early schooling. Very near to Wellesley House stood St Clare, a preparatory school of excellent report. It had originated in Hastings, moved to Walmer in 1891, and occupied a large house built in 1806 by a Norwegian merchant named Andrew Gram. It is pleasant to record that the school is still operational, though now teaching only girls. Cecil John was solicitor to Alexander Elder Murray, the proprietor and a kinsman on the Yates side, useful things to be when fees were considered, and Willie was duly entered in 1894. Nine, the age at which Josiah had gone to sea, and John Dimsdale to Eton, was rather old to begin, but the early years had not been wasted. Harriet seems to have made his first lessons her particular charge; when Berry muses about one of his earliest recollections, that of an old lady with a star-sapphire ring in which she would invite him to find the star ('it gave me infinite pleasure, as it did her') he is almost certainly using the voice of Willie. Grandmother Harriet received her reward. There are few more attractive characters in the books than the Lady Harriet Touchstone.

St Clare in the Nineties was still a small school, but Mr Murray had taken pains over the selection of his staff. H. C. Peck, late of Westminster School and University College, Oxford, was everything that a preparatory schoolmaster should be, a scholar, an athlete and a man instinctively on the same wave-length as small boys. It was he who kept Willie's nose down to the irksome business of parsing and analysing, tasks necessary to a proper understanding of the English language, and who grounded him in the classical essentials of a gentleman's education. At games he was less successful, rather to his

17

disgust; Willie played cricket in some fashion but for everything else he displayed neither aptitude nor zeal. Peck, resigned to the fact one cannot have everything, concentrated on *mens sana*, for this was obviously rich soil for him to plough. His early death in 1897 was a tragedy for the school as well as for Willie, but the seed had been sown. After Peck's death, St Clare gained another pupil who would make a name for himself in time to come; to be accurate, two names. Graham Seton won acclaim as a novelist; Lieutenant-Colonel Graham Seton Hutchison, DSO, MC, a founder-member of the Machine Gun Corps, did more than most men to break the Kaiser's Army. His classic work, *Machine guns: Their History & Tactical Employment*, outweighs any number of novels.

When, years later, Hutchison came to write his autobiography, *Footslogger*, he devoted much space to St Clare, remembering it 'with peculiar joy':

> It was a great, rambling, creeper-clad house with some thirty acres of gardens and playing fields . . . Mr Murray was a grey-haired Scots of wee free predilections. A narrow lane between high brick walls separated the school from a convent; and we never ceased to be told of the iniquity of the Catholics. As our minds grew in knowledge, so we imagined all the horrors of the Inquisition taking place on the other side of the wall.

Though Murray and his sister, Miss Charlotte, 'loathed the Inquisition on the other side of the wall', they drummed into their small charges a firm, even a harsh, faith in the Protestant variety of Christianity.

Hutchison tells of regular Saturday evening lectures, often given by the Headmaster himself with the aid of a magic lantern; and speaks approvingly of the food. However, dinner with the Murrays was a pleasure that he found mitigated by the thought that 'God was hovering over the table in the presence of the penetrating clear blue eyes of Miss Charlotte, enormously magnified behind her glasses'.

Alexander Elder Murray, after the fashion of good preparatory school headmasters, exercised an influence over Willie Mercer that remained with him throughout his life. In addition to possessing the ordinary attributes of a scholar and a gentleman, he had strong literary connections for, as his name suggests, he was akin to the great publishing houses of Smith

Elder and John Murray. Coming from such a background it was natural that he should lead his young charges onto the paths of good writing, and at that period there was plenty of new work that merited their attention. Stevenson was recently dead, and W. H. Hudson came a little later, but Conan Doyle, Stanley Weyman and Anthony Hope were all turning out some of their best work. The habit of reading good books for sheer pleasure was firmly imbued. All of these are mentioned by name in Mercer's own works; his observations on Epstein's statue of Rima, the heroine of Hudson's *Green Mansions*, are firm. 'Rima was Amaryllis, the most delicate child of nature that ever was known. The illustration in marble is as revolting as it is indecent, and it was unveiled by a Prime Minister of Great Britain. Surely, on that memorable day, the ramp or swindle of modernist art touched its high-water mark.' Something of Rima certainly went into his own creation called Jill. He nowhere mentions Thomas Hardy by name but his own style suggests that he was well-read in Hardy's books. By the end of his prep school days Willie Mercer, thanks to Alexander Elder Murray, had acquired a taste for the English tongue that he was to carry to the end of his life. It was a useful attribute at this period of it, for no Mercer was anxious to mix with Deal and Walmer society at a time when skirts had a habit of being pulled in at the approach of anyone of that name. Willie kept much to himself, and the books of other people provided him with an alternative world in which he was completely happy. Almost all of the fictional characters who became his daily companions were persons of quality. Only a few late Victorian writers followed George Moore in writing about the lower orders, and such Willie ignored.

Towards the end of his time at St Clare, Willie's parents took a decision of great importance to him and of great credit to themselves. During the twenty-five years just passed, a number of new public schools had opened their doors in Kent, each a carbon copy of Dr Arnold's Rugby. In the nature of things, they had not yet had time to make reputations for themselves, but the majority of the sons of the professional middle class, whose parents had never looked above their local grammar school, were rapidly filling up all the places they had to offer. Cecil John and Helen aimed higher. Even though it would put a great, perhaps an unendurable, strain on their finances it was to Harrow that they determined Willie should go. Possibly

19

there was an element of what is now called 'one-upmanship' about it, for Walmer society was almost entirely of the haute-bourgeoisie; in the main it was the purest unselfishness. Willie had a good brain, he aspired to being something better than a solicitor, and it was right that they should change their lives completely to create this opportunity. If, as seemed likely, he had an eye to the Bar then Harrow had a strong tradition of that kind and he would make useful friends there. Dr Wood, the Headmaster, was an old Manchester Grammar School boy, and would understand. He did, and Willie was duly entered.

Ways and means were the next question. After making his calculations Cecil John concluded that the only course open to him was to cut completely adrift from East Kent and move both home and office to the school gates. He sold his share in the practice at Ramsgate and Walmer to Whitehead; it continued under his name until 1912 and still exists, although neither Mercer nor Whitehead appears in the present title. West Lea was also sold, and a lease taken of Northwick Lodge in Harrow. A small London office was at 61 Carey Street, a makeshift place with an ominous name, from which Cecil was to remove to Temple Avenue in 1905. Willie became what was known as a home boarder; Cecil John, rising fifty, nailed up his plate at Northwick Lodge and invited clients to present themselves. Whether they would do so in numbers sufficient to underwrite his and Helen's gamble remained to be seen.

2

Harrow and Oxford

Picture then, if you can, the Willie Mercer of 1899, rising fourteen years old and poised to enter the forbidding world of Harrow School. He was well grown for his age—in maturity he measured a respectable five feet ten or so—even though his build was slight; to the end of his life he was to remain on the lean side. His mind was well stocked, and not only with the Shakespeare, Caesar and Euclid that might have been demanded of him, but with additional fodder. He had been born into a golden age of new romantic writing and had grabbed at everything that had come his way.

The year 1894 was one that deserved to be marked with a white stone. Robert Louis Stevenson died, leaving a legacy that is still enjoyed, but he had successors. In the same year Anthony Hope, barrister and son of a parson, delighted the bourgeoisie with the *Dolly Dialogues*. His characters were strictly of the upper class, but one, Samuel Travers Carter, gives the definition which may still do duty. ' "Bourgeois", I observed, "is an epithet which the riff-raff apply to what is respectable, and the aristocracy to what is decent." ' After Dolly (whose dimples are subject to comment of a sort often found in the short stories of Dornford Yates) came Arthur Conan Doyle with *A Duet, With An Occasional Chorus*. Here were books of a new kind; social satire, no doubt, but gentle and almost affectionate. Two other men, Stanley Weyman, a not very successful barrister, and his friend Hugh Stowell Scott, a Lloyds underwriter better known as Henry Seton Merriman, were also breaking new ground. Scott had been firmly advised by James Payn, editor of the *Cornhill Magazine*, that 'the insular nature of the ordinary Briton made it, as a general rule, highly undesirable that the scene of any novel should be laid outside the British Isles'.

Though he greatly valued Payn's judgement Scott held him, in this instance, to be mistaken. In company with Weyman he travelled extensively in France, especially in Bearn, in Spain, Germany, Corsica and Poland. The 1894 vintage produced from him *With Edged Tools* and from Weyman two fine books about the wars of religion. *A Gentleman of France* and *Under The Red Robe*. The last named deals with the exploits of Gil de Berault, sent by Richelieu to hunt down a fugitive in the marches of Spain. Weyman's descriptions of scenery in the Pyrenees can be laid alongside those of Dornford Yates and it would be hard to tell who had written which.

Anthony Hope made a deep impression on young Mercer, as he did on many people. Even Mr Asquith was not above pirating the scene with Rhadamanthus in the last chapter of *Dolly*; the little play he wrote in 1914 comes straight from it. At least half a dozen lesser writers took a fancy to Ruritania, but it was not only in the lower reaches of authorship that the idea of an anonymous Central European kingdom set the typewriters to work. Even one great man, P. G. Wodehouse, in his salad days when he was green in judgement, told of it in *The Prince and Betty*. Thomas Cook must have been inundated and the Orient Express crammed with heavily moustached gentlemen in Norfolk suits, Inverness capes and deerstalker hats. In years to come John Buchan not only based his novel *The Dancing Floor* on Hope's *Phroso*, but devised his own kingdom. It looks as if at some time, perhaps in 1919, the last Elphberg must have been driven out and the country partitioned between Riechtenburg and Evallonia.

Written in a different tone but still romantic, came the first important work by a writer of another kind. Maurice Hewlett took his readers on a journey, not to Ruritania, Neopalia or to Hope's alternative-kingdom Kravonia, but on a time-trip to some unspecified part of the High Middle Ages. His style, like his period, comes somewhere between Chaucer and Ben Jonson by way of Edmund Spenser, and most people either were captivated or repelled when *The Forest Lovers* appeared in 1898. Mercer acknowledges his debt in so many words, but the acknowledgement was hardly necessary. If Prosper le Gai did nothing for him Isoult la Desirous (so spelled) was another matter. She was the daughter of a countess, no less, who for rather unsatisfactory reasons was abandoned early in life to care for herself in the great forest. Naturally enough she became a part of woodland life, beautiful, virtuous and capable of finding provender for her exhausted master by milking the wild does. In his absence she presses into service a tree—not an elm but a pine—to whom she addresses herself regularly during the time of her stay at the convent called Gracedieu. Prosper seldom addresses her other than as 'child' and the last words of the book, telling of events soon after their formal marriage had been made reality—the earthy Mr Hewlett did not shrink from this—are 'It was, after all, but a rosy child that Prosper kissed.' Regular Yates readers will have no difficulty in identifying either the quotation or the prototypes of two characters, Boy and Jill. There was nothing wrong with Willie Mercer's memory.

Harrow made no attempt to exorcise these things, and it was right that it should leave them be, for here were the heirs to Charles Lever, Dickens and Thackeray. Willie Mercer took his place with all this outlandish material, supplied by St Clare, neatly compartmented into his excellent brain along with heavier things. He was one of those fortunate beings who never forgot anything that he had once read. It is not necessary here to rely on assurances from his friends. His writings proclaim it loud and clear.

Every new boy enters his public school with his heart in his boots and, for Mercer, the experience was worse than for others. The world into which he was moving was as mysterious as the dark side of the moon, for he had never met another boy who had undergone the same experience nor, save for an occasional glimpse of the Lord Warden and amongst the Dimsdales, had he ever encountered a member of the upper classes. He had no talent for games that might bring him a respectable position in life; there was always the outside chance that somebody might know about bad Great-Uncles George and James; worst of all, he was not at all sure where he stood vis-à-vis his father. There was always the awful possibility that on some great occasion Cecil John might turn up in a panama hat and banana-coloured boots.

Willie Mercer was never one to make friends easily, nor had he any gregarious instincts. To the end of his time, although he was a member of several clubs, he remained an unclubbable man. It was inevitable that he should be lonely, an inevitability made more certain because his status as a home boarder necessarily excluded him from some of the most important parts of a schoolboy's life. It was upon his brain and his personal agreeableness that he must depend to see him through. The only surviving photograph, of a black-browed young man with a rather wary look under the straw hat exactly positioned suggests self-sufficiency.

He arrived at Harrow during one of its best periods. Dr Wood, who had just succeeded Dr Weldon, was no Arnold; he was, above all else, a gentleman and a scholar and he treated his charges as potential scholars and present gentlemen. Wood had been an assistant master at Tonbridge School at the time of the Edwards trial and, as Maidstone and Tonbridge shared a common local newspaper, it is almost certain that he knew more about the background of the new boy than he would ever let on. Very probably Mercer was treated with unusual gentleness as a result. Certainly he found himself in excellent hands. Norman Kenneth Stephen had come to Harrow in 1888 and one of his earliest tasks had been to gain the interest of the young Winston Churchill in Latin prose. It was hardly through any lack of diligence on Stephen's part that he failed, for Churchill had not been fortunate in his grounding. With the English language it was another matter. There can be little fault found in a man who taught so unwilling a pupil to understand and to love his mother tongue. Mercer acknowledged a debt every bit as great. 'He was a tall, good-looking man perfectly groomed and always point-device. Scrupulous to a hair, he commanded great respect. His ready wit was brilliant—there is no other word.' Two books, *Blind Corner* and *Wife Apparent*, are dedicated to him. Plainly he set the schoolboy an example he strove to copy.

But even making the most generous allowances for the forty years on it is hard to take at its face value an exchange between Berry and his form-master, 'a man of the rarest wit'.

One morning Berry, who had been requested to translate a passage from Juvenal, stumbled through a line and a half and then stopped dead. 'Go on, Pleydell.'

Berry looked up apologetically. 'I'm sorry, sir, but the English equivalent of the next phrase has for the moment escaped me.'

'Can you construe?'

'I—I don't believe I shall do the satirist justice this morning, sir. To-morrow, perhaps . . .'

'The artistic temperament?'

'You're very understanding, sir.'

It may, of course, have been so, though it was not the common experience of young mankind.

Stephen, who lived long enough to be writing to Mercer in 1944 explaining how best to avoid a flying bomb, took pity on the boy and learnt very soon that he was deserving of more than that. Chaucer, who has it in common with Hewlett that you love him or hate him, came early on the agenda and Mercer was enchanted by the Prologue. It is unlikely that the elegant extracts in the two autobiographical books, *As Berry and I Were Saying, B-Berry and I Look Back*, are accurate renderings of passages between master and boy, but there is no reason to question their tenor. Stephen treated Mercer, and others besides him, as if they were not quite contemporaries, but still something approaching equals. Conversations between gentlemen are, after all, not regulated by considerations of age. Not all the masters were Stephens. His form-master at one point was 'a painfully pompous man. He'd married a lovely wife who was very rich. And he couldn't get over that.' It suggests that he had little time for the unimportant Mercer.

Towards the end of Mercer's years at Harrow the School had a visit from Stephen's former disciple who seemed to be confounding the gloomy forecasts about his future which had accompanied him on leaving. Winston Churchill had charged with the 21st Lancers at Omdurman. He had also written a book about it, and a very good book it was. Everybody was agreed about that, but there was still something about Churchill at twenty-six that held many back from whole-hearted approval. He was a medal-hunter, a regular soldier who behaved unlike other regular soldiers. The *Malakand Field Force* might have been taken as the one bite allowed to every dog but he had now bitten again, looked as if he was going to continue biting, and had made some very impertinent criticisms of his seniors. Mercer cared for none of these things. Young Winston, kinsman to a Duke, son of an American mother of interesting lineage and plainly master of English, remained in his memory with photographic clarity long after more famous lecturers were gone and forgotten. From that day onward Churchill was the Superman and even when his standing in the country was at its lowest he had one uncritical admirer. To be like him would be a splendid thing but it was far beyond the range of the son of an attorney.

Harrow, in all probability, was responsible for guiding

25

Mercer into the patterns of life that he was to follow and it may be that his parents had rendered a doubtful service by sending him there. Outside its gates he was nobody, the son of a new-come and little-regarded practitioner of a profession that did not command general admiration. Inside he was determined to show himself at least the equal of young men whose homes were of a more elevated style and to compel them to accept him as one of themselves. It was the beginning of a life of which a good part can be identified with the Flanagan and Allen song, 'On the Outside Always Looking In'. The difficulty was in finding some aspect of Harrow affairs that might make him worthy of notice. Games were out; even hard work that eventually brought him membership of the Twelve, the intellectual élite, did little to enhance his prestige beyond that of a clever home-boarder. Only one thing remained. As befitted a nursery of future public speakers of one kind or another, Harrow had a Debating Society; it met regularly in the Vaughan Library and was the preserve of more prominent boys; the opportunity of addressing it was something to be sought after and Mercer sought harder than most. At eighteen he could speak fluently and well, but his standing in the school never sufficed to bring him an invitation to hold forth. Eventually, in 1903, he abandoned the unequal struggle and took counsel with the Headmaster. Wood was neither able nor willing to influence the Society; the best he could do was to give his blessing to an alternative—one could hardly call it a rival—organization. The 'Friday Evening Debating Society', held in an empty class-room, came into existence. As Emerson says, an institution is but the shadow of one man and on Willie's departure later in the following year this one seems to have gone quietly out of business. No other trace of Mercer's four years at Harrow remains.

Towards the end of them the Mercer family lifted up its eyes to the spires of Oxford of a Golden Age, of Tommy Case at Corpus and Herbert Warren of Magdalen. It was only a few years later, in November 1911 to be exact, that Lord Derby was writing to the King on the subject of a suitable college for the Prince of Wales. The answer was firm. 'There appear to be three in the running—Christ Church, New College and Magdalen. New College I should not like as according to the Archbishop of York there is much trouble there . . . Christ Church is a large college apparently where all the nouveaux riches go, and where the sole object seems to be to spend money and prove themselves men instead of being what they are—boys. Magdalen would appear to have none of these disadvantages . . .' For Cecil John and Helen Mercer the amount of the Caution Money and probable size of battels was of more consequence. University College may not have figured in the royal short list, but it was ancient and relatively cheap. Anyway, no other college could boast that a former Master had fought at Agincourt, as Edmund Lacy had done. Willie Mercer duly matriculated there in 1904, a part of his emancipation coming in the trimming of the loathed Willie to plain Bill. You may already have noticed that none of his better-class of character admits to having been at University College. All are either Christ Church, New College or Magdalen men with the first well ahead of the field. A fourth ancient foundation gets an occasional credit, for many years were to elapse before the sight of Paul Robeson's sweating paddlers would bring from cinema audiences the cry of 'Well rowed, Balliol'. Nevertheless, there are three characters named Lacey in the novels, and all of them are good men.

Young officers, on being introduced to the North West Frontier, used to be told that 'the eye of the tribesman is always watching you'. So, until the autumn of 1904, had it been with Bill Mercer. His parents had been models of all that good and ambitious parents should be, but never for a moment had the eyes of one or other of them been lifted from him. Now came his chance to lead an independent life and he resolved to seize it with both hands. His status as an old Harrovian was unassailable, his brain of a quality to make future examinations nothing to be dreaded. There would be all the time in the world in which to enjoy himself, to make such friends as he might and to do the pleasant things that do not come the way of schoolboys. Later on, when he came to write *Blind Corner*, Mercer summed up his views and put them into Jonathan Mansel's mouth. 'The only place in the world where a man may eat his cake and have it too, for the years he wastes there are beyond measure profitable.' Mercer addressed himself to such years. During his first one he paid a visit to his old prep school and took part in a cricket match. The young man in the photograph that still tells of it bears little resemblance to the patrician figure on the back of the dust-jackets. Behind old-fashioned pads with gaps between the ribs stands a young man unsmiling, not

over tidy and with hair bleached by a summer sun. The wary
look remains, for this was Walmer and many people there still
regarded the name of Mercer without enthusiasm.

The freshman began to look about him for some form of
activity in which he might shine. Music meant little to him; *La
Bohème* and *Tosca* are the only pieces mentioned by name in
his writings, apart from 'Printemps qui Commence' and some
of Shakespeare's songs, and Puccini was at the height of his
fame. Such politics as he had were a little to the right of those
of Mr Balfour whose administration was tottering towards its
end. Had he arrived a year earlier he would have crossed with
another University College man named Clement Attlee, himself
son to a solicitor, who might have loosened his extreme views a
little; but probably not. There remained one unexplored field
that might have possibilities. Compton Mackenzie, who was
still up, wrote about it in *Sinister Street*.

> The OUDS was at the opposite pole from Vincent's, and if it
> did not offend by its reactionary encouragement of a supreme
> but discredited spirit, it offended even more by fostering a
> premature worldliness. For an Oxford club to take in *The
> Stage* and *The Era* was merely an exotic heresy. On the walls
> of its very ugly room the pictures of actors that in Garrick
> Street would have possessed a romantic dignity produced an
> effect of strain, a proclamation of mountebank worship that
> differed only in degree from the photographs of actresses
> on the mantelpiece of a second-rate room in a second-rate
> college. The frequenters of the OUDS were always very
> definitely Oxford undergraduates, but they lacked the
> serenity of Oxford, and seemed already to have planted a
> foot in London. The big modern room over the big cheap
> shop was a restless place, and its pretentiousness and
> modernity were tinged with Thespianism . . . It had the
> advantage of a limited membership.

Possibly it was this last characteristic that Mercer found
most attractive. His outward aspect was already inclined to the
stiff and formal, he had no competitive instincts and he did not
make friends easily. Not many people were likely to outshine
him, largely because few were sufficiently interested to want to
try. The OUDS was the place for him. To mark his joining
he bought a motoring-cap; a modern thing to do; the ordinary
run of caps was still that now reserved for club cricketers and

schoolboys; the new fashion, now universal, was very slightly snob. Thus attired he might enter into the spirit of things; perhaps even, for a time, be on the inside looking out.

The Society was of no great antiquity. It had come into being as recently as 1885 and was the creation of two then undergraduates, Arthur Bourchier of Christ Church and Cosmo Gordon Lang of Balliol. Bourchier, son of a cavalry officer and Old Etonian, had fancied himself as a Shakespearean actor and it was he who had persuaded Vice-Chancellor Jowett of the respectability of his enterprise. Lang took his talents into the Church and during Mercer's time up he was the young and pushful Bishop of Stepney; his memorial is to have gone down in history as the 'Old Swine Lang' of the Abdication crisis. The memory of his cousin, Matheson Lang, is more fragrant, even though his best remembered part is as the sinister Chinaman in *Mr Wu*. Both Bourchier and Matheson Lang were familiar figures in OUDS circles and Mercer came to know them well. It was pleasant to think that a man could be an actor and yet be received in society. Each deserved cultivation and was duly cultivated. In the year of Mercer's Oxford début Lang was playing Benedick to the Beatrice of Ellen Terry, a great improvement on Mrs Langtry who had played the part in America. Mercer saw him and was captivated. Acting of this quality must surely rank as one of the fine arts. Beside it Jurisprudence had some economy of charm; and both Lang and Bourchier, in spite of the latter's monstrous conceit, were such extraordinarily nice men. In the nature of things he saw more of them than of the actresses and was spared Dr Johnson's unseemly emotions at the prospect of so many white bosoms and silk stockings. Gentlemen did not allow themselves to become so affected. The founding fathers of the OUDS, still only in vigorous middle age, were regular visitors to the city and stern critics of their successors. As often as not they brought their friends, and most of the big names in the theatre were to be seen at one time or another about the Oxford streets and hotels.

Dress was an important matter to an Edwardian undergraduate and nobody was better aware of this than Mercer. At nineteen he now had a scout, almost a gentleman's body-servant, and he became immaculate in all his accoutrements up to the limit of his father's means. He makes Berry tell of a young man whose trousers were cut for walking and in which he refused to

sit; the other end of the spectrum was to be seen in Oxford in
the shape of 'the Britter'—a diminutive of British Working
Man—a Hebrew coach whose garments were designed only
for sitting as he claimed never to walk anywhere. Two triangles
of cloth, base uppermost, contrived to produce the desired
result. It was regarded as mildly amusing but not seemly. A
gentleman should wear only sealed-pattern clothing, as Mercer
invariably did.

His friends at the OUDS were two, Gervais Rentoul, son of
a judge and destined for the Bar, and Paul Rubens, the composer. Rubens, whose early death was a loss to the theatre,
wrote a good deal for the smoking concerts to which senior
members of the colleges were invited. Possibly his best remembered piece was the song which contained the unforgettable
lyric, 'She was fat, she was fat, she was awful, awful fat; She
weighed at least some twenty stone in nothing but her hat'. The
Principal of BNC, Heberden, was reputedly strait-laced; it
was surprising to hear him murmur to his neighbour, 'What I
like about Paul Rubens is that he is so amusing without being at
all vulgar.' It was not his best work.

The OUDS productions stood on a higher plane, regulated
by the Vice-Chancellor's Charter. Under its terms, four out of
the eight plays produced during an eight-year cycle had to be
by Shakespeare, one was unavoidably Greek, and the remainder
might be chosen from any authors of classical standing. Mercer
had the misfortune to arrive during a Greek year. He did not
come badly out of it, for he played Strepsiades in *The Clouds* to
the Philippides of Compton Mackenzie. The *Isis*, in its number
for 4 March 1905, spoke well of their efforts. After saying how
much harder a task this generation had than the 1892 vintage
had suffered with *The Frogs*, the writer went on to add that, 'It
is all the more creditable to them to have produced a show
which is really worth going to see . . . The credit is principally
due to Mr C. W. Mercer, who gets all the fun possible out of
the bantam-turkeys and the occasional successful search for
smaller animals on which Aristophanes mainly relies for his
comic relief.' Mercer still felt aggrieved fifty years afterwards
because an unsympathetic producer had not allowed him to
deliver six hundred words in patter at express speed. There was
a respectable precedent. Eighteen years earlier A. E. W. Mason
had played Heracles in the *Alcestis*. He was beginning to find
himself amongst the great and famous. Sir Hubert Parry

prescribed oysters and stout for his voice. From Aristophanes he moved over to Shakespeare with a small part in *Measure for Measure*, followed by 'Pedant' in *The Taming Of The Shrew* and lastly Demetrius in *A Midsummer Night's Dream*. The language soaked into him; scratch any of his work and out it comes.

So complete was his dedication to the OUDS that he was made Secretary in 1906, and took his duties seriously. Still more of the great and famous came his way, for the top men of the professional stage were all on excellent terms with the Society. There was Hugh Allen, who conducted the Bach choir and 'shoved in organ-stops with his head'; Dion Clayton Calthrop, Byam Shaw ('he looked just like a bookie who had had a good day') and even Rudyard Kipling whom Mercer had to bear-lead around Oxford. 'I was frightened to death. But he seemed more frightened of me. I couldn't get over that.' Mercer admired Kipling's work above that of almost any other man.

Commem balls, with beautiful women, beautifully gowned and gloved to the armpits, waltzing to Archibald Joyce's band through the long nights of summer were all very well, but for William Mercer the play was the thing. In 1907 he was promoted to President of the OUDS and with that he was well content. It might not have been a position of first importance in University life, but it was undeniably something. He was a personage at last. 'Mercer? Univ man? In with all those theatrical johnnies?' was not quite the same thing as being Mercer, stroke of the Oxford Eight, or Mercer, President of the Union, but it made his name known and lifted him above obscurity.

During the vacations he fleeted the time as they did in the golden world; Cecil John Mercer had probably never been as far afield as Calais, but his son was going to see what he could of foreign parts while the opportunity was still there. It was neither difficult nor expensive, with passports almost unheard of and excellent railway systems, created to enable the armies of France and Germany to get at each other most advantageously, affording cheap and swift journeys nearly everywhere. Details of his travels are vanished, but something can be gleaned from the writings. Berry speaks of seeing unspeakably fat men in Marienbad in 1905, of a visit to Wiesbaden, and of Paris. Boy reminisces of the table that winds down through the floor in *Perishable Goods*, borrowed from one of the pleasing conceits

31

of Ludwig II of Bavaria, and asserts that of his own knowledge the statement (in *Blind Corner*) that before 1914 a duel could have been fought with Lewis guns in certain parts of Austria without attracting attention was true. Mercer, in any number of letters, asserts that all this is autobiographical and there is no reason to disbelieve him. Only when Berry tells of Parisian adventures in 1902, inferentially unlikely for a seventeen-year-old of Mercer's background unless the Dimsdales had taken him there, does one suspect that he is drawing on the doings of somebody else. Plainly he got to know Europe passably well, and Germany better than France. His travels did not lead to any love for our Teutonic cousins. 'Elizabeth' of the German Garden gets very short shrift, and her dreadful German husband provides the raw material for a number of instructive stories. Germans, mirroring their Sovereign, were not delightful neighbours in the years before 1914.

To be an Oxford undergraduate in the reign of King Edward was very heaven. A few years later, Douglas Jerrold tells us, every schoolboy knew of the German strategic railways and there was not a cadet in the OTC who expected the German armies to attack through the Belfort gap. In Mercer's time nobody gave a thought to such things. Splendid fellows of eighteen and twenty punted happily on Isis and Cherwell; although the summer of 1904 was one of the beastliest in memory, the sun always seemed to be shining. The Union owned some of the best and wittiest speakers in its history, most prominent being Hugh Kingsmill, whose 'The speaker entertained doubts, but not his audience' might well have done duty for Berry. There were also notable snobs about. Dr Warren of Magdalen has had many stories fathered on him, the favourite being his reception of Prince Chichibu of Japan. On being told that the name meant 'Son of God', Warren is reputed to have answered with much satisfaction that 'You will find that we have the sons of many other distinguished men in this College.' Mercer had nothing against honest snobbery. For him aristocracy was a word that would bear literal translation: the best. It would take a mean mind to grudge them their brief flight in the sun for many did not live to see thirty. The obligations of *noblesse* were fully as real as its privileges.

There were men other than speakers and eccentric dons who claimed his attention and who were to provide fodder for writings to come. F. J. V. Hopley, for instance, an Old

Harrovian who was the best amateur light-heavyweight boxer of his day and whose feats would in due time be transferred to Jonathan Mansel.

Ellis Robins, son of an officer in the little-esteemed army of the United States, was the first Rhodes Scholar to represent the State of Pennsylvania and he gave a glimpse of a wider world, tempered by a proper attitude towards the eternal truths. Lord Winterton, the only undergraduate of recent years to be elected to the House of Commons, had gone down from New College shortly before Mercer came up to Oxford. Robins soon joined him as Secretary to the Anti-Socialist League of Great Britain, a very suitable post for an American who would live to become an English colonel and an English peer. Mercer came to know him well and their friendship lasted throughout their joint lives. It may well have been from Robins that he picked up the pre-1914 American slang that appears from time to time in his writings.

Mercer rejoiced in particular at the Englishness of it all. This becomes apparent in his feelings towards that royal phenomenon King Edward VII. Everybody knew the monarch to be a classic case of satyriasis; the French, reputedly lax in such matters, had turned against Henri Quatre when he kept up into advanced age the gallantries which had once been endearing. The English, reputedly Puritan, took exactly the opposite view; the King, like Lord Palmerston before him, became even more popular as he continued to manifest that age had not caused the decline of his powers. Mercer, taking the essentially proper view that it is not for a subject to criticize his Sovereign, wrote of the King's courteous demeanour in public in terms only just on the south side of sycophancy. 'He was worshipped because he was worshipful: loved because he was lovable: however well you felt, the sight of him made you feel better than you had felt before' may be true; but 'So long as he lived Germany dared not make war' is hardly an opinion likely to command much support. Yet there is no humbug about either passage. Each represents Mercer's honest view of the matter. The nobility, genuine nobility of respectable ancestry spanning centuries, ranked only a little lower than the fountain of honour himself. Mercer greatly admired the work of John Singer Sargent; the portrait of Lord Ribblesdale shown at the Royal Academy in 1902 must have given him immense pleasure, for here was the quintessential *milor anglais*. The very thought of anyone addressing a being so august as Tommy would have seemed an indecency. This was no mere vulgar social climbing, nor was it in the least discreditable. The middle-class Mercer was fascinated by the upper class; the current tendency is to go in the opposite direction. If a man wants to identify himself with a kind of people other than his own it is at least as good to look up at the stars as to look down into the mud. Nor are respect and admiration yet entirely vile words. The upper classes of the first decade of this century were, on the whole, innocently engaged in perpetuating the manner of life that had been the way of their fathers and grandfathers.

No doubt Society had its faults; any body of people number-ing some thousands can hardly fail to contain every degree from the near-saintly to the notoriously sinful. The fact remains that the aristocracy of England was not merely unresented by the rest of the King's subjects but, taken in the round, it was respected and even admired. Jacqueries and tumbrils have never loomed large in English life, rather to the disgust and incredulity of Continental neighbours. There is a famous *Punch* cartoon showing an ex-Communard of 1870 standing alongside a working man by the side of Rotten Row doing his best to inspire Republican sentiment by asking whether the sight of so much wealth and privilege did not arouse his indignation; the Englishman's answer is simple and to the point. 'Bet you 'avent got 'orses like them in France.'

From the King and Queen, by way of such men as the Yellow Earl of Lowther Castle down to the lower reaches of the upper classes, they were welcome figures on all public and, in particular, on all sporting occasions. The reason was not merely whimsical. The territorial magnates for the most part dwelt on their estates and looked after their dependents with more than a grudging duty. Their fine houses, their family coaches, their strings of racehorses and squads of liveried servants excited no envy; men felt rather that they themselves were all a part of it, each a thread in the tapestry that portrayed an England so soon to end in flame and thunder. Many people knew, or at any rate suspected, that some of the nocturnal goings-on in the great house parties would not have stood close examination but it was left to their grandchildren to dwell on these things with an unseemly relish. The general view was that expressed by an adjutant to his new subaltern. 'I don't care a damn what you do in private, provided that you do it behind closed doors.' Scandal was the only real sin; at the first hint of it, society instinctively formed a ring as rugger players do around a man who has lost his shorts. The rise of Labour was to be due in great part to officers who came back from the war captivated by the unsuspectedly fine qualities of the working man in khaki and who were determined to do all they could to help him to enjoy the better life that he so well deserved. In the 1900s few people would have regarded a kitchen sink crammed with unwashed crockery as a suitable back-drop for popular writing. Stables and grouse moors were far more alluring.

Part of this allure came from the curious structure, if structure it was, of the aristocracy; it was a bizarre mixture of the exclusive and the open door. Society knew its own members without the need for any nominal roll but it was continually changing. Wooden shoes clattered up as fortunes were made; silken slippers pattered down as they were lost. More than one beautiful peeress whose white arms lifted coronet to brow at the Coronation had not long since displayed them to almost equal advantage in the front row of the Gaiety chorus. More than one broken peer was learning to shear on an Australian sheep run. An outsider, provided that he had a modicum of cash and knew how to behave himself, could usually find means to join as a temporary member. He must, of course, be a gentleman; this useful word, then as now, defied definition. It might be compared to elephant, in that you would be hard put to explain it but would recognize one without difficulty. The English gentleman was, by common consent, a superior person whether at home or abroad. From time to time a character of Mercer's, accosted in some Continental spa with a rhetorical question about nationality, replies that he has the honour—now and then the great honour—to be an Englishman. The turn of phrase may cause lips to curl today, but it sounded perfectly natural and proper long after King Edward had been laid in his grave. Duties walked hand in hand with privileges. The gentleman must at all times dress correctly, be courteous to all comers, be scrupulous in money matters and tip generously. His speech must be grammatical, his accent pure and he must on no account suffer liberties from any man; women were another matter; they could treat him as they pleased and he must never retaliate. All these things had been well understood in Walmer, but Harrow and Oxford were needful in order to provide the proper glossy finish. By 1907, the year in which he became President of the OUDS, Bill Mercer was fit to be presented to any company. Thanks to the industry of departed Walls and Yateses his mother was well enough off to set him up in modest style and he was willing and able to entertain useful and amusing people as a gentleman should. Cecil John's practice in the Temple was bringing him into touch with the common-law Bar, and the Boltons district, where he had taken No. 3 Coleherne Court on leaving Harrow, suited Bill very well.

It was his interest in the theatre that gave him the entrée to new places. The OUDS was only twenty years old and a good many of the founding fathers have moved on to the professional stage long enough since to be now standing at its head. Most of these magnificoes still found pleasure in returning to the scenes of their youth and Mercer found them to be men whose company gave enormous enjoyment. They seem to have liked him, for, according to one who knew him at about this time, Bill Mercer was good value. Already he had grown a shell that might easily discourage strangers into thinking that they had found a pompous prig, but it was egg rather than tortoise shell. He was a kindly young man and blessed with a sense of fun more civilized than was common in undergraduates.

The years 1905 and 1906 saw the planting of the bushes which would eventually bear fruit as Berry. Many men, the biggest men in the profession made their contribution. There was Arthur Bourchier, of the OUDS, and his old enemy Beerbohm Tree. It was at the Oxford Pageant, organized by Dion Clayton Calthrop as Master of the Robes, that Tree and Mercer first met; they lunched together, and at Tree's request set off for the pageant-ground in a landau. Mercer had done Tree well over luncheon and he was ripe for mischief, asserting loudly that in all his visits to Oxford he had never seen a good-looking girl. Mercer replied that this circumstance was hardly surprising. Tree, announcing that should one appear he intended to rise and salute her, mused on to the effect that even the Cities of the Plain were able to produce one good man. Mercer was on pins, for he knew his companion's reputation and, as he pointed out, he would be still in Oxford long after Tree's departure. On Magdalen Bridge the dreaded moment came. An uncommonly pretty girl, dressed mediaeval-style for some part in the pageant, hove into sight. Tree staggered to his feet, supported himself on the other man's shoulder and made theatrical obeisance; the young woman looked suitably startled, Mercer wished for the earth to swallow him up and Tree resumed his seat while pondering richly on the chances of meeting her on the train home. Mercer could never bring himself to speak of Tree with whole-hearted enthusiasm. His trouble, apparently, was that he soon became bored with any part he was supposed to be playing and showed it after the first few performances.

Tree and Henry Ainley, Arthur Bourchier and Harry Irving—son to Sir Henry—were the friends of a season, but two men met in the OUDS days remained Mercer's friends for life. The Canadian-Scot Matheson Lang, always called Tristram, and the Australian Oscar Asche, along with their respective wives, were excellent company and never did embarrassing things in public places. Lang is probably best remembered now as 'Mr Wu', and *The Chinese Bungalow* was a fine play: Oscar Asche's name is synonymous with *Chu Chin Chow*. Neither man would be grateful for so narrow a remembrance. Mercer calls Asche 'the best producer before the first war' and claims his productions of *The Taming of the Shrew*, *As You Like It*, *Kismet* and *Count Hannibal*—another of Stanley Weyman's Henri Quatre pieces and produced in 1910—to have been 'as near perfect as possible'. He thought little of *Chu Chin Chow*—'a lot of scantily dressed ladies and the war was on'. Asche and Lang, each a dozen years older than Mercer, were well known to each other and had learnt their business together playing Shakespearean parts in Frank Benson's company. At the time of their descent upon Oxford and Mercer, Matheson Lang was playing Benedick in *Much Ado About Nothing*, while Asche had just taken over management of the Adelphi. Obviously they all found the company congenial; it was not long before Mercer was off with Oscar Asche and Lily Brayton, his beautiful wife—herself a memorable Rosalind—to enjoy a caravan holiday in the New Forest. When he treats of caravans—the horse-drawn variety, of course—Mercer seems to be suggesting that the pastime lacked much enjoyment but the Asches were to become important figures in his life. Nor had he seen the last of Matheson Lang.

The gipsy life in the high summer of 1907 was his introduction to the Forest and the spell of it never quite left him. Plodding slowly along roads frequently unmade, stopping for drinks and necessary shopping in villages unchanged for centuries and glimpsing an occasional great house, already of a respectable antiquity when men were piling up brushwood for the Armada beacons, was a revelation to a man whose England so far had comprehended only East Kent and the Home Counties; the Forest in the 1900s was very different, in aspect, in tempo and in its scents, from anything he had experienced before. Waggoners and ploughmen, verderers and woodmen, all went quietly about their businesses in slow and amiable fashion. Roads were places where men might, and did, linger for a gossip without fear of being mown down, and the smell of thyme and wistaria was not yet overlaid by the stink of diesel oil. It was governed by strange laws all its own, as ancient as the *fueros* of the Basques. Mercer was just in time. Only a few years were left before the England that Arthur Conan Doyle had painted in *The White Company* vanished for ever. Mercer, incidentally, puts a spoof version of the bowman's song into Berry's mouth very early in his writing, in 'The Order of the Bath'. His choice of reading matter was always excellent. Though he had not yet begun to consider himself as a writer, he had found the *mise-en-scène* for nearly all that part of his future work which did not concern itself with foreign countries.

A few years earlier, in about 1901, he had a brief encounter with a cousin already famous. Hector Hugh Munro was in London for a spell and Bill Mercer visited him at the home of John and Mary Dimsdale in Phillimore Gardens. It is a pity that no more than a few casual observations have survived upon which to build some account of a meeting so important. 'Saki' had come to notice through his short stories in the old sea-green incorruptible, the *Westminster Gazette*, and the discriminating were anxiously waiting for more.

Mercer was mightily taken by his exotic cousin. Though his reputation had not yet reached its peak 'Saki' was already a name that the more literate kind of reader was mentioning with respect, and his talent in using words was plain to see. In time a good deal of it was to rub off on the younger man, especially in that choice of proper names that hall-marked both of them. Consider Clovis Sangrail, Virgil Pardoner, Bertie van Tahn, Piers Marriner, Crofton Lockyer, Comus Bassington, Jonathan Baldric, Odo Finsberry, Pomfret Tudor, Arlington Stringham and Mrs Drinkabeer Stoat. You may not be able to tell without a moment's thought which is Munro and which is Yates, but you can have no doubt that all of them came out of the same stable. The habits of speech peculiar to Clovis and his friends do not occur in the writings of any other Englishman of the period but they are interchangeable with some of the allocutions of Berry a few years later. It is indeed the Englishness of both men that shines out of their work. Munro was Highland on his father's side but the blood of Josiah Dornford and Samuel Mercer appears undiminished; not even Hector Munro would have thought in terms of Merrie Scotland, nor is there any tune known to music as England The Brave. None of this greatly mattered to Mercer in 1907. The eye of the tribesman was off him, his term as a gentleman of independent habit was barely half run and he had no plans for becoming an author. Nor, for that matter, of becoming anything else. Jurisprudence, the Science of Law, was creeping nearer but there was urgency neither about that nor about a career. Pageants and stages were, for the present, of much greater importance.

For William Mercer, as for most of the young men of his age and background these were best years. An almost exact contemporary who had the misfortune to be a member of the other University would, in 1914, put them into something imperishable under the name of 'The Great Lover'. Mercer indeed merited the title for he loved the England he saw, the good-natured Englishmen who inhabited it and even the humble artifacts of England. Berry's braces, that he bought for eighteen pence in 1912 and which served him faithfully for near on a quarter of a century, button precisely on to Brooke's 'good smell of old clothes and others such'. It was in 1906 that there first appeared something in the higher reaches of craftsmanship that caught his imagination as the supreme example of English genius and refined workmanship. Some captious men still insist that King Alfonso's tulip-wood Hispano-Suiza was the most beautiful motor-car ever made, but for Mercer, as for most people, the Rolls-Royce 40/50 h.p. stood apart. So delighted was he by the first specimen to come his way that for ever afterwards he wrote of it as the only vehicle fit to carry an English gentleman, especially in foreign parts.

His world was a small one, but it was a smaller England inhabited by some thirty million men and women—little more than half today's total—nearly all of them from a common stock. The ruder part of it he had yet to see.

In Shakespeare he soaked himself, but for his next needs a familiarity with the Sonnets was of no more use than an ability to tame wild rabbits. The Schools had no intention of going away and waited for no man. It became disagreeably plain in the spring of 1907 that Jurisprudence now demanded more than a nodding acquaintance and that its arcana were not of a kind to be easily mastered nor long remembered. So far he had done just enough work to keep himself out of trouble but now heavy concentration could no longer be put off. Mercer found himself at only one remove from despair. Whether in compelling Berry to enter into a voidable contract with the Devil—six months of his life against an Honours degree—bore any resemblance to his own preparations seems doubtful. The Devil would never have behaved so shamelessly in the execution of his part. Much more likely is it that he hired himself a crammer, for his acquaintance with crammers and their habits described nearly fifty years afterwards was plainly an exact one.

The habit of permuting and combining questions posed by examiners over the past couple of decades was established and respectable. With luck, or by diabolic intervention, the aspirant might find himself faced by ten questions from which three could be answered with confidence; with the odd seven he must take his chance. Mercer's luck was not in. His academic dress and white tie were beyond reproach, his brain was churning with half-digested precepts of Justinian, some of which he might have rendered into intelligibility. They were the wrong ones. He was lucky to leave Oxford with any degree at all. The manner in which the news reached him did nothing to soften the blow. Not only was it a very wet day, but it was also the day of the Pageant, at which he was appearing in the character of Friar Bacon. For some reason he travelled by motorcycle, skidded on the damp grass and was cast into the river. As he surfaced and dashed the hair out of his eyes the doom-laden voice of his scout reached him. 'You've got a third, sir.'

This was a very serious matter. Cecil John and Helen had confidently planned a sound and respectable future for their only child. He was not likely to want to become a solicitor; hope could hardly triumph over experience as far as that; the obvious place for him was the Bar, but for that highly competitive profession a third was no flying start. Mercer, who had a conscience, cannot have enjoyed his home-coming. For his father he had no particularly strong feelings, but his mother was something different. Helen Mercer adored her only son, and was adored in return; those who best remember her are at one in calling to mind her devoutness and that it was rare for a day to pass without her attending some church service of the higher Anglican kind. The ambition for her Willie was perhaps a little prejudiced; such a paragon deserved to reach the heights of any occupation that he might choose and it was bitter to learn that he had made so poor a start. Cecil John was obliged to take a further look at his son's prospects. His own little practice in Temple Avenue barely sufficed, along with Helen's money, to keep up the appearances needed to a family in good standing. He had been resigned to the fact that he would have to carry his boy as a passenger for some time to come, for puppy-barristers seldom earn their keep for the first few years after Call. The questions now was whether he would be called at all, let alone chosen. The sooner Bill, who may very well have grown a little too grand for his father's taste, was put to honest work and earned something the better. There was one possibility. Helen and Cecil John sounded out their Yates relations, still in business as City merchants of substance and people who could probably find him a job.

The first six months of the year 1908 cover Mercer in something of a London fog for it was a time about which he never reminisced. It is certain that he worked in the City; it is probable that he was some sort of a clerk in or near to Crutched Friars. Characters in the novels speak of the place without affection. Ward Lock & Co., a name to be heard again, were inclined to agree. Their *Guide to London* observes it to be 'a crooked street deriving its name from a former monastery of the Friars of the Holy Cross. Commercial, and almost squalid as is all this quarter now, it is to be remembered that when the Court was in residence at the Tower, the nobility and gentry had mansions hereabouts and the great religious houses gave it an ecclesiastical importance hard indeed to realize today.'

3

Set to the Law

Picture then Cecil William Mercer, late President of the OUDS, as he appeared in the part of an aspiring, if unenthusiastic, captain of industry. As he stepped aboard the tube train carrying him from Kensington to the City he looked everything that such a man should be. His morning coat without fault, his boots varnished and in the forenoon his spats fell neatly over their uppers. Spats, you will not need to be told, were not worn after luncheon. His silk hat glistened, his hair was cut to a nicety and his face, like most civilian faces of his generation, clean shaven. On arrival at his destination he moved into a world undreamt-of at University College or at Harrow. The warehouse still abounded with the commodities brought daily by Mr Kipling's big steamers and the air was fragrant with cheese and figs and bacon. The men who ordered their disposition were successors to many generations at the same business, men of strict honesty in their dealings, but without any affectation of fastidiousness when it came to talking money and striking bargains.

Here was the solid foundation of the prestige of England. Here came the exotic and the spicy products of hotter countries without which the English table would have been even without such flavour as it possessed; not for nothing do the Germans call groceries 'kolonialwaren'; lacking the provisions purveyed by what the English persisted in calling Italian warehousemen, Mr Cooper of Oxford could never have concocted his noble marmalade nor Mr Colman his mustard. There was romance and peotry in the business. Mercer did not perceive it. A little over thirty years were to go by before he set out his well-remembered feelings about being in trade on the very first page of *Shoal Water*. His alter ego for the purpose, Jeremy Solon, tells of how, determined to be worth his salt, he got down to the job. 'No man ever worked harder than I did . . . The business was so well established that, fortunately for me, routine duties were all that had to be done; but these were numerous. I laboured early and late, and, except for an odd week-end, I had no holidays . . . and, most important of all, I honoured a list of rules which must, I think, have been printed before my father was born.' It has the sound of autobiography.

Distance may have lent some enchantment, but there is no reason to doubt the substantial truth of his account of the matter. Mercer was still chastened by his inglorious departure from Oxford and was firm in his resolve to demonstrate his aptitude for higher things. His pleasures were few. The craving for romance was already there but the means of satisfying it did not exist. On a clerk's wages he was in no position to give much thought to girls; the idea of two tube tickets, two seats in the back row of a cinema—kinema it was usually spelt then—followed by an inexpensive if nourishing meal at Lockhart's or Pearce-and-Plenty's had a basic lack of charm. Until he could fittingly entertain a young woman with taxicabs, two stalls at Daly's and a discreet little dinner at the Carlton Grill or somewhere such, young women would have to wait.

Cecil John and Helen probably never intended that their only son should continue for long at a task that he reckoned below him. The ambition of many solicitors to see their sons installed in what was commonly reckoned the higher branch of the law was widespread, more especially amongst those who had no great practice to hand on. There happened to be a back door to the Bar, little used, but serviceable, and Cecil John determined to give it a push. He was not without friends and one of these was H. G. Muskett, himself son to a solicitor and by now head of the famous firm of Wontners in Bedford Row, solicitors to the Commissioner of Police for the Metropolis. The back door might lead through his office, for a regulation existed under which a prospective barrister might, before Call, serve a turn in a solicitor's firm as a pupil without going through the formalities of being articled. Not many people took advantage of this, but Cecil John had inherited something of the determination of his naval ancestors and he sought out Muskett with his proposition.

Though Muskett was several years junior to Mercer in point of admission he was a very senior man and his standing in the profession was of the highest. He had never before taken a pupil—few solicitors had—and he had no enthusiasm for the idea. His staff was adequate, his coach needed no fifth wheel and a young man of whom he knew nothing tailing along behind him everywhere offered no advantages. Eventually, though upon what terms nobody can now know, he allowed himself to be persuaded, and in the autumn of 1908 William Mercer presented himself at Bedford Row, engaged to serve as a pupil for one year. A decade earlier John Buchan had done the same thing in another office in the Row. 'Being a stern man he naturally regarded me with grave suspicion.' Mercer asserts that 'this I contrived to allay, and we soon became good friends and I went with him everywhere! . . . The first day I came, Muskett said, "You will see and hear many things in this office which you must never repeat." He stopped there and looked at me. Then, "I never speak twice," he said.' Mercer acquired a great respect for Muskett, but he could not resist a dig at him. 'His short address to the Magistrate could hardly have been bettered by some counsel briefed for the defence. Yet Muskett had never been at Oxford and had never had any of those things we call advantages.' For the son of an unimportant solicitor to speak thus of another solicitor's son who was at the top of his profession is barely on the south side of impertinence. Sad to say it was not just an isolated lapse; Mercer held firm always as an article of faith to the demonstrable superiority of Old Harrovians and Oxford men over any others of God's creatures. It was to Muskett more than to any other man that he owed not merely his admission to the rank of barrister, but his seat in Treasury Chambers. For the time being, however, Mercer was immersed in his part of the industrious apprentice and he played it well. It can never have occurred to Muskett that his pupil was condescending to him. Had the thought ever crossed his mind William Mercer would have been back in the warehouse with the speed of light.

His first encounter with a rougher side of England came with his introduction to the militant suffragettes. This phenomenon kept newspapers busy for a number of years and for those of us who were not there to witness the extraordinary events that marred the tranquillity of England it is hard to be dogmatic. The movement started innocently enough, organized by women of high quality and with a cause that was by no means unarguable. Because they did not immediately get their own way they allowed the business to get out of hand. In its early days there was some sympathy with the idea amongst members of a new Liberal Government dedicated to reform, but the slashing of paintings beyond price, the smashing of shop windows by the score and the antics of a self-advertising few soon forfeited any claim to public tolerance, let alone public goodwill. They had, of course, their champions. Women, more often than not, are smaller than men, especially are they smaller than policemen. It is hardly possible to take into custody a violently struggling woman, shrieking out words that she has no business to know, without laying hands on some portion of her anatomy, nor is it difficult so to contrive matters that the arrester seems to be conducting himself unseemly. The experts knew exactly how to bring this about and even men of the calibre of H. W. Nevison were persuaded that the police were really rather enjoying it. The resulting publicity was exactly what the ladies hoped for.

Mercer had a grandstand view of it all, for Muskett was charged with the duty of appearing for the Commissioner when the offenders came up at Bow Street. The most notable occasion was on the June evening when Mrs Pankhurst, whose statue now adorns a garden by the Houses of Parliament, announced her intention of leading a mob from Trafalgar Square to that same House. Muskett decided that it would be expedient for him to see things for himself and his faithful pupil accompanied him. With the Commissioner himself making a third they took up station on a traffic island in Whitehall just by Parliament Square and under strong police guard. The constables were all on foot, as experience had shown the ladies to have the habit of animating police horses by judicious use of the hat-pins they all wore. By then it was after eight o'clock and the street lights were on. The monstrous regiment flowed down Whitehall; as they approached the police cordon, the valiant Inspector Jarvis stepped out and halted them. Mrs Pankhurst demanded the right of passage; on being met by a courteous refusal she took a swing at the Inspector and knocked his cap off. This sounded the Charge and, as she was decorously arrested, the mob went for the police.

It was a shocking scene, and, had I not seen it, I never would have believed that educated women could so degrade themselves. Indeed, I declined to believe that any woman, however

45

low and vile, has ever so behaved unless she was drunk. And these women were not drunk. Arrests were made right and left, and a constant stream of women was flowing to Cannon Row. Some fought and struggled, demanding to be 'let alone': others went quietly enough. Police reinforcements filled the gaps in the cordon and were assailed in their turn. After about half an hour we left the scene. In that time I only saw one woman roughly used. She had been arrested and was resisting savagely. The constable who was taking her to Cannon Row took her by the shoulders and shook her. He was immediately reproved: but he had my sympathy. The woman had laid his face open from temple to chin.

Mercer's story is corroborated by another eye-witness. P.C. Ryan was a talkative man off duty; when, in 1914, he was transformed into Leading Signalman Ryan of HMS *Bacchante* it was his custom to end every conversation by holding up his thumb and observing, 'See this scar? Bitten by Miss Sylvia Pankhurst, I was, while trying to arrest her.' It is not wonderful that Mercer's view of the sex, hitherto elevated, underwent modification.

He was at Bow Street the next morning carrying Muskett's bag when nearly a hundred women appeared to answer charges. Inevitably Mrs Pankhurst and her friends turned the place into a circus, demanding between their sandwiches that the Home Secretary and the Chancellor of the Exchequer, neither of whom had anything to contribute, be brought to testify. The Magistrate, unwisely, indulged them. Herbert Gladstone, not an admired figure, behaved surprisingly well but 'the figure Lloyd George cut was almost contemptible. His demeanour was craven, and he tried to be funny and failed—and laughed at everything he said. Nobody else did.' Mr Lloyd George started with a double handicap; not only was he a radical politician, he was also a solicitor. All the same, Mercer was not alone in his view of the matter.

The proceedings brought one lighter and more instructive moment. Whilst lunching with Muskett at the Gaiety Restaurant, Mercer was careless enough to leave his wristwatch—a new-fangled thing in 1909—in the wash-room. On getting back to Bow Street he told Superintendent Wells of his loss. Wells listened to him, spoke quietly to Inspector Jarvis—the only words Mercer caught were 'Go yourself'—and twenty minutes later, 'he laid my watch beside me with a quiet smile'. Mercer had sense enough to ask no questions. Possibly Falcon and Sweaty and The Wet Flag were born in that moment.

With Muskett for guide Mercer saw a good deal of the goings-on of some part of that world that lay below the surface of Edwardian England. He has been accused, along with John Buchan and 'Sapper', of anti-semitism. There is truth in this, but it was not uncommon amongst men who knew anything of the world of crime. Alien immigration, mostly by Jews originating from Central Europe and especially Russia, was then a subject that troubled some Englishmen nearly as much as black immigration does others today. It was commonly believed that the tongue of many of the worst criminal societies was Yiddish, and indeed one judge (Sir Albert Bosanquet) was heard to observe that 'a characteristic of this language is that it cannot be used for telling the truth'. The sale of women into prostitution was a thriving business; when, years later, Mercer came to treat of the subject in *Shoal Water* he was writing of things he well understood.

It was not only the vilest of ordinary criminals, men of the stripe of Cammy Grizard, Stinie Morrison and the brothers Reubens, who infested the Jewish section of the underworld; terrorism is not a modern invention and the murders of three policemen in Sidney Street—no great distance from the Old Bailey—on 16 December 1910, followed by the siege, brought to a head matters that had been long suppurating. The unhallowed names of Gardstein, Svaara, Trassjonsky, Luba Millstein, Nina Vassileva, Duboff, Rosen, Hoffman, Federoff and Peter Piatkow or the Painter did nothing to warm hearts towards the ancient race of Israel. Mercer saw Jewry at its worst, and the common knowledge that some shady solicitors were of the same race did nothing to mitigate his feelings. They were not peculiar to Mercer and the other two writers. Every-body who knew anything of these matters felt the same. It was hard on decent, hard-working Jews who had made their homes here, but life goes on in that fashion.

The outside world, Mercer was learning, was very different from the world of Oxford. Muskett's own office, for a start, seems to have been a thought behind the times. By 1909 typewriting machines—a typewriter was the young person who pounded it—had been in use for something like twenty years, but not at Wontners. Mercer, after speaking of the quiet of Bedford Row, goes on to tell how every letter was still written by hand and every indictment in copper-plate on sheepskin. Their clerks worked all hours and, surprisingly, there was always laughter about the place. His position was a curious one, something like Hans Andersen's duckling in its early days. He lived amongst solicitors but not only would he never become one, he would before long be translated to a stratum which had little enough time for such people. While he was there, however, he took pains to learn all he could of their ways. The London solicitor and the country solicitor were poles apart. As the King of Siam sent ambassadors to Louis XIV, but Louis XIV sent no ambassadors to the King of Siam, so the country man was obliged to keep an agent in London in order to deal with such of his affairs as might come inside the metropolitan boundary. A London practitioner engaged in country business could do what he pleased.

The great men of the profession inevitably plied their trade in certain traditional areas; not even their names were commonly known, for those on the brass plate outside were nearly always of founding fathers long gone to their account. The country solicitor, however, was not a poor relation. Quite recently a long-established firm in Canterbury, being pressed for space, threw out a load of ancient ledgers. A quick glance before the dustman arrived showed that in the first years of this century no partner earned less than £4,000; tax, of course, was negligible. The money came, for the most part, from the harmless non-contentious businesses of conveyancing and probate. Litigation was not usually welcomed; if it could not be avoided then the London agent must earn his keep. A man could make a decent living, even a modest fortune, without ever entering Court.

London was another matter, though plenty of firms there eschewed any sort of Court business. Solicitors came in all shapes and sizes, about half the admitted men in the Kingdom having their offices in the capital. The best known in the 1900s was, without doubt, Sir George Lewis. Such was his fame that Sir Arthur Conan Doyle pressed him into service with a throwaway line in Sherlock Holmes' *Adventure of the Illustrious Client*. Holmes, speaking to Watson of his fictional Sir James Damery, observes that 'He has rather a reputation for arranging delicate matters which are to be kept out of the papers. You may remember his negotiations with Sir George Lewis over the Hammerford Will case.' That is exactly the reputation Lewis enjoyed, the tidy disposal of skeletons. Those who recall him remember best his rudeness, especially to those unable to answer back. He married a German lady, and his son, heir to the baronetcy created in 1902 as one of the first acts of a grateful King Edward, despite strong opposition from Mr Balfour, was to do so in his turn. At the other end of the London ladder was Arthur Newton, whose manners were more pleasing, but who ought to have been in gaol. It was not fitting that an old boy of Shrewsbury should have acquired such skill at the subornation of witnesses in criminal cases that the entire staff of Marlborough Street Police Station had to be changed every month for fear that he might have corrupted them. Newton was a rogue, but he was a far more amusing man than Sir George Lewis. Without him Sir Edward Marshall Hall's fee-book would have been much slimmer.

Between these misty flats the rest drifted to and fro; men of high professional skill and the strictest honour controlling vast sums of other men's money shading down to those who counted themselves lucky to remain on the Roll. Should anything in this book lead any possible reader to form an unfavourable opinion of solicitors as a body he might do worse than pay a visit to the Members' Common Room in the Law Society's Hall. There, around the walls, he may read 1127 names. Of these, 669 are those of solicitors who laid aside their papers, went out to fight for their King, and did not come back; the remaining 458 are articled clerks who died in battle before they had been granted the time to present themselves for the Final Examination. It is not a contemptible record.

In this world Mercer was a bird of passage, seeing little but criminal practice of a kind by no means typical of all solicitors' work. In his spare time he got down to his books once more. The Bar Final had few terrors for him. No doubt men have failed it, but there can hardly have been many of them for it was not regarded as particularly searching.

In Muskett's company Mercer saw the Bar from the outside, both the best of it and the worst. A notable figure was the notorious Mr Abrahams who, misliking the name, changed it to Abinger; the first Lord Abinger, once Sir James Scarlett, had been one of the most distinguished men of his day, both at the Bar and on the Bench. The gentleman who became his namesake was reputed to keep a picture of Lord Chief Baron Abinger prominently displayed in his Chambers in order that those having business there might draw conclusions unwarranted by fact. Abrahams made a very reasonable fortune by the exercise of the two talents with which he was blessed, skill in touting for business in the hall of the Old Bailey and pertinacity in attacking all prosecution witnesses in all circumstances. Muskett doubtless obtained a dry pleasure from this convincing demonstration that malpractice was not confined to the solicitors' branch. Abrahams, the 'thieves' lawyer', had not even Arthur Newton's redeeming feature for there was no wit in the man. Dr Johnson says somewhere that no man is on oath in a lapidary inscription, but Abrahams' *Times* obituary was to raise fury in Mercer. 'Any layman reading it would have sighed for the passing of a great man. And in fact he was a disgrace to his profession, and he spent his life obtaining poor men's money by false pretences.' Mr Abrahams was not the only one of his kind. His familiarity with the law was that of necessity; his professional scruples conspicuous only by non-existence. Happily he was one of the last of a dying race.

One of the most important of Muskett's lessons was in the matter of language. In Shakespeare's hands this could be a chaplet of pearls; with Muskett it became an industrial diamond. There is hardly a word in English of more than one syllable that has not at some time been dissected and interpreted by some judge. Precision in use was the daily task of the lawyer and Muskett's indictments were the work of a master of the English tongue. Mercer took kindly to it all; it would be tedious to go into details, but his works are peppered with the well-understood verbal shorthand that was part of the stock in trade of the legal profession. More important, you will be hard put to it indeed to find a single word of which the use cannot be strictly justified. As he grew older Mercer became more and more fussy on this subject. His particular bugbear was the over-worked word 'nostalgia'; never did he weary of pointing out that it has but one meaning, 'home-sickness', and admits of no other.

As 1909 passed from summer to autumn so did Muskett's year pass into history. His examinations behind him and his dinners eaten, Cecil William Mercer answered his call and at Michaelmas he was dubbed barrister by the Honourable Society of the Inner Temple. Muskett had plainly liked him, for he rendered a last service of inestimable value by persuading Travers Humphreys to take the young man as his pupil into Treasury Chambers. The fact that he was found a billet there shows that a very decent spirit prevailed at the Bar. Charles Gill, you will remember, had appeared for the defence of Great-Uncle James and Archibald Bodkin had prosecuted him. Travers Humphreys, son of the distinguished London solicitor C. O. Humphreys, must have known all about the Mercer family skeleton, but he and the others put themselves out to be friendly to the new recruit; the sins of uncles and great-uncles were not his sins, although Mercer's first visit to the Nisi Prius Court at Maidstone, housing the dock from which one such had been taken down, cannot have been an agreeable experience.

It was plain to the well informed that Humphreys was a man with a distinguished future ahead of him and Mercer was fortunate indeed to have such a pupil-master. Cecil John, as well up in these things as any man, doubtless paid over his hundred guineas with a light heart. Becoming Humphreys' devil was a far better bargain than the other doubtful one that had paid only with a miserable third.

All this promised well for the days that were to come, but put no immediate money into the pocket. For the moment it was necessary still to be a charge upon the family resources, but there were compensations not to be despised. The new-hatched barrister found himself at large in a world very different from that of his school-fellows who had chosen another path. The fresh-gazetted subaltern soon learnt that he was less than the dust beneath the wheels of the Maltese cart that carried the Mess stores. His seniors, should they unbend enough to address him, did so as 'wart' and emphasized his failings and his insignificance; the Royal Navy did something of the same kind in its own fashion and no doubt assistant curates had their tribulations. The Bar, however, went to the other extreme. The young man soon learned that, as a full member of a sodality in which all were equal, he should address famous men, his elders not by years but by decades, with the familiarity of bare surname. He must also learn that the less he had to do with those other ranks of the law called solicitors the better it would be for everybody. Travers Humphreys, like Mercer and many other barristers, was the son of a solicitor; such misfortune could be lived down so long as attention was not drawn to it. Mercer had more difficulty than most, for it was less than twenty years since Mercer & Edwards had crashed, leaving many people in and around Walmer poorer than they should have been, and the reverberations had not quite died down.

Relations between the two branches of the profession were carried out with a measure of well-mannered humbug. 'Attorney hugging' was the sin against the light, but only attorneys could provide the Bar with the means of paying the rent and the grocer. Here the barrister's clerk entered his kingdom; no professional body troubled itself with his daily doings, his income rose or fell in proportion to the fees his master attracted, and it was his duty as well as his interest to keep in with the managing clerks of the solicitors who held the tap that governed the flood or the trickle of briefs. There was a story current before the South African war of the cavalry subaltern's answer to the question whether he was happy in the service. 'The Army would be all right if it were just the Mess and the band: no bloody men or horses.' Reading 'Courts' for 'band', 'solicitors' for 'men' and 'clients' for 'horses', many a barrister might have said the same. In an age that knew nothing of Legal Aid beyond the Poor Prisoners' Defence Act 1903, it was next to impossible for a man to earn a living income during his first few years. The Criminal Bar, though it was the branch most likely to get its members' names into the newspapers, was notoriously ill-rewarded. The best thing about it was that it held some prospect of being other than a blind alley for a man who could stay the course. A young solicitor could never hope to become more than an old solicitor; for the moderately senior barrister there were prizes in the shape of judgeships in their varying degrees.

There is room for criticism of the Bar system, for it reverses the natural order of things. The head boy of the preparatory school becomes the junior fag; the head prefect becomes the freshman. The new graduate, like the newly commissioned cadet, commonly becomes an underling to be cursed and punished all over again. Only at the Bar is the recruit treated as a person of consequence, the peer of the oldest hand. His opinion is heard respectfully; any difference from it is couched in unhurtful language. Should his head be in the least swollen to start with, it will swell further yet. The subaltern or midshipman, reviled and subjected to indignities, is, for a season, prevented from becoming pleased with himself. The barrister, by contrast, is encouraged; there is room for suspicion that William Mercer needed no such encouragement.

He came into the profession at a time when it was changing fast. For many years now the public had regarded it with a distaste that had much to justify it. Far too many barristers, inside a world familiar to them but alien to outsiders, habited in the dress of Queen Anne's day and apparently supported by the grim figure on the Bench, had had things far too much their own way. Though they gracefully referred to each other as 'learned', few had any real claim to the adjective. No man pretended to know all the Laws of England; it was enough to have acquaintance with that section of it that earned his daily bread. There were, of course, some men of brilliance in every generation, but the majority, compared with men of the stamp of Rutherford or Marconi, were journeymen. The great art was to be able to bully witnesses, a thing not too difficult with men and women already overawed by the ancient majesty that was new to most of them. A generation before Mercer's call the Abrahams had dominated and no honest man would permit himself to be exposed to the rude hectoring that was a witness's portion if he could by any means avoid it. Though the Bar was well pleased with itself, the country was less pleased with the Bar. The simple pleasure of the folk knew no bounds on the famous occasion when Marshall Hall, hired to cut down Lord Alfred Douglas, was himself beaten into the ground: and Lord Alfred was not the most popular of men.

It was difficult indeed for a barrister to make himself a name were he unwilling to stoop to these practices and they were becoming increasingly distasteful to the Bar itself. Nevertheless their living came from what Arthur Hugh Clough called 'the horrible pleasure of pleasing inferior people'. Though all but the Abrahams behaved honourably, there was a tendency to regard the business as a game; the man who paid the bill was a long way down in the batting order. Mercer related with obvious amusement a tale of Lord Tiverton, the son of former Chancellor Lord Halsbury. 'Tivvy's practice was a slight one, limited in the main to appearances in country Magistrates' Courts in the days before Kipling ridiculed them in *The Village That Voted The Earth Was Flat*. For want of other employment Tiverton passed much time turning over the dustbins of ancient precedent and blinding the Justices with erudition. Inevitably he secured many acquittals: equally inevitably the joke wore thin and a day came when he was taken to the Divisional Court. The story of the setting-down of 'Tivvy', unable to begin to sustain his arguments before professionals, was held to be vastly entertaining. The victim, who, properly advised, would have pleaded guilty and endured a small fine, was saddled with the costs of all the proceedings. He, and the solicitor who had to explain why he needed to write so large a cheque, found it less risible.

All tides turn sooner or later, and a clean new stream was now flowing in. It was Rufus Daniel Isaacs—embarrassingly for some a Jew—who began it and he was followed by men of the calibre of F. E. Smith and Edward Carson. Under such leadership the quality of advocacy rose to forgotten heights. The manners of gentlemen came to replace the crude tactics of the bully and it soon became clear that the rapier was far more effective than the cudgel, as well as being less messy. Humphreys was a man of the new dispensation and Mercer was taught his art well. No trickery, no cheating, but the painstaking collection of evidence and its presentation in a fashion at once courteous and deadly.

It was invaluable, but it was not lucrative. Many a young man at the Bar was compelled to look around him for a means of augmenting a slender income and there were accepted methods of doing this. Lecturing, the writing or editing of legal text-books and private coaching were well understood ways of passing the vacations, but these were over-subscribed. Writing of any kind, provided that it could not be called advertising, was permitted; the highest form of this was generally reckoned to be articles for *Punch*. Mercer turned his eyes towards the famous round table, where Linley Sambourne was still presiding in his last days.

The reputation of *Punch* in the years before the Great War stood at its highest. Mercer himself regarded it with awe. When he wished to emphasize the high quality of a rapscallion standing shabbily before the Court on some charge, he observed that 'In his way his record was brilliant. He had contributed to *Punch*.' It was not so much the quality of its jokes that made *Punch* supreme. Take away excruciating puns, the ignorance of the lower orders, the aspirations of the new rich and the uncouth vocables of babies and you will find little left. The glory of *Punch* was its artists. The roll call includes names that must be amongst the immortals. Bernard Partridge and E. T. Reed for the political cartoons: for social commentary, E. H. Shepard, F. H. Townsend, G. D. Armour, L. Raven-Hill, G. L. Stampa, A. Wallis-Mills and Lewis Baumer, the creator of, amongst others, the appalling 'Oofy' Goldberg whose activities did little to mitigate any lurking anti-semitism in anybody. The immaculate men, morning-coated, spatted, top-hatted and monocled; the beautiful, subtly-corseted women, the hansom cabs and the hunting field give as perfect a picture as one could wish of a vanished age. There is more to be learnt from *Punch*, especially from its illustrators, than from any number of printed books. What our parents wore, their tricks of speech, the way they worked, shopped, travelled, worshipped and amused themselves and the manner in which they furnished their houses, all are there, drawn and described for immediate consumption but caught in mid-flight and preserved for ever. Ina Garvey's letters—usually headed 'Park Lane' but occasionally 'Deauville' or 'Monte Carlo'—always beginning 'Dearest Daphne' and ending 'Ever thine, Blanche', tell of the doings of such mythical beings as Poppy, Lady Ramsgate (alas, not Maude, Lady Littlehampton); as Edwardian society found them true to life it is fair to assume that they were. It is not difficult to guess where Mercer's Daphne had her origins. The book reviews were reckoned by publishers and authors to be the most authoritative going; the theatrical criticism, usually by Owen Seaman, was just as highly regarded. Seaman and E. V. Lucas were the judges of whether a contribution was good enough for the paper and Rhadamanthus himself could have judged no more sternly.

Mercer was determined to have a try. It was not only the money that mattered; having appeared in *Punch* would raise his status in the Bar Mess and make him something more than a nameless junior. He was in luck with his first attempt. The piece, entitled 'Temporary Insanity', occupied a whole page, save for an unrelated drawing in the middle, for the issue dated 25 May 1910 and for the first time the world saw the name 'Dornford Yates'. It was an excellent one for the purpose, the long preceding the short as in the Latin foot or hallowed fictional ones like Abernethy Pike. One is compelled to admit that the article was not very funny. In the days of the National Telephone Company crossed lines were a commonplace. 'I picked up the receiver and put it to my ear. "Number, please".

"Double it, add seven——." "Number, please". "What are the Mayfairs like this morning?" . . .' and so on. The heavy-handed teasing of men accidentally or otherwise brought to the telephone is nowhere near Berry standard, nor does the annoying of an over-worked operator greatly amuse. Mr Yates had still a great deal to learn. Lucas seems to have felt the same way, for no other *Punch* work over the Yates name ever appeared. Mercer tried once more, just after the war, but his offering was rejected. This was hurtful, but nothing could now take away the fact that he had appeared in *Punch*. It was a kind of nursery slope. The contributions of P. G. Wodehouse at about the same time are not particularly funny either.

The year 1910 was amongst the fullest in Mercer's life and it is convenient to leave his professional activities aside for the moment. His fascination by the theatre never left him and he became a member of the Old Stagers, the longest-running amateur dramatic society in the country. His friend Gervais Rentoul was already a member and the Old Stagers have a traditional association with the Bar. He was not the only man there whom Mercer knew, for Paul Rubens had been one of their number for some time and had indeed written one of the plays to be presented during Canterbury Week, the highest point in the Old Stagers' year. Mercer went down to stay with the rest at The Fountain, the splendid coaching inn that for the past forty years has been a hole in the ground, and joined happily with the party around the piano that always seemed to coalesce whenever Rubens appeared. Two shows were put on, beginning on 10 August with *Lovely Woman*, by Paul Rubens and Harold Whitaker. The text seems to have vanished, but the cast list remains, including 'Mr Frank Bailey, an Insurance Official: Mr W. Mercer'. The account of it in the local newspaper makes no mention of either. The second play was more rumbustious stuff, Stanley Weyman's *Under The Red Robe*. Gil de Berault, broken gentleman and gamester, is called out in a Paris pot-house by a young Englishman who has caught him cheating at cards. Berault kills him and his sentence of death is commuted by Richelieu on the condition that he undertake a dangerous mission in the Pyrenees. Before the duel Berault (Mr Rentoul) is reprehended by the Marquis de Pombal (Mr Mercer). Having observed, 'Shame on you, Berault, he is a mere boy,' de Pombal quits the stage. Berault has three acts in store for him. The local reviewer spoke generously of

Mr Rentoul's performance. Mr Mercer gets not a word. Oscar Asche's company were just going into rehearsal for another Weyman play of a similar kind, *Count Hannibal*. When it was presented a few weeks later Owen Seaman observed unkindly that 'I love to watch Mr Oscar Asche striding about in clattering armour with pistols in his belt, a sword at his side and a dagger lashed to what was once the small of his back.' Asche might have been thickening a trifle but he was in an excellent position to advise how de Pombal should be played. There is no record of Mercer ever acting again; for the future he continued to exercise the actor's habit of 'marking' people, in tube trains, in the street or wherever he happened to be. From these time-killing amusements sprang all his minor villains, Punters, Bunches, Goats and the like, for with such types London abounded. Mercer was observant, and he forgot nothing.

And so, day by day, he continued to learn his trade; the journey between Kensington and the Temple was easy enough on the Underground and by this demotic means a barrister was allowed to travel, but the custom of his profession forbade him to enter a third-class compartment. The work-places of father and son remained for several years within shouting distance of each other, but their intercourse was minimal.

Travers Humphreys was a painstaking master and he seems to have taken to his pupil. Crime of all sorts flowed into Treasury Chambers and there was work for the lowliest devil to do. Mercer joined the South Eastern Circuit at an unusual moment in its history, for it cannot have often happened that both the Clerk of Assize and the Circuit Butler appeared in *Debrett*. The former, Arthur Denman, was there as the son of a High Court Judge and grandson of a Lord Chief Justice of England, circumstances that weighed heavily upon him; he was a figure of a dignity so immense that it could without straining language be called pomposity. When he reprehended Mercer for addressing the Court with one hand in his trouser pocket the reproof was accepted with a becoming, if un-characteristic, meekness, for Denman had seen Great Uncle James sent down. Alfred Smither, the Circuit Butler, achieved his small piece of immortality and provided raw material that would be used in the novels of Dornford Yates. His little daughter Jessica had grown into an uncommonly beautiful woman and, being minded to make a career on the stage, she came to the conclusion that the castaneal name she bore did not lend itself to the purpose. Jessica Smither thus became Denise Orme, the star of Daly's, both bright and particular. Captain Yarde-Buller of the Scots Guards had been through the Divorce Court in June 1908 by reason of his adultery with the wife of the Colonel of the 12th Lancers. It was generally expected that the Captain would do the right thing, send in his papers and marry the lady. When, in April 1909, she read in *The Times* of the marriage at Kensington Register Office of Captain the Hon. John Yarde-Buller to Jessica, daughter of Alfred Smither, Esq., Mrs Atherton promptly issued a writ claiming damages for breach of promise. Sir Edward Carson appeared for the plaintiff, Mr Rufus Isaacs for the defendant; the plaintiff succeeded and was awarded £20,000 damages. Being both rich and disdainful she never claimed the money. On the death of Yarde-Buller's father, Lord Chilston, two years later, the title passed to him and Jessie Smither, as was, became a peeress. The unhappy Mrs Atherton, after several lawsuits and other mis-adventures, eventually put the muzzle of a shot-gun in her mouth and blew her lovely head to pieces. Smither, says Mercer, appeared to think well of him and they saw a good deal of each other. They had a common interest in the stage, and it is difficult to condescend to the father-in-law of 11,000 acres. Humphreys calls him 'a friend to every member of the Circuit, as good a judge of a glass of wine as he was of the likely length of a case'. He was also quite a notable pianist.

The Circuit comprehended the Assize towns of Maidstone, Lewes, Guildford and Kingston and to each of these Mercer was occasionally dispatched in order to consent to applications for adjournments or the grant of bail or some other unimportant matter. Humphreys, in time to become one of the great lawyers of his generation, did his best for him, but the scope for an under-devil was limited. Though his appearances on his feet were few, Mercer saw a good deal of the paperwork that lies behind the detection of crime and the bringing of the criminal to retribution. It is not necessary to go through all the cases he mentions in the near-autobiographies, but a few of them were so notable that they cannot be ignored. For example, there is the one which he begins to describe with the words 'A man of means dwelt at his country place'; he goes on to recount how the man was shot by an intruder, and how a suspect was arrested, tried and most surprisingly acquitted by a jury. Later on, another man, strikingly resembling the first, was arrested and acquitted in his turn. This is a faithful account of the affair known as the Gorse Hall Murder. It was tried by Austin Jones, J. who, many years later, told the story to another judge who passed it on to this writer. Nobody, including Mercer, knew the full oddity of it all. The first man had been out burgling and ran a false alibi; he was, in all probability, guilty. The second was acquitted largely, because someone else had been previously accused and eyebrows had been raised at his acquittal. It was dramatic stuff and went to fortify a theory picked up by Mercer in his OUDS days. Two men of strong physical resemblance, no matter how far apart in other respects, will act in the same fashion. It may well be that no scientific basis for this exists, but to Mercer it was an article of faith.

Edwardian England owned some very hard cases amongst its crooks. Mercer was in Court when the greatest 'fence' of his generation—possibly of the century, but 'fences' are shy creatures who do not boast of their feats—was sent down. It is hard to find anything in 'Cammy' Grizard that justified his existence. It was 'Saki' who first used the phrase, borrowed later by Berry, 'Waldo is one of those people who would be enormously improved by death.' The same might have been said of Grizard. It probably was, though not quite in those words. Grizard lived by terror and had a fine house in Hampstead complete with butler, carriage and coachman. In appearance he was the crime novelist's dream, a big, powerful Jew, dressed to the nines and well pleased with himself. The police, as he knew perfectly well, had been after him for years, but could prove nothing. No lesser villain would have dared to say a word against him. Mercer's account of the matter is that the trial was conducted by the Common Serjeant, Bosanquet, that Grizard was defended by Charles Gill, and that the charge was that of harbouring a thief. He asserts that the conviction came about, because Gill put an unnecessary question to a witness, Grizard's known enemy, who blurted out, 'I only know that he's the biggest receiver in London—and so does everyone else.' For some inexplicable reason the trial was allowed to proceed; after that, whatever the judge might say about disregarding what they had heard, the jury could not fail to bring in a verdict of guilty. As the charge was only a minor one Grizard received no more than a sentence of eighteen months' imprisonment. This was the beginning of the end for him. After coming out of prison, he went back into business and appeared to be prospering, though narrowly watched by Scotland Yard. In 1913 came the Great Pearl Robbery—the third in twenty years—and this time Travers Humphreys nailed down his coffin.

Mercer, who had no hand in the matter, describes the trial from the standpoint of an outsider and he was certainly well informed about it. Newspapers had made their readers familiar with the great receiver's appearance and reputation and it is a fair surmise that the good men and true summoned to the jury had his measure irrespective of anything said in Court. Grizard this time came before A. T. Lawrence, J., later Lord Trevethin, who had no hesitation in sending him to prison for seven years. Mercer was fascinated by 'Cammy', for he was a figure straight out of E. Phillips Oppenheim and would have made on the stage a part of which an actor might dream. He bears a strong resemblance to Ellis in *Blind Corner* so far as aspect and attire go and might have added something to Mercer's theory of similarity. 'Cammy' and Ellis were certainly two of a kind.

There was no lack of material for bad characters to be found at the Central Criminal Court. Mercer was present at the setting-down of the notorious Reubens brothers and tells the story, at any rate in part. Inspector Wensley was the model of what a police officer in a tough district ought to be. When the dead man, William Sproull, was found by the road near Leman Street Police Station in a pool of blood, Wensley and the constable who had made the discovery went straight to the house where the brothers were known to be and arrested them. Sproull, second engineer of a ship just arrived from Australia, had died hard and one of the exhibits at the trial was the front door, taken off its hinges and still displaying the bloody print of his right hand. Only Mercer makes any mention of one of the two girls who had lured Sproull and his companion to the house; 'for all her tawdry finery she looked what she was—a lady born', and how the judge, Jelf, observed to the jury, 'Gentlemen, this is a sight to make the angels weep.' There is no reason to suppose that Mercer was romancing. The story of Katharine in *Shoal Water* shows that his mind was affected by the fact that such things could and did happen. The screaming and struggling of the convicted men in the dock disgusted all who saw it, but Wensley was later to say, with truth, that from that date, 'robbery with violence grew unfashionable in East London and few unaccountable dead bodies were found in the streets'. Mercer greatly admired Wensley, as he did Wells and Jarvis. The criminal classes were terrified of him, but his dealings with them were dead honest. During the Great War he got into trouble in arresting a gang who had robbed a warehouse of furs. When one of them tried to make a break through a window at the Old Bailey—he did not get far—Wensley walked up and down in front of the prisoners shouting, 'Bloody foreign Jews.' He told Humphreys that 'I had just heard that the second of my two sons had been killed in action, and the sight of those young, strong men who could find nothing better to do for the country than make money out of stolen furs made me lose my temper.' Such were the men whom Mercer came to know, and from an amalgam of them came Inspector Falcon and the others. They were no imaginary figures.

He saw the trial of Stinie Morrison, another 'great big Jew . . . his hands were enormous, I have never forgotten his hands'. Morrison, like the others, lived on women and had a long record of violence. His conviction for murder almost justified the existence of the 'thieves' lawyer'; any normal counsel would have known that by attacking a prosecution witness he would be giving the prosecution an opportunity to prove his client's previous convictions. Such refinement went too deep for the knowledge of Morrison's advocate; he pitched into a policeman, in accordance with custom, and an interested jury listened to Stinie Morrison's record. There was little more to be said. With experiences such as these behind him, is it really surprising that in Mercer's vocabulary 'Jew' was synonymous with pimp, bully, parasite, thief and killer? It was not then regarded as an eccentricity. On the other hand, the King numbered many of them amongst his closest friends; Rufus Isaacs was a future Lord Chief Justice and Viceroy of India; but a few rotten apples badly let down their ancient race.

The prosecution that affected Mercer's mind far more than any other had nothing to do with foreign Jews and it began for him whilst he was still playing de Pombal at Canterbury. Travers Humphreys was the first to hear of it, without enthusiasm for he was enjoying a needed holiday with his family. Hawley Harvey Crippen was not one of the classic murderers, but August is a slack time for newspapers and they took him up enthusiastically; a disgusted cartoon by Bernard Partridge in *Punch* shows a mudlark plying his trade, bearing a board reading 'Home Life of the Female Prisoner. Full Details.'

and calling out, 'Here you are, gents, chuck us a few more coppers and I'll roll in it.' Thus the name of Crippen became imperishable.

There is surely no need to recapitulate more than the barest facts. Crippen—often called Doctor, because he was agent for some hell-brews called Munyon's Remedies—suddenly vanished from his home in Hilldrop Crescent, hard by Holloway Prison; his typist, Ethel le Neve, also disappeared. Mrs Crippen, according to her husband, had gone some time previously to visit her sister in America; later on he announced tearfully that she was dead, one of the few true statements he made. Miss le Neve moved in to comfort him, the neighbours began to talk, and one of them eventually called in at Scotland Yard. Chief Inspector Dew visited Hilldrop Crescent and told Mercer about it at a later stage. 'The moment I entered that house I felt there was something that shouldn't be there. And I was troubled.' Crippen insisted that his wife was dead, both then and on Dew's second visit the next day. On his third call the house was deserted and all the signs pointed to sudden flight. A detailed search turned up nothing of interest. 'Now what immediately follows Dew told me himself. So far as I know he never told anyone else—outside the Yard.' The substance of the tale is how he was still persuaded that all that remained of Mrs Crippen was there, in some overlooked place. A kitchen-poker was lying about and with it Dew levered up some bricks in an almost empty coal-cellar. There he found what he was seeking. 'If Crippen had taken the trouble to order a ton of coal, he'd be a free man today.'

On 25 July, the Master of S.S. *Montrose* wirelessed to London that he believed two of his passengers to be Crippen and the girl. Dew embarked in a faster ship and joined *Montrose* off Quebec. On 1 August the papers were full of the arrest and Mercer, his duty to the Old Stagers finished, hurried back to London. It was long odds that Humphreys would be instructed for the Crown and he was determined to be in on this act; very sensibly, for it might well be the opportunity of making a name for himself amongst the horde of nameless juniors. He had no status in the matter. Travers Humphreys was not Senior Treasury Counsel—that was Richard Muir—and Mercer was, as Philip Guedalla put it in another context, 'between the devil and the deep K.C.' He arrived in Chambers on the Monday morning and had the run of the papers until Humphreys appeared on the Friday. By ancient tradition he had established his right to a brief and it never occurred to him to think otherwise. Beyond question he and his master worked very hard, usually up to eleven at night. Crippen, inevitably, was represented by Arthur Newton. Only he could explain how he came by his instructions, but he got them.

The preliminary hearing was little more than a formality. Humphreys says that Newton took no serious part in it. Both Mercer and Humphreys went to Hilldrop Crescent, presumably in company, but each came back with a different mental impression. Humphreys was angry with Dew who had left a number of the exhibits intended for use at the trial still lying about the house. He also misled Humphreys about the evidence available regarding the purchase of the pyjamas worn by Crippen whilst engaged in the task of dismembering his wife. Mercer's only memory was of Crippen's toothbrush, 'with the toothpaste still on the bristles, waiting to be used'.

At the Bow Street hearing Mercer feverishly noted the evidence, a vexing job for a man who does not write shorthand, but he found time to watch the prisoner intently. Crippen had some medical knowledge and had poisoned his wife with hyoscin, then a little-used drug. When Humphreys used the name in opening, 'Before my eyes the blood rose in [Crippen's] face, as I had never seen blood rise into a face before.' As Arthur Newton was bound to fight like an unscrupulous tiger it was necessary to do a great deal of earth-stopping. The defence would be bound to take the point that the *disjecta membra*, lacking a head, were not proved to be those of Mrs Crippen. All the great pathologists of the day, Willcox, Spilsbury, Pepper and Luff, had been pressed into service, for a cardinal point was the identification with the deceased woman of a portion of her anatomy bearing an operation scar which would, in due time, be passed around the jury box on a platter. Newton would certainly enlist his own expert who would say that it was something else. Here Fate dealt Mercer an unkind blow. In such a case as this the Treasury always allowed a brief for a second junior and Mercer had the customary right to it since he had been the first to get his hands on the papers. Muir, by ill chance, had a pupil, Ingleby Oddie, who was a qualified doctor of medicine; probably the only one in the ranks of the junior Bar. With such a man at his disposal, and with the obvious desirability of having somebody to tug his gown should he stray into a medical trap, Muir cannot be blamed for prefer-ring Oddie to Mercer. He and Humphreys both tried hard to gouge a third brief from a skinflint Treasury, but without success. Mercer, though he puts a good face upon it in his book, was bitterly disappointed and furiously angry. The chance of a lifetime, the kind of case for which every junior prayed usually in vain, had been snatched from him by a freak circumstance. Oddie behaved well, as was to be expected of him, but the wound was a deep one and it never quite healed.

He was present throughout the trial at the Old Bailey, but only in the capacity of pupil to Humphreys. This at least gave him the opportunity of watching everything and everybody without the distraction of having a hand in the game, and his account of the trial is essential reading for anyone misguided enough to want to become better informed about the end of Hawley Harvey Crippen. He never forgave Muir; the only characteristic Mercer shared with Horatio Bottomley was a lack of appreciation of the skill of a man whom Humphreys called 'as good a lawyer as any of the Treasury Counsel since the time of Poland'. Bottomley, in *John Bull*, put it differently. 'As for Muir, how can anyone be angry with him? He is just a dear old Almanac.' He was certainly a man of immense thoroughness.

Crippen for ever afterwards stuck in Mercer's memory, though he was never given the accolade of having a character based upon him. Stinie Morrison, 'Cammy' Grizard and the Reubens were viler by far than this unremarkable murderer. Yet who remembers their names now? Equally, who does not remember Crippen? He came near to breaking William Mercer's professional heart.

Crippen's appeal was dismissed in October 1910. Shortly afterwards Mercer, his year of pupillage over, left Treasury Chambers.

4

The Floating of the Company

Christmas of 1910 found William Mercer in an unhappy frame of mind. He was free to practise his profession but he had no place from which to do it. The devilling in Treasury Chambers had brought in some small fees but his prospects were none too bright. In blessed ignorance of the fact that the world he knew had less than four years to live, he saw his future stretched in front as immeasurable as it was bleak.

Mercer was not without friends and his ill-luck over Crippen was common knowledge. Charles Gill, a highly respected man, offered him a place in his own Chambers, but the bulk of Gill's practice was in conducting prosecutions for such bodies as gas and water companies, dock companies and local authorities. Mercer had had enough of work of that kind, and he looked around for such broader horizons as the Common Law Bar could offer. He did not have long to wait, and it may well be that he had Gill to thank. Rowland Harker was moving from Harcourt Buildings to become head of a set of Chambers at 1 Brick Court, the same address as Gill but on a different floor. Early in 1911 he offered to take Mercer in with him, and Mercer gratefully accepted. Twenty years earlier the same building had housed a tenant whose influence on the newcomer was already making itself felt. His uncle had been the famous Mr Justice Hawkins, but he is better remembered by his two Christian names, Anthony Hope.

Harker's was not one of the biggest names at the Bar but he had a respectable practice and some of it would almost certainly rub off on the younger man if the clerk was worth his keep. There would still be a measure of criminal work, but some part would now be civil litigation in the King's Bench Division with excursions from time to time to Assizes in the four south-eastern towns. By the time he had paid his share of the rent and

65

the clerk's wages, however, it was not likely that there would be much left over. In 1910, Cecil John, insisting that his son become joint ratepayer, moved from the flat in Coleherne Court and into 79 Victoria Road, W8, off Kensington Road and almost opposite the Palace. There they remained for the next four years. It was a considerable come-down, but it could not be helped. William Mercer's actor-manager friends maintained a satisfactory flow of complimentary tickets and he was able to keep up with his theatre-going; this gave him the opportunity to become acquainted with Mr George Bernard Shaw's works, to which he took a violent dislike.

In Harker's Chambers Mercer turned his hand to anything that came his way. He mentions having once or twice appeared as junior to Edward Marshall Hall, Arthur Newton's favourite counsel, but gives no details. Once he was let loose before Eve, J., in the Chancery Division, a very close borough where a common lawyer stood out like a choir-boy at a coven. He tells of a number of famous cases in his reminiscences, but usually adds wistfully that he was not concerned, but only happened to be there. It was plain that something had to be done to fortify an income insufficient even for the most modest kind of London life. He had neither talent, nor inclination, for lecturing or coaching, but already he felt that he had it in him to write. *Punch* deserved nothing more from him, but there were other periodicals that might be worth a try.

Practically everybody who has expressed an opinion about Mercer's attributes has included the word 'ambitious'; there can be little doubt but that it was justified. The scandal that had done so much to poison his childhood deserved to be wiped away by the reputation of a man who had become an acknow-ledged success in some activity or other, and Mercer was determined somehow to make a name for himself. It did not seem likely that the Bar would provide the means, for competi-tion was fierce and the chances of an unimportant junior becoming a person of repute outside the Temple were slim. Practice of the law, however, was not a waste of time. The man who could write a lucid opinion and settle a complicated pleading with both clarity and economy of words could turn his hand to other writing without diffidence. Mercer's reading of the better kind of fiction published during the last few years had furnished him with the outline of some simple plots; his acquaintance with men of wit, especially among his stage friends, had given him a fund of amusing comment from which it was not too difficult to write entertaining dialogue. It was to this art that he addressed himself in the beginning. Hope's *Dolly Dialogues* and Conan Doyle's *A Duet With An Occasional Chorus* had proved palpably successful and they had had no followers. His own experiences in the company of men drawn from a rather higher stratum of society than his own, but to which he was set on gaining admittance, was sufficient for him to be able to tell of their doings and sayings without fear of solecism. As he was an occasional visitor to his old preparatory school, a fact proved by photographs, it seems likely that he took counsel with his old headmaster, for Alexander Murray had many friends in the higher reaches of publishing and would have been able to advise him. It can only be supposition, but the likelihood is strong that it was Mr Murray who suggested that he try his hand at a story for one of the monthly periodicals which were the nurseries of the aspiring young writers.

Apart from his reading, Mercer had heard many tales from his older friends about their own early days that might be turned to account. Oscar Asche had been a ship's cook, and when he first arrived in London he had slept on the Embankment, earning coppers by calling cabs. Tree had a talent for irony that made him one of the most amusing men of his day. The story lingers of how he once said to an actor, 'I want you to suggest—well, you know, don't you?—a cross between a whitebait and a marmoset.' His habit of pulling the legs of strangers was notorious and some of it rubbed off on Berry and his tribe. With his own magazine well stocked with such ammunition Mercer sat down and drew from it as much as he needed for his first story.

The monthly magazines, the kind made up of short stories and articles by authors of varying degrees of fame, were an established part of London life. Conan Doyle had begun his career in the *Strand*, but Mercer had no thought of running a rival to Holmes. A possibility seemed to be the *Windsor Magazine*, set up in 1895 by the publishers Ward Lock & Co. and generally well regarded. The *Windsor* and its competitors were railway children; their habitat was the station bookstall from which they were purveyed by boys in peaked caps with a kind of butler's tray slung round their necks. The *Windsor*'s object was to provide the variety of reading needed to enliven a train journey, and its public was immense. Many of the best writers were glad to be contributors. The stories were invariably well written; some were funny, others were serious, but there was a factor common to them all. The *Windsor Magazine* treated of romance, not the boy-meets-girl stories of lesser periodicals for the simpler orders, but lady-meets-gentleman in circumstances fit for drawing-room reading. Mercer knew as much about girls as he did of Chancery procedure, but he had got his will of Eve there and he could try again.

His first story appears, in a slightly modified form, in *The Brother of Daphne* as 'The Busy Beers' and provides much scope for uninstructed psychology. Mercer, an only child, had never lived in a family bigger than three in number, at least not since the death of his grandmother long ago. He had the good fortune to be free of sisters, but the price was an ignorance almost complete of the ways of young women, especially in their tyrannical aspect. His experience of life as it was lived outside a town was bounded by the caravan holiday in the New Forest along with one visit to Cornwall, and it is doubtful whether he could have told a pheasant from a kingfisher. His powers of invention, he found, were more than equal to the task ahead and amply made up for lack of personal experience.

First he had to invent a family and to find names for its members. Pleydel is so spelt in the first book, acquiring a double 'l' in the next. It is suggested that, as Mercer is known to have set store by Lockhart's *Life of Scott*, this might have derived from High-Jinks Pleydell in *Guy Mannering*. Since Buchan says that 'Pleydell was admittedly based on Adam Rolland for demeanour and learning while the "high-jinks" side of him was suggested by Andrew Crosbie, one of the heroes of the old Crochallan Fencibles', this seems hard to support. It does not sound like Berry. It may be mere coincidence but Pleydell-Bouverie is the family name of the Earls of Radnor, who owned Folkestone, and one of them was in practice in the Temple at the time. It is a right-sounding name and was readily at hand. Daphne, the senior lady, was almost certainly Ina Garvey's *Punch* creation, well-born, elegant, beautiful, nice and not conspicuously bright. The Boyes, Boys or Bois were amongst the oldest families in East Kent, though fallen from their knightly estate to being solicitors and suchlike. As to Bertram, there was a Bertram Mercer, son to Robert Mercer of Rodmersham, but the relationship if, indeed, it existed was distant. As well seek the ancestry of Mr Wooster. Mercer spent a very long, briefless time polishing up his

Pleydells until he had produced an identifiable tribe. His fashion of writing, not yet fully developed into anything that could be called a style of his own, shows traces of the influence of Walter Pater, who may also have provided a name for the cadet branch of the family; 'the late Dean Mansel (a writer whose works illustrate the literary beauty there may be in closeness, and with obvious repression or economy of a fine rhetorical gift)' suggests himself. One should not complain that now and then reality breaks in. Of the two authors of the *History of the Fifteenth (Scottish) Division*, John Buchan made one. In an appendix he names one of the artillery reconnaissance officers as Lieutenant R. M. Mansel-Pleydell.

Then he set himself the task of finding them a suitable dwelling place. It had to be in or near to the New Forest, for he knew no other piece of country that lent itself to his kind of people. It had to be somewhere ancient and it had to be substantial but there was as yet no suggestion of White Ladies being any more than that. 'The Busy Beers' tells us only that it boasted a drive, lodge gates and a stable clock, that the family kept a brougham and a car, that no inhabitant seemed to be older than about twenty-six and that all their parents appeared to be dead. In later stories Mercer warms to his work and White Ladies becomes, by degrees, something far more considerable. By the time of 'The Love Scene' the place has grown big enough to house, in addition to the family, seven actors taking part in a play; elsewhere you may find clues to its latitude and longitude: fifteen miles from Southampton and ten from the sea. To set to work with ordnance map and dividers would, however, be wasted labour. Mercer says very firmly in more than one letter to admirers that he had no particular place in mind. 'I am afraid that to identify any of the houses or villages I mention in my tales of England is impossible. Most of them are really composite photographs,' may surely serve as a sample. At the time of 'The Busy Beers' his family had not quite formed itself in his mind. Boy has an elder sister—'If she had not been the stronger of the two, we should have played with the same toys'—and a brother-in-law by inference a little older than she. Jonah gets a passing mention, but one character has yet to appear. Since Berry says just after the Armistice, 'little Jill is actually twenty-two', she was probably still at school.

The first story was of very high quality, quite unlike anything that readers of the *Windsor* were accustomed to getting for their sixpence a month. Arthur Hutchinson, the editor, advertised that 'Some magazines are devoted chiefly to masculine interests, others are frivolously feminine. The *Windsor* stands alone as the Leading Magazine for the general reader who wants the best work of every kind.' He did not often get pieces where the male characters regularly deliver allocutions that sound like a summing-up by Mr Justice Darling. 'It is, I suppose, not impossible that, although I am not actually invulnerable, my sterling qualities may yet be so apparent to the bee mind that, even were I so indiscreet as to lay hands upon their hive, they would not so far forget themselves as to assail me.'

The story follows the *Dolly Dialogue* pattern, much pithy talk but little action. Hope's Mr Carter, like Mercer's Boy, is a rich and well-bred bachelor though he lacks flirtatiousness and is exceedingly decorous in his dealings with the Countess Dolly. When Boy first addresses a girl as 'Lass' one fears the imminence of some Laurentian influence but none follows. The devout Mrs Mercer would not have tolerated anything approaching it. The bee idea may have been given by 'Saki', for 'The Story of Saint Vespaluus', one of *The Chronicles of Clovis*, had just appeared.

With memories of his limited success with *Punch*, Mercer wrote 'Busy Bees'—the original title—as a one-off piece of work and thereby he laid himself a stymie. The magazine version ends with a paragraph plainly meaning that Boy and Madrigal had been married for a year, for they were encouraging toads and named one monster of hebetude and gluttony 'Berry'. It would hardly have been seemly for Boy to engage again in his customary poodle-faking and a year was to pass before the next adventure enlivened the *Windsor*. Madrigal is not mentioned and Boy is palpably unattached. In later years Mercer found a summary way of dealing with characters surplus to establishment. He killed them off ruthlessly in air crashes. As 1911 was not yet ready for such executions he merely dropped Madrigal and left the reader to judge for himself in what manner she had met with misfortune. Two more stories were published during 1911, 'Punch and Judy' and 'A Drive in The Dark', later renamed 'When It Was Dark'. They were well enough received, but Mercer was still not an important contributor. Years later, in *Berry and Co.*, he marries her off again. There was no story in 1912. The first one had, however, been accorded the honour of line drawings by Wallis Mills of *Punch*; as most of them are back views, save for Daphne who is all instep-length skirt and bee-keeper's veil, they do not add a great deal.

Mercer was immensely taken by his creations. From now on he was able to lead a double life simply by closing his eyes. Then Kensington and Brick Court, with their unromantic inhabitants, ceased to exist and the briefless barrister became at once the young squire driving his high-wheeled dog-cart through lodge gates to the high-class orphans' co-operative called White Ladies, where the favours of young and lovely women could be had without conscious effort. The fantasy was harmless enough and went far towards healing the wound dealt by the late Dr Crippen. It was fairly clear that he had a talent for writing saleable work and he did not intend to neglect it.

During ordinary working hours he continued to haunt the Courts and 1912 brought him once more to the fringes of a notable trial. His friend Gervais Rentoul, as lacking in briefs as himself, had a stroke of good fortune. Amongst his friends was a newly admitted solicitor, named Mr Saint, with a tiny practice in Islington. One day there came to Mr Saint's office the Superintendent of the London and Manchester Industrial Assurance Company, who had a tale to tell. He and his wife had, of the goodness of their hearts, taken in as lodger, a Miss Barrow, a spinster of forty-nine. Miss Barrow had died rather unexpectedly, an inquest was to be held and Mr Saint's client desired representation. Saint, inexperienced in these matters, decided to brief junior counsel, the only one he knew personally being Rentoul. For a modest guinea Rentoul agreed to appear at the inquest on behalf of the witness, a Mr Frederick Henry Seddon. In the course of the proceedings before the Coroner it became painfully clear that Miss Barrow had died from the administration of arsenic over a period of time and that the only candidates for the part of murderer were Seddon and his wife. Both were arrested on leaving the Court.

This was too heavy a business for Mr Saint and Mr Rentoul. As Seddon seemed to be comfortably off they arranged that he should be defended by Marshall Hall, with Rentoul holding a brief for the lady. Travers Humphreys appeared for the Crown, led by the Attorney-General, Rufus Isaacs. By long tradition, poisoners are always prosecuted by the Attorney himself. Soon the prosecution found itself in a difficulty. Miss Barrow had been poisoned by arsenic, the doses having been administered over something like a fortnight. Nobody but the Seddons could have done it. The husband had got everything Miss Barrow had owned in exchange for a promise to pay her an annuity. The case seemed deadly, but for one thing. There was no evidence that either accused had ever possessed arsenic. This Travers Humphreys told Mercer during a chance encounter in the underground on their way to the Temple. Humphreys went on his way to Paper Buildings, Mercer to Brick Court; there he received a message. Rentoul wanted to see him at once. He knew as well as any man of the gap in the Crown's case, but he had a theory that he wanted to try out on his friend. There were fly-papers *chez* Seddon; was it true that these useful articles could be marinated in water and that a toxic draught would result? Mercer spoke of chemists' poison-books and advised him to forget fly-papers. The rest of the story is well known. Seddon himself had been the first to speak of fly-papers, telling his solicitor that 'the old girl must have drunk some of the water' in which they were soaked. Saint pointed out that chemists would only supply fly-paper against a signature. Seddon, as was his nature, knew better; he sent his small daughter to a chemist's shop to buy some. The chemist was having none of that and sent her away; but, it transpired, she had made another, earlier, purchase from another chemist. This clinched the case for the Crown. Mercer's version of it is curious, very different from that of Marshall Hall. He tells of Miss Seddon being a friend to Mr Saint's daughter and of how they went together to a chemist's where Miss Seddon spoke of having bought fly-papers six months previously—the date given is 4 June—and of having signed the poison-book. As her mother was only thirty-four it seems doubtful whether any chemist would have accepted the signature of so young a buyer and the date given at the trial was 26 August. Nor does the name of Miss Saint appear elsewhere. Mr Saint being just twenty-two, it seems unlikely that she was of an age to sign poison-books either. Mercer, admittedly, was writing forty years after the event; he seems to have muddled his facts somewhere. Be that as it may, Seddon was hanged. 'I ask myself what could be done with such a fiend except treat him as a poisonous snake at large or a mad dog is treated,' wrote Humphreys. There was little money to be made at the Criminal Bar, but one did meet interesting people.

It also left some of its practitioners with time for nobler things. Mercer began to devote more to his writing and he was beginning to find his length. White Ladies and its inhabitants were as much to the taste of *Windsor* readers as they were to his own and he began to develop his characters. Five tales of their exploits and their dialogues enlivened the magazine in the course of 1913, one of them—'A Point of Honour'—giving an air of permanence with the cry of 'Oh, I believe you're one of Berry and Co.' In order of appearance they were 'A Private View', 'There Is A Tide'—to become 'Clothes and the Man'—'A Point of Honour', 'A Lucid Interval', and 'The Love Scene'. The burden of them all is similar, but their backgrounds are not confined to White Ladies. 'There is a Tide' tells of a holiday in Cornwall, 'A Lucid Interval' in Munich.

All, of course, are illustrated. The earlier ones have drawings by several artists, but at the end came the celebrated Mr C. W. Wilmshurst. Either he and Mr Mercer never met, or the former did not quite understand that he was to be identifying the author with his creations. Boy, by Mr Wilmshurst, bears no relation to the Mr Mercer pictured on the back of his dust-jackets. He appears in various guises; in a Norfolk suit, with breeches and puttees; in evening dress; in a bathing costume. Always the sitter has the same appearance; something of a bruiser, with a Neanderthal brow, a big nose and a face devoid of expression save for such as can be given by varying the wrinkles on the forehead. If he is only twenty-six then he is old for his age. A man to whom you would entrust your daughter, and in doing so you would be safe. As for the girls, such as can be seen between big hats and boots, they look strong and healthy, every one of them fit to advertise Ovaltine. The interest shown by writers of the day in the female foot—'He glanced at her feet, being an old stager. She was perfectly shod', Hugh Drummond was to put it in his time—did not suggest unseemly thoughts. Faces apart, when neither shadowed nor veiled, there was nothing else to look at. Mr Wilmshurst's ladies would be good, if tiring, company on a long country walk; but they are to a great extent anaphrodisiac. Even Mermaiden, winsome in her 1911 bathing-costume, suggests nothing more than that she could give the rather dim-looking Boy a long start to the raft and still beat him by several lengths. Such was the style of the *Windsor Magazine*. Good, wholesome reading for young and old alike, above or below stairs.

Mercer, for the last couple of years before the deluge, led a wholly agreeable life. His professional duties were not exhausting, and he seems to have kept up his holidays abroad, probably with the help of the Dimsdales. One cannot trust the quasi-autobiographies too far, for it is sometimes difficult to work out whether the narrator is William Mercer of No. 1 Brick Court or Boy Pleydell of White Ladies. He writes of Madeira—unaccountably called Rih—and a letter written in 1932 says unmistakably that he had visited the place at some time before the war. Austria, however, he certainly did get to know, along with some part of Bavaria. The accounts of it to be given in the next batch of stories are fairly detailed, sufficiently so to invite derision from the travelled if they did not ring true.

It was not, however, a life entirely dedicated to the arts. Harker and his clerk between them kept him supplied with enough work to enable him to see something of the administration of justice in England. He writes knowledgeably of judges, though his opinions of some of them are not those generally held by posterity. There was Phillimore of the heavy moustache, the vermiform side-whiskers and the Puritan mentality; Eldon Bankes, whom he tells us to have been made by Sir George Lewis; William Grantham, whom he loathed so much that he gave him the alias of Weston Gale; Horace Avory, of the immitigable countenance, is held by most knowledgeable people to have been one of the greatest of criminal lawyers, but Mercer thought him a show-off, a view one would imagine to have been strictly his own. He greatly admired Channell, as did all who remember him, but his favourite was always Mr Justice Darling. Comment on this is now almost impossible, for Darling's wit came and went with the wind. Very probably a swift mind was needed to take it in, and an instructed mind at that. It is Darling's son, a distinguished cavalry officer, whose pleasantry remains. When invited to complete the customary form from *Who's Who* and faced with the heading 'Publications', he solemnly wrote 'Squadron Orders; at frequent intervals'. Blood will always tell.

The junior Bar had little opportunity of seeing His Majesty's Justices *en pantoufles*, but the chance came Mercer's way when Channell's son, a Harrow contemporary, went sick and invited him to go marshal with his father. The office was an important one, for the Justices in Eyre were formidable men wielding vast, if undefined, powers. The theory used to be that the Judge was the Monarch's alter ego, with all the royal power of a mediaeval kind. Should a subject so forget himself as to show mild disrespect to the King there was little or nothing His Majesty could do about it. Not so his doppelgänger. Any fancied contempt could be, and was, swiftly visited. A judge of the present time has told the writer of how, long ago, he went marshal to a future Lord Chief Justice of England. As was proper, the High Sheriff met the party at the station with his fine Rolls-Royce. During dinner he asked to be excused attendance at Commission Day for some compelling reason and it was granted. In the morning, as the Judge was making ready to leave, the High Sheriff's car arrived for him. Not the Rolls of the previous day, but a black and yellow Daimler, vast but of formidable antiquity and suggesting that it had seen service as a fowl-house. On being shown this, the Judge observed in a terrible voice, 'Marshal, pray inform the High Sheriff that if that object be not instantly removed and the Rolls-Royce substituted for it, I shall fine him £500.' As he would have done, had there not been just sufficient time for obedience.

Channell, J., and Coleridge, J., were men of different qualities. Mercer acquitted himself well enough, his phenomenal memory enabling him to get the long oath to the Grand Jury word perfect without crib. The knowledge of how judges spoke and conducted themselves off parade was to come in very useful in the future. When Coleridge invited his opinion whether, should he become a judge, he would feel able to order that a man be flogged, he did not understand Mercer's measure. For some crimes flogging was the only punishment possible and he would never hesitate to order it. Coleridge's mild rejoinder that he could never do such a thing as he would feel the pain himself, was greeted with contempt; unexpressed, of course, but contempt. Hanging and flogging were very necessary weapons in the armoury of the law. As Jonah was to manifest, the law was the least essential factor. It is improbable that Coleridge knew of the bond between himself and the acting marshal, but Mercer was painfully aware of it. In 1893 the Judge's father had sent the marshal's great uncle to serve a long term of penal servitude and had made some sharp remarks from the Bench in the process.

Small briefs in small matters in minor Courts kept him in trim, but in the course of 1914—or of such months of that year that remained to the old world—Mr William Mercer, of counsel, inexorably made way for Dornford Yates, author. By the beginning of the year Boy Pleydell had trifled with the affections of eight different young women; another seven were still waiting their turn. Mercer, as Hutchinson realized, had

75

struck a rich vein and there seemed no reason why it should ever run dry. How much he received for the stories can now never be ascertained, for all the records were destroyed by bombing in the last war. It was certainly more than the pitiful sums he had earned at the Bar.

The Bar, however, had provided useful training. In no other calling could he have learnt to write of the curious use of language made in Courts, and its proper antidote: 'Counsel wagged a menacing finger. "I put it to you that he did." "You can put it," said Berry, "where you like, but—".'

In the spring of 1914 the Mercers moved from Victoria Road to their last London home. No. 22 Elm Tree Road lies near to Lord's cricket ground, and Mercer took a considerable fancy to the place. When, in 1922, he came to write *Jonah & Co.*, he began with a dedication. It is to 'B.S.M.', the initials of his first wife, and it deals at some length with his feelings as he is about to leave the house for the last time. After telling of the study, the garden with the high walls, the birds, the lilies and the laburnums, he goes on to say that 'Nine years ago there was a farm upon the opposite side of the road—a little old English farm. Going out of my door of a morning, I used to meet ducks and geese that were taking the air. And horses came home at even, and cows lowed.' It seems rather surprising, but Mercer is at pains to give the address and he would hardly have invited ridicule from those who knew the neighbourhood. The neighbours, incidentally, included his old friends Oscar Asche and Lily Brayton. Elm Tree Road was a rung or two higher than Kensington.

Mercer avows more than once that he was always a slow worker. The magazine stories took a good deal of ingenuity and the writing of a new one every few weeks inevitably occupied the greater part of his time. Gone were any dreams he might ever have had of becoming Mercer, J., but the new world was more entrancing. He could tailor it to his own liking, and that he set out to do. His characters began to emerge as real people, for he had a talent for creation that has seldom been bettered. Boy, although he is the prime mover, is the least important; his goings-on are those of any young man of the day and his speech is that of the recently enlarged undergraduate who has been an active member of the Union. He arrives on the scene full-grown and does not develop as do the others. Jill gets a passing mention in the second story, 'Punch and Judy', misses the third, 'When It Was Dark', but appears as a regular member of the group in 'There Is A Tide' and remains unchanged for the next four decades. Daphne also has a consistency about her; the acerbity of an elder sister, mitigated by her other aspect, that of the elegant wife who controls her household to perfection. Jonah, during this phase, occupies a rear seat. His time is still to come. The master creation of them all is, of course, Berry. It is more than fifty years since I first encountered him, and the number of times I have read all of his doings and his disquisitions is beyond counting. He remains the only character in English fiction who can still make me laugh aloud. Many other people say the same.

For a writer to contrive a character or set of characters so popular that more and more is demanded of them is to make a rod for his own back, as Conan Doyle found out with Holmes. Mercer was always careful to avoid being led into absurdities that might be detected. When, in *Jonah and Co.*, Berry is invited to give the gendarmerie the date of Jonah's birth for comparison with his passport, he answers 'The date is December the fifteenth, 1885'. This makes Jonah twenty-two when, in 1907, he buys the first Rolls-Royce. A little on the young side, but no matter. As the years pass this makes him rising fifty when he is compassing the destruction of bad men in the early 1930s. Mercer is careful to put this right. Later editions of *Jonah and Co.* put the date of his birth on to 1891. By the time of *The Berry Scene* the damage has become irreparable and the reader must accept the fact without argument that Jonah bought his Rolls at the age of sixteen. Readers are not expected to be too clever by half. If they are, they must suffer the consequences.

Berry is old England. When he and Daphne teamed up in 1907 the things they did and the words they used were beyond calendars. One feels that it would have been much the same in 1807, 1707, 1607, or even 1507. With luck, it may be equally true of 2007. Berry is bone-idle, but he is no lily of the field. He is a thread in the cord on which the pearls of England and Englishness are strung. He gives employment to many, he is a conscientious trustee, a level-headed junior member of a bench of magistrates and a support to his vicar. There were Berries in plenty in King Edward's day, and in those of the first years of the following reign, but only one is amongst the immortals.

The *Windsor* stories are all much of a piece and to dissect them would make as much sense as carving a butterfly. Two, however, deserve mention. 'Fair Exchange', later renamed 'Adam and New Year's Eve', ends with Jonah reading out a telegram from 'Henry Fairie, the man I met at Pau last Easter'. The place name seems to have been taken at random but it will be heard again. 'Which To Adore' came out in the summer of 1914, by which time the magazine was announcing each story as about to be followed by others in the same series. Hutchinson had cottoned on to the idea sufficiently to have them copyrighted in America and for this one he invited Wilmshurst to produce a double-page illustration showing all the members of the Company. It is a good picture, for Wilmshurst was a competent artist, but one feels that Lewis Baumer would have been better fitted to bring out their different characteristics. Boy remains, as ever, more suited to the prize-ring than to the boudoir; Daphne and Jill, big-hatted and long-skirted, Daphne wearing button-up boots, are half way between professional beauties and health-food poster pictures; Jonah, natty in the elastic-sided boots called 'Jemimas', looks like Sherlock Holmes' young brother. Only Berry looks right; trim moustache, well-cut suit and cap-à-pie from Lock to Lobb. The pre-war gentleman par excellence.

The group likeness, however, is not a success for it has the air, at best, of a suburban tennis club gathering; at worst it looks like a collection of waxworks. Lewis Baumer's people in his illustrations to Ian Hay's *The Lighter Side Of School Life*, published at about the same time, are very much better. Baumer's men and women are unmistakably members of the upper classes and one can almost hear their well-modulated voices. It is better by far to cling to one's own mental picture of the young Berry & Co. and to leave Mr Wilmshurst on one side.

Early in 1914 Hutchinson, satisfied that he had found a man capable of turning out an inexhaustible supply of stories exactly suited to the magazine, took counsel with Wilfred Lock; the result was an offer to Mercer to have the first fifteen of the stories published between hard covers together with all the illustrations. This Mercer accepted with alacrity; not only was he saved the need to hire an agent—a genus described by somebody as 'men who are paid ten per cent in order to make bad blood between publishers and authors'—but he was assured of a wider public without any effort on his part. About the illustrations alone does he seem to have been unenthusiastic. Mr Wilmshurst's name is nowhere mentioned in the first edition.

His good luck, as so often happens, was balanced out by a stroke of bad. While the book was still in the hands of the printers the Kaiser got in first. It might be convenient to run ahead of events just this once and tell of the first appearance of *The Brother of Daphne*. *Punch* reviewed it on 19 August, and was kind.

Mr. Dornford Yates, whose name I seem to recall as a contributor to the magazines, has written a book of the most agreeable nonsense which he has called *The Brother of Daphne*. For no specially apparent reason, since Daphne herself plays but a small part in the argument, which is chiefly concerned with the brother and his love affairs. The brother, addressed as Boy, was a bit of a dog, and an uncommonly lucky dog at that. The adventures he had! He apparently could not go out for the simplest walk without meeting some amiable young woman, divinely fair and supernaturally witty, with whom he presently exchanged airy badinage and, towards the end of the interview, kisses. What distressed me a little at first, till I tumbled to the spirit of the thing, was the discovery that the charmer was always a fresh one, and in consequence that these osculations had, so to speak, no matrimonial significance. Perhaps, however, Boy recognised an essential similarity in all of his partners. He may, for example, have been deceived by the fact that they all talked the same sort of Dolly dialogue—light, frothy and just a little more neatly turned than in the common intercourse of mortals. You know the kind of speech I mean. It is vastly pleasant and easy to read; but I must decline to believe that any young man could have the amazing fortune to meet fifteen pretty girls who all had the trick of it. Still, that by no means lessened my enjoyment of an entertaining volume, notice of which would be incomplete without a word of praise for the illustrations of Mr. C. W. Wilmshurst, a favourite black-and-white artist of mine, whose name is unaccountably omitted from the title-page.

Wilmshurst was omitted for reasons entirely accountable, but one other person was not. The dedication reads: 'TO HER, who smiles for me, though I essay no jest, whose eyes are glad at my coming, though I bring her no gift, who suffers me readily, though I do her no honour. MY MOTHER'. A dedication merited, honest, and untainted by humbug.

5

Mars and Venus

At the beginning of August 1914 Mercer had been five years at the Bar and, although he had achieved no great success there, he had no thought of giving up the profession. His writing was beginning to develop, he had several more stories finished or on the stocks, and it is possible that had events not overtaken him he might in another year or so have turned into a full-time author. It is equally possible that he might have run out of inspiration, for his experience of the world was of necessity limited. Without hesitation, however, he put these things on one side and chose the man's part. His King and country should not have to ask twice.

The Bar, as a whole, did not show up to advantage in 1914. The young men, like young men everywhere, put on their stoutest boots and formed up at the recruiting offices, having first confided their practices to their friends. Nor was it only the young men who left. F. E. Smith, Major in the Oxfordshire Hussars, went unhesitatingly down the path of duty. Other Silks eagerly agreed to take over his abandoned briefs and to pay him half the fees. Of these only two, Marshall Hall and one other, kept their promises. If Smith's family had a hard time as a result—and they did—it must have borne a lot harder on the juniors. Many a lucrative practice started in a thinned-out Temple, to the disgust of those of its members who had gone off to fight.

It was not fitting that an Old Harrovian should merely accompany men into battle; it was his business to lead them. Though Josiah Dornford's brass telescope hung on the wall and Admiral Sam's miniature looked squarely at him, the sea did not call. William Mercer decided to fight his war on land and as it was not seemly for a gentleman to fight on foot he chose to do so in the cavalry. The only horse he had so far encountered socially was the one that had pulled Oscar Asche's caravan, but such obstacles could be overcome. The 3rd County of London Yeomanry had a good name and their headquarters were conveniently situated at Saint John's Wood Barracks, no distance at all from Elm Tree Road.

At the same time a young man of twenty-one named Geoffrey St George Stedall, far away in Trinidad, was thinking on the same lines. He had hunted from childhood and on board the ship that brought him home, he too learned that the 3rd County of London Yeomanry was a Regiment in which a man might take a pride. Amongst those he met at Saint John's Wood Barracks was William Mercer, eight years his senior but a companionable enough man. On a number of occasions Mercer took his new friend to Elm Tree Road where he came to know Mrs Mercer, Oscar Asche and Lily Brayton quite well; of Cecil John he has no recollection at all, for he seems never to have put in an appearance.

The first-line of the Yeomanry left early for Egypt and an additional regiment was formed in which both men duly received their commissions as 2nd lieutenants on 5 October 1914. The Commanding Officer of the new unit was Oliver Haig, nephew to Sir Douglas, and he had for Adjutant Dandy Beatty, brother of the Admiral and already famous as a trainer of racehorses. Their Squadron Leader bore an equally famous name, Algernon Edwyn Burnaby, late of the Royal Horse Guards. Burnaby, the Squire of Baggrave Hall, Leicestershire, and joint-Master of the Quorn, had had to leave the Blues long ago as the result of an indiscretion, and had meantime been a Captain in the Westmoreland and Cumberland Hussars. At forty-six he was a little elderly for the command of a squadron of horse, but he knew his business and was well-liked. Stedall, with his hunting credentials, got along famously with him; Mercer, knowing nothing of horses, found it less easy, but he marked Burnaby as he marked everybody who crossed his path. One need look no further to find the original of Hubert de Guesclin in *Lower Than Vermin*.

Apart from his new friend Geoffrey Stedall, Mercer found amongst his brother-officers an old one of Oxford days. Ellis Robins, the sometime Rhodes Scholar, was with the first-line Regiment and they met fairly regularly during the first months. How an American citizen came to be holding the Commission of King George is not our business. The new cornet's first duty took him a little time. King's Regulations, ever since the Crimea, had laid down that 'the chin and under-lip will be shaved. The upper lip will not be shaved. Whiskers, if worn, will be of moderate length.' This held good until after the battle of the Somme. Mercer obediently added a moustache to the rest of his equipment. It pleased him and he retained it ever afterwards.

Windsor Magazine stories continued to appear during the first few months of the war; 'A Bébé In Arms', 'Contempt Of Court', 'Every Picture Tells A Story', 'The Judgment Of Paris', 'What's In A Name', 'A Sister Ship' and 'To Seat Four', along with his one war story—in the October issue as 'And The Other Left', the tale of a drive in a car loaded with explosive through the German lines—in due time formed the first part of *The Courts Of Idleness*. Although Mercer asserts in one of the autobiographical novels that during the war he wrote 'Never a line. I had neither inclination nor opportunity', it is Boy Pleydell speaking. The stories continued until the middle of 1915. The last, 'And The Other Left'—its name was changed in the book to 'Interlude'—seems to have had its origin in the adventures of either Toby Rawlinson or Flight-Commander Samson. It could not possibly have been written long before publication.

William Mercer was not the only one of Admiral Sam's grand-children to see plainly what a man must do when his country is at war. Hector Munro, in his forty-fifth year and now a famous name in writing circles, did not want a commission, at any rate not until he had learnt thoroughly the whole business of an infantry soldier. When Mercer met Stedall at Saint John's Wood, Private Munro, H., A. Company, 22nd Royal Fusiliers, was swinging along the roads around Horsham, pack on back, rifle slung over shoulder and determined to stick out the full twenty-three miles of the route march. He did, of course. 'Saki' was that sort of a man. When he was offered a commission in the Argylls at the end of November, he wrote to his sister Ethel that 'I would not accept it, as I should have so much to learn that it would be a case of beginning all over again and I might never see service at all. The 3½ months' training that I have had will fit me to be a useful infantry soldier and I should be a very indifferent officer. Still, it is nice to have had the offer.' He had been in the House to hear Sir Edward Grey's speech on 3 August and had written it up for the *Outlook*. Next day he had joined up.

The 2/3rd County of London Yeomanry, once it had completed its tally of recruits, moved to Hurlingham in order to
begin its training. 2nd Lieutenant Mercer, as many a man before
and since, found himself introduced to the horse and under the
necessity of getting upon terms with it as quickly as possible.
Geoffrey Stedall, who knew more about the subject than did
most men, says that 'he could hardly be described as a horseman
or cavalry officer type. How he learnt to ride I do not know, as
he had no lessons at Hurlingham. He could ride up to a point,
but he had never hunted or ridden in point-to-point or played
polo or the usual things done by cavalry officers.' All the same,
he seems to have acquitted himself well enough to get by.

The Hurlingham year was uneventful, but one thing about it
deserves mention. Mercer was at pains not to identify himself
with Dornford Yates, the man who wrote romantic fiction. It
was not a credential that would have appealed to Algy Burnaby
and his hunting friends and, although he was mulling over in
his mind how to end the series of yarns eventually to appear as
the second half of *The Courts of Idleness*, he put the business
firmly on one side for the duration.

The use of cavalry during the Kaiser's war was a subject of
much argument. When the British Expeditionary Force went
to France in August 1914, it contained a strong element of
horsemen, the best mounted troops in the world; South Africa
had taught the lesson, unappreciated by other armies, that the
cavalry soldier must not only know his trade as a man whose
weapon was sword or lance and who must be able to get the full
benefit of the shock action of a cavalry charge; he must also, at
need, get off his horse, hand it over to somebody else, take his
short Lee-Enfield from its bucket and fight with it on his two
feet. Dismounted cavalry made up the only reserves available at
First Ypres and, lacking them, the line would almost certainly
have been driven in. It was, however, wasteful. By the time
enough men to care for the horses had been taken out of the
ranks the remaining fire-power of a few hundred men and
some Hotchkiss light machine-guns was barely half that of an
infantry battalion. The amount of fodder needed to keep the
horses in any sort of condition was enormous, but it was
unavoidable that a body of mobile troops be kept in being, and
no other existed. The number of regiments of horse needed in
France and Flanders was, however, limited and some other use
had to be found for the new units and formations that had come

into existence. Most of the Yeomanry found themselves packed off to Egypt, where their maintenance was less expensive and training facilities better. The 2/3rd County of London Yeomanry marched aboard the troopers during the summer of 1915 with no clear idea in anybody's mind of what was to become of them. The first Gallipoli landings had been made on 25 April; the fresh one at Suvla Bay took place in August. One or other of these beach-heads seemed a likely eventual destination.

Mercer, Stedall, and another Leicestershire fox-hunting man named George Herriot, shared a cabin throughout the long slog across the Bay and through the Mediterranean. It was a pleasant enough voyage in fine summer weather, little disturbed by rumours of submarines, and in those happy days unlimited drink was available at staggeringly low prices. Mercer and Stedall, both sensible men, appreciated it; Herriot did more. Everybody liked him, whilst regretting his inability to control his elbow, but there was no denying that he could, in drink, be rather a nuisance. They did not allow it to spoil their journey. Rupert Brooke had been dead some months, but his spirit was very much with them still. They were young, they had a good regiment around them, and they were going to war. There is such a thing as joy of battle; at any rate, there used to be.

They arrived at Alexandria and were soon encamped in the shadow of the Pyramids, with forty centuries looking down. The heat was something outside their experience, but Mercer loved it. He was always something of a salamander. The photograph of him and Geoffrey Stedall, taken at Ayan Musa on the Suez Canal, shows an unusual view of Mercer, sloppily dressed in 'muck order' and grinning like a schoolboy. Stedall charitably observes that 'We both look pretty awful. To be fair, he did look a little better than this.' Very rarely did the fastidious Bill Mercer allow himself to be caught off guard in this fashion. The sun was less welcome to George Herriot, who fell into a depression. Late one night he shot himself.

The Yeomanry Mess was a good one and Mercer fitted happily into it. The 'most popular boy in the Remove' figure is almost unknown in the Army and if a man can live in company for a decent period without incurring actual dislike, there is probably not much wrong with him. Mercer was cheerful, kindly, amusing and attentive to his duties. By the 'Yeoboys' he was liked well enough, though he did occasionally irritate them by an excessive pernicketiness over things that did not much matter. There is no guesswork about this statement. Geoffrey Stedall has a very clear recollection of it all.

Early in October came a signal from the Suvla battle front. Casualties amongst the Yeomanry engaged there had been heavy, the more so amongst officers, and replacements were needed. A party of the 2/3rd under Burnaby was detailed to go to Port Mudros in the island of Imbros and there to stand ready to embark for Suvla at short notice. Both Stedall and Mercer were included. On arrival at Mudros they were, however, not expected and left largely to fend for themselves. Stedall, a resourceful man, boarded the notorious SS *Aragon*, Sir Ian Hamilton's floating HQ on board which Staff officers were believed to live in Capuan luxury. There he had the good fortune to run into an old friend, Captain Alec Campbell, RN, of HMS *Prince George*, who mentioned that he would be going ashore at Suvla in a few days time and would Stedall like to come too. A luncheon 'like Claridges' followed aboard Campbell's ship, something that seldom came the way of a junior subaltern. Burnaby agreed to let Stedall go provided that he too was included in the invitation. Campbell agreed, but it would have been pressing fortune too hard to suggest adding another to the excursion. Bill Mercer was left to roam round the dusty island while his brother officers passed some interesting days in the trenches. In the event, no business resulted and none of them was posted to any of the units of IX Corps. They were well out of it. Within weeks the Suvla plain was flooded by torrential rain and snow; within a few more the evacuation took place. The party returned to Egypt and sunshine.

During this time their Regiment was encadred with others into a new Mounted Brigade, the 8th, for which work would soon be found.

The opening of a new front in Macedonia was the joint effort of General Joffre and Mr Lloyd George; Joffre, because he needed to find a job for General Sarrail as far from Paris as possible, Mr Lloyd George for vague strategical reasons of his own connected somehow with the rescue of the valiant pig-farmers of Serbia who had fought like Trojans and were in bad trouble. After some complicated arrangements with the Kaiser's brother-in-law, King Constantine, approval was given to the landing of an Allied force in Salonika under French command. The 10th (Irish) Division of the New Army was the first to go, followed by others and eventually by the 8th Mounted Brigade, in which 2nd Lieutenant Mercer had been appointed to command the Signal Troop. In a short time he mastered Morse and was initiated into the mysteries of the DIII field telephone.

The 8th Mounted Brigade disembarked in Salonika, a place well known to Hector Munro from his earlier journeyings, but to hardly anybody else, on 16 November 1915. It was not a pleasant experience. In the first place the numbing cold of a Balkan winter hit hard at men who had become conditioned to extreme heat. In the second, the campaign was not going well. It had followed the usual precedent. General de Lardemelle's Frenchmen had advanced quickly, walked into a German-Bulgarian army stronger by far than they had bargained for and had retreated hurriedly, the British element following suit. By late November a line of sorts had coalesced and Mercer's Brigade was moved up behind the infantry near Lake Doiran. Brigade HQ, where Mercer dwelt, was at a village whose name was pressed into service later. It was called Irikli. The place must have impressed itself upon Mercer more than upon others, for it is hardly mentioned in the histories, official or otherwise. Indeed the doings of the Army in Macedonia at this time are very scantily recorded anywhere and it is only from the recollections of survivors that one can gain any picture at all.

The Brigade was spared the experience of cavalry in France, for it was not sent into the trenches to do the work of infantry. Only Ward Price, the official correspondent, has anything useful to say about it. 'Mounted troops with headquarters at Kilkish were keeping daily watch upon the Bulgars and the Germans by Lake Doiran, and eastwards along the line of the Krusha-Balkan. I spent some time with them, going out with their patrols which played a game of hide-and-seek—the "seek" chiefly on our side—with the German Uhlan cavalry, who were reciprocally full of curiosity about us. A lovely country for the Balkans was this debatable land into which we rode, a region of wooded, irregular hills, from whose heights could be seen mile upon mile of the Struma plain, with its shining river on the one side and the hilly country beyond Lake Doiran on the other.' It was also hellishly cold in winter and as the weather warmed up it became infested with a virulent kind of malaria-carrying mosquito. Everybody hated the place.

This was hardly surprising, especially for a romantic. Mercer had come forward ready and willing to fight the Germans.

Instead of speaking with the enemy in the gate he found himself bogged down in a beastly country where no substantial
operation seemed likely; nor could any such operation have
achieved anything useful even had the means for it been there.
It was a pointless, debilitating business with no future and
never a word of recognition. By comparison with the Western
Front it was the poorest of poor relations. Geoffrey Stedall, of
the same mind, contrived to get himself transferred to the
Royal Flying Corps where more worthwhile adventures were
to be had. Mercer, in his thirty-first year, had no such hope.
He became wretchedly ill and the cold and the wet forced their
way into his bones. Rheumatism, that curse of armies, began to
work in him. Burnaby had long gone and the work of the
Signal Troop kept him away from his friends in the Regiment.
In the summer of 1917, just at the time the Army had finally
decided to give up the pestilential Struma valley, he was plainly
unfit for duty and was sent home. That was the last that Bill
Mercer saw of the sharp end of the war. A more miserable piece
of luck could hardly have been imagined. Out of things at
thirty-one, with not even a wound-stripe to show for it. The
bitterness he felt appears several times in his writings. Jonah
limps from an honourable wound, 'a present from Cambrai';
Boy, though never forthcoming about his war record, speaks
several times of having been kicked on the knee by a cab-horse
in Boulogne. There is self-mockery in this. Boy comes by his
disability in the most inglorious way possible. To be kicked by
a cab-horse would be bad enough; to have it happen in a place
so far in the rear as Boulogne doubles the humiliation. The
injury is still sufficient to disable him years later; possibly this
was a part of the gibe, for Mercer was plagued by his rheumatism for a long time to come. It is for Berry, however, that he
reserves the ultimate ignominy. Though he achieved field rank,
apparently without seeing active service of any kind, Berry
ends by being awarded the MBE. As Mercer perfectly well
knew, for he read his *Punch* assiduously and would not have
missed Owen Seaman's scathing poem on the subject, the OBE
and its derivatives were then regarded as disreputable; an invention of Mr Lloyd George and conferred upon some very
odd people for some even odder reasons. Soldiers asserted it
to stand for 'Only Base Experience'. It was all a part of Mercer's
self-flagellation at the unheroic end of his military career.

He was back in London, living once more in Elm Tree Road,

by the autumn of 1917. There can be no doubt about the seriousness of the rheumatism that wrecked him, for it was a time when
any trained officer not completely disabled would have been
packed off by the War Office to some unit somewhere; if he
were not yet fit to fight, at least he might be fit enough to instruct
or to administer. No such appointment was found for him.
Instead he was taken out of the Army in everything but name
and seconded to the Ministry of Labour in a quasi-civilian post,
manning an office. Though worse casualties even than those of the
Somme were yet to come and as comb after comb went through
the fur to pick out anything useful that might still lurk there, the
War Office never wanted him again. Once more William Mercer
was in a world but not of it. He wore uniform, he was given the
acting rank of Captain, but except when he happened upon an
old friend the Army knew him not. With every breakfast *The
Times* brought its seemingly endless list of fallen officers and
Mercer would have been more than human if he had not, once in
a while, given quiet thanks that he was at least safe.

It was not only officers whose names brought a pang. Before
Mercer had reached London, Lieutenant Josiah Dornford and
Admiral Samuel Mercer, along with Colonel Munro who had
seen the storming of Delhi, were joined by a kinsman. Hector
Hugh Munro, now a highly respected and trusted Lance
Serjeant within a month of his forty-sixth birthday, formed up
in the freezing darkness of the morning of 16 November 1916
with his Fusiliers for the attack on Beaumont Hamel. At 3 a.m.,
somewhere in front of Pendant Copse and the Quadrilateral,
up to the knees in mud, 'Saki', during a brief lull, sat himself
down in a shallow crater, leaning comfortably against the lip.
His last words were 'Put that bloody cigarette out'; then came a
single rifle shot. So ended a splendid life, and many empty
glasses were turned down. Mercer's grief for his admired cousin
went deep. As was his habit, he waited until the chance came to
write of him, in his usual form of semi-fiction. You may read
an account, partly coloured up in the Yates fashion, of a man,
forsaking his high position and of his own free will fighting as a
private soldier, within the pages of *Lower Than Vermin*. It was
Mercer's tribute to the man of whom he wrote in the dedication
to the second near-autobiography.

To the memory of that brilliant novelist 'SAKI' (H. H.
Munro) whose first cousin I had the honour to be. It was a

true honour. Gently bred, aged forty-four, Hector enlisted on the outbreak of the first great war. A very fine linguist, more than once he was offered a commission and an appointment to GHQ, but he preferred to fight and die a corporal, in the front line.

There come moments when mere safety does not seem a thing to be greatly prized. The year 1917 began with a terrible cold, the cold that bites into a man's bones. In France it was recorded that a soldier who filled his water-bottle with hot tea at stand-down half an hour after dawn found himself only a few hours later to be carrying round a solid block of ice. It was little better in England and it did nothing for a man suffering from muscular rheumatism. Nor was there much else to make life more pleasant. The U-boat sinkings reached their culminating point and food was shorter than ever before. The cold weather showed no inclination to go away; Bullecourt was fought in a snowstorm and it was still snowing when Allenby's men took the great bastion of Vimy on Easter Day. For Mercer, safe though he was, it was a miserable time.

He had gone off to war as an Englishman should, willing to endure certain hardship and prepared at need to suffer wounds or death. The ribbon of the 1914/15 Star above his breast pocket proclaimed that he had been no hang-back, but it was not pleasant to be young and unwounded as men younger still, many of them now conscripted into the Army, carried the torch forward to Messines, Ypres and Cambrai. He joined the Cavalry Club, though he seldom if ever visited it. The 8th Mounted Brigade moved over into Palestine and the 3rd County of London Yeomanry had at last a chance to show the mettle of its pastures. Colonel Wavell, of Allenby's Staff, put it into print. Near Gaza, on 27 October 1917, 'when the London Yeomanry of the 8th Mounted Brigade (temporarily under orders of the 53rd Division) held this line, the enemy suddenly attacked it in great force. The Yeomanry put up a gallant and desperate resistance. The post on Point 720 was overwhelmed by a mounted charge after beating back two dismounted assaults; only three of the garrison survived. The post on Point 630 held out until relieved by the advance of the 3rd Australian Light Horse Brigade and the 53rd Division, when the Turks withdrew.' Ellis Robins was there, soon with the ribbon of the DSO to add to his Star; Geoffrey Stedall was flying overhead;

one gentleman of England then abed must have cursed himself that day he was not there. He had borne his part during the black days and it was cruel that he should have no share when they turned to gold. In old age he was to write to a cousin that 'I am used to hard knocks' and of 'the rude philosophy that experience brings'. This knock was hard indeed and called for all the rude philosophy he could muster.

Having no place in the battle he addressed himself to the uncongenial duties of a recruiting officer for a civilian ministry, duties of which little trace remains. His leisure was spent in rebuilding old friendships and it was lucky that there were those about him who could take his mind off the doings of his regiment. Oscar Asche, his neighbour in Elm Tree Road, had gone from strength to strength in partnership with his wife Lily Brayton. Asche had long had a taste for exotica. *Kismet* had been followed by *Mameena*, *Mameena* by *The Spanish Main* and *The Spanish Main* by the longest running show before *The Mousetrap*. *Chu Chin Chow* had opened at His Majesty's in August 1916 and it exactly fitted the mood of the moment. Mercer, long afterwards, attributed its success to the facts that a war was on and it contained lots of scantily clad ladies. There was more than that to *Chu Chin Chow*, for it continued its run long after the war was over and its tunes are still amongst the most familiar in the language. Such things do not happen by accident. He can hardly have spoken slightingly of the show to Asche and his wife, for they remained on terms of close friendship.

The bad year of 1917 dragged on; whatever may have been happening in the world outside it was for Mercer a dreary time. At Christmas came the flash of sunlight when Allenby's men took Jerusalem, but for Mercer joy was mitigated by a further reminder that he was once more on the outside looking in. Nearer home, his beloved mother's health was showing signs of failing. By the New Year she was plainly very ill and on 10 March the unfortunate lady died in a nursing home at Dorset Square from 'inflamed uterine fibroid and cardiac failure'. Her son was with her throughout the pain-racked last stages and with her died the one woman in his life so far. Helen Mercer was only fifty-nine. Had she lived for a few more years this story might have taken another course.

Helen Mercer, heiress to some of the Wall family money, had always been the financial mainstay of the family. When

her estate was sworn for Probate all that remained was
£443 12s. 11d. It went to show to how great an extent expendi-
ture had been exceeding income for quite some time. Cecil
John and his son continued to live at Elm Tree Road, looked
after by the housekeeper Beatrice Barnham who had been with
them since 1912. It was galling to know that Helen's sister
Emma, still living at Coleherne Court, was well endowed with
Wall and Yates money.

Ten days after Helen Mercer died there came a distraction
that must almost have been welcome. After a barrage the like of
which had never before been heard, the new German armies
released from Russia began the offensive that nearly ended the
war. Every man fit to bear arms was rushed to France and the
finest-toothed comb of them all was applied to the Army's
fleece. Captain Mercer, still filling in forms, cannot have escaped
it and the fact that he remained at his desk while men barely
recovered from their third or fourth wound went back again
must surely put paid to the ungenerous suggestion that he
'skrim-shanked'. In April 1918 any man on the strength of
Home Forces who avoided the last round-up must have been
either a dedicated and skilful scrounger or thoroughly sick.
Since his old comrades continued to treat him as a friend it
is unbecoming in those who can, of necessity, know nothing
about the matter to hint that he was less than willing to risk his
skin once more. It may be convenient just this once to avoid
strict chronology and remind of what he himself was to write,
in an oblique fashion, about his condition. Berry, as you will
remember, was plagued by muscular rheumatism. It brought
him up all standing in Bond Street and it nearly broke down the
arrangements for the journey across France described in *Jonah
and Co*. It is commonly believed, largely by reason of the
statements made by Mercer about the autobiographies, that he
depicted himself as Boy. This is an over-simplification. In a
letter written three years before his death Mercer explains his
view of the matter. 'No, I'm afraid Berry and Co. are all
creatures of my imagination. As all the tales are written in the
first person, I suppose I have introduced into Boy Pleydell
something of my own personality. But all of them are, let us
say, composite portraits of people that I knew.' The man who
wrote of Berry's then troubles knew all about muscular
rheumatism; all the male characters, beyond much doubts,
reflect some facet of their creator.

91

The vacuum left by the death of his mother cried out for filling and it was not left long empty. At the Elm Tree Road home of the Asches, Mercer went with Geoffrey Stedall to a Christmas party and was introduced to a girl who was playing a small part in *Chu Chin Chow*. Bettine Stokes Edwards—she enjoyed also the name of Athalia, though this emerged only at her death—was an American and an actress. Her father, described as a captain in the American Army, was dead and Bettine, along with her sister Josephine had been benighted in Europe as a result of the war. Oscar Asche had been much taken by her skill as a dancer and had signed her on in his own company. Everybody liked Bettine; she was a dark beauty, lively, amusing and excellent company. She played a good game of tennis, was a devout Catholic and possessed an American accent just strong enough to allure. Mercer, his emotions empty, was captivated. The only person who seems not to have approved was Cecil John; with the end of the pause that had followed the breaking of the German offensive, it began to seem that the war might really end some day and his son would have to think seriously about earning a living before turning his mind towards setting up a home of his own. Apart from that, the Mercers and the Walls had always been strong Anglicans, and he had no enthusiasm for the Church of Rome.

The war came to a sudden end, just at a time when people were bracing themselves to endure one more frightful winter. The relief it brought was tinged with shock and men who had been for so long living on their nerves began to look about them and take stock of what was left. For years death had been everywhere and now that it was suddenly plain that many old friends and relations were really not coming home a kind of feyness set in. Barrie probably began it in 1917 with *Dear Brutus*; Sir Arthur Conan Doyle had made spiritualism respectable, so far as it amounted to efforts to communicate with the beloved dead. Mercer, still grieving for his mother, his cousin and many old friends, caught the prevailing infection and carried it with him for the rest of his days. The supernatural had always intrigued him; Berry's tale of meetings with the famous palmist Count Hamon, commonly called Cheiro, is almost certainly telling of an incident in Mercer's own life.

His demobilization was not immediate. His commission was not a temporary one but a permanent Yeomanry appointment, terminable only on resignation or the reaching of retirement age. In any event, he was in no great hurry to give up an assured income in favour of a blank future. During the first months of 1919 he remained at his desk, but there was time enough on his hands to begin writing again. First he took up the stories that he had left unfinished in 1915. His party of young people had been abandoned in Madeira and it was necessary to round off their adventures, later to be published as *The Courts of Idleness*. The manner in which he did it shows one of the compartments of his mind at work. During their mild frivolities his characters are disturbed by a sudden noise; the girls hear it as a ship's siren, the men as the explosion of a heavy gun. Time moves on. The men, conveniently serving in the same unit in Macedonia, again are interrupted by a sound. They hear it as a ship's siren, their orderly as a gun. A second later all are dead in the crater of a great shell. It was ingenious, original and slightly sinister. Hutchinson was glad to have it and in June 1919 the first part came out in the *Windsor Magazine*.

In April 1919 he was released from the Army and transferred to the reserve. He could, of course, have returned to the Bar, where work in plenty was available in a depopulated Temple, but he had had enough. No man, at the end of a war, can be quite the same as at its beginning; Mercer saw more clearly now that the law was not just an occupation for gentlemen, but a trade or business like any other in which a man must push and shove to get and keep ahead of his brethren. His ambition was to become a professional writer and ambition drove him hard. Muscular rheumatism was a thing he had to live with and it would be more bearable in some vocation in which he could work in a fashion of his own choosing. To seize up in court would be one thing; to suffer an attack in his own study quite another. Hutchinson encouraged him and he was not alone.

Oscar Asche and Lily Brayton were his closest friends and Asche plainly saw talent in the younger man. *Chu Chin Chow* was doing so well that he could afford to take a small risk with another production; he suggested that he and Mercer should between them write a musical comedy, which he would have staged in London. The ex-President of the OUDS jumped at the idea, although he had had no experience of writing for the theatre. On the whole, he did not make a bad job of it. *Eastward Ho!*, lyrics by Dornford Yates and Oscar Asche, music by Grace Torrens and John Ansell, opened at the Alhambra on 9 September 1919; the leading parts were played by Violet Loraine and a very young Ralph Lynn. Geoffrey Stedall, home from the wars, went to see it and his old friend appearing on stage in his capacity of author. *Eastward Ho!* ran for 124 performances and closed on 13 December. Not a smash hit, but not a flop. A picture of the scene aboard S.S. *Osterley* appeared in the *Stage Year Book* for 1920. Like the *Punch* article, however, it was not followed by another.

During the time that the play was in rehearsal Mercer wrote a strange little story obviously inspired by the long, dancer's legs and soft voice of Bettine. The tale appears in none of the books. It tells of Sir Richard, engaged to the beautiful Valerie; her origin is unknown and, on the eve of their wedding, she disappears. Sir Richard, assisted by a witty friend called Bertrand, finds out that her trustees have defaulted, all her money is lost and that she has gone abroad. He pursues her across Europe, eventually running her to earth, 'dancing for her bread' in a sleazy establishment in, of all places, Salonika. She is half starved but impregnably virtuous and all ends as a *Windsor Magazine* reader would wish.

The year 1919 brought a rush to marry amongst the young men and maidens who had been kept hard up to the collar throughout the war years. The *Daily Mirror* strip cartoon 'Archie In Search Of A Wife', the daily account of the exploits of a young demobilized officer in search of domesticity, was one of the best things the paper ever did, and it commanded a large following. Bill Mercer, disliking the thought of spending more days than necessary with an uncongenial father, caught the spirit of it. He knew nothing of women, less even than Boy whose well-built lady friends might have made up a platoon of their own in the Land Army. His acquaintance had been limited to a possessive mother, Mrs Oscar Asche, to whom he had been decorously attracted, and hardly anybody else. Bettine fascinated him; for her part, she was twenty-nine, unattached and only too willing to make a match of it.

On 22 October 1919 William Mercer, Captain, 3rd County of London Yeomanry, married Bettine Stokes Edwards, spinster, at St James', Spanish Place. Geoffrey Stedall was best man, and was presented with a handsome inscribed stick from Briggs in St James's Street; the bride's sister Josephine was one of the witnesses. A disapproving Cecil John stayed away. Bettine's address is given in the marriage certificate as the Langham Hotel. Almost exactly nine months later, on 20 July

1920, their son Richard was born. As the register shows the birth to have taken place at No. 6 Elm Tree Road it may be that the Asches took Bettine from the womanless No. 22 for her confinement. The houses were re-numbered at about this time. No other child followed. A neighbour, who many years later was to become Mrs Diana Barnato Walker, speaks of Bettine at this period of her life. 'She was always most kind to me and used to let me play tennis on her court. She was a tall, delightful person and extremely kind to young people. She was obviously very much in love with her husband.'

Mercer was plainly of the same mind, but he was in other respects not on top of his form. His father moved out from Elm Tree Road to live alone in Chambers in Temple Avenue, a biscuit toss from his little office. The *Windsor* stories continued month by month, but Mercer's future was precarious and under the pressures of poor health and financial uncertainty his temper began to wear thin. The Berry family, now enriched by Adèle-Bettine, came back into circulation, and his Egyptian experience proved useful in rounding them off. Early in 1920 Ward Lock put all the published tales, except 'Valerie', into another book. Mr Punch had been hardened by the war, for he was something less than enthusiastic about it.

> The main object of the characters in *The Courts of Idleness* was to amuse themselves, and as their sprightly conversations were often punctuated by laughter I take it that they succeeded. To give Mr Dornford Yates his due he is expert in light banter; but some three hundred pages of such entertainment tend to create a sense of surfeit. The first part of the book is called 'How Some Passed Out Of The Courts For Ever', and then comes an interlude in which we are given at least one stirring war incident. I imagine that Mr Yates desires to show that although certain people could frivol with the worst, they could also fight and die bravely. The second part, 'How Others Left The Courts Only To Return', introduces a new set of people but with similar conversational attainments. Mr Yates can be strongly recommended to anyone who thinks that the British take themselves too seriously.

It was not very kind, not very generous, and it hurt.

6

Early Days at Pau

The world of 1920 was very different from the world of 1914 but this was a fact that Mercer was slow to accept. The change that had come over *Punch* was symptomatic of the whole. New characters were appearing; the profiteer, hard-faced and obese, who had done well out of the war, but was weak on his aspirates; the ex-officer—invariably DSO, MC—working as a farm hand or chauffeur; the dancing-mad flapper, lightly clad and heavily made-up, the brutal-looking striker and the mad-eyed revolutionary. Most frequent apparitions were those of the New Poor, in the main men and women of Mercer's own kind. Most writers decided to lower their sights and to tell stories of people down on their luck. It was not so with Bill Mercer. The shell-shocked ex-officer, hard up but still a gentleman, certainly appeared prominently in his stories, but he was not the only kind of man whose adventures came to his mind.

The aristocracy had, on the whole, emerged from the war with credit. In a world of soaring prices, a fearsome housing shortage, much unemployment and a good deal of misery, he concluded that his readers would prefer to be taken out of themselves and to be transported to a gracious world rather than be told of the sad adventures of those much like themselves. He was perfectly right. Berry and his Company had broken surface again in *The Courts of Idleness*, but that was a hang-over from the war. In the *Windsor Magazine* stories that appeared later between covers he expanded his theme. White Ladies grew from a substantial country house into a genuine stately home, complete with Rolls, butler and the rest. Boy, a little old for a *jeune premier*, slowly retired to the sidelines and Berry became the unchallenged leader. His tricks of speech may read eccentrically now, but they were genuine period stuff. The style, somewhere between the Pentateuch and the Bard, was not all that uncommon. Kipling had started it long ago in *Stalky & Co.* and it was not peculiar to Mercer. 'Sapper', Lieutenant-Colonel Cyril McNeile, uses it just as effectively. Hugh Drummond, driven by his enemies to take shelter behind a sky-light, utters one of the classics of its kind. 'Here am I, even upon the roof, with a liver of revolting aspect.' Mention of 'Sapper' raises another point. Mercer after the war clung to his title of Captain, and for this he has been much criticized. A word of extenuation seems called for. All demobilized officers, provided that they had behaved themselves, were furnished by the War Office with a piece of paper giving them 'permission to retain the rank and to wear the prescribed uniform'. Not many took advantage of this but for some years to come the practice was not regarded as bad form. 'Sapper', the most Regular of Regulars, begins *Bulldog Drummond* with the advertisement of an ex- —and thus not Regular—officer seeking excitement. All through his books 'Sapper' refers to his hero as Captain Drummond. What was good enough for 'Sapper' was good enough for most people, but as the war became a more distant memory men accustomed themselves to their civilian status and became plain Misters. It was largely through the activities of a commercial kind by gentlemen whose claim to any military title at all were doubtful that the retention of rank got a bad name. During the early 1920s genuine Captains, Majors and Colonels abounded and nobody thought the less of them for sticking to titles they had honourably won. It was a lot more respectable to be a captain than a KBE; at least no money had passed.

The great triumvirate of the time consisted, in alphabetical order, of Buchan, 'Sapper' and Yates. Mercer always resented the comparison of his works with those of other writers save only for Anthony Hope, and the likenesses are but superficial. One thing, however, was common to them all; their women were not as real women were. The war had done far more for the status of the female of the species than ever did Mrs Pankhurst. Girls born in the last years of Queen Victoria had become familiar with wound-dressings and bed-pans, the driving of tractors and the filling of shells whilst their brothers broke the German armies. For all that, they wanted to become women again and not eccentrically shaped men. Skirts were shortened, legs became visible and few remained able to claim that they could sit on their hair. For Mercer also there had come revelations. Rather late in life, he had discovered sex and found it not disagreeable. Romance, it seemed, had for its background music not only the sob of a distant violin, but the cheerful twanging of bed-springs. The thought was, however, stridently indelicate and should on no account be hinted at. His young women might be permitted to drive cars, even to smoke, but there must be no suggestion of indecorum in thought, let alone in action. A glance out of the window at Richard's towelling garments drying on the line reinforced this. Babies, by no stretch of imagination, could be considered romantic. With one short-lived exception his pleasant characters remained obdurately childless.

The stories that were to be bound up as *Berry and Co.* all came out in the *Windsor Magazine* during 1919. They were longer and much funnier than the earlier tales and Hutchinson had found him an illustrator more on his wavelength than Mr Wilmshurst. Norah Schlegel entered more into the spirit of the thing than he had done, and her sketches show something much more like the Dornford Yates people of one's imagination. In a world of 'old beans' and 'old things', Berry and Daphne, Jonah and Jill, Boy and his current companion are all unmistakably ladies and gentlemen. There was more to the book than the invention of pleasing characters and the contriving of amusing situations. The style of writing, even if a thought pedantic, is excellent and the choice of words fastidious. Even now, two full generations after he put his pen to paper—which is exactly what he did—*Berry and Co.* is as fresh as the day it left the printers. The reading public of the time revelled in it; their grandchildren still do; very probably the same will be said by their own.

Mercer, from the very beginning, makes it clear to the reader where he stands and in what sort of company he finds himself. Every one of the eleven stories opens with a short observation by somebody, beginning with ' "Who's going to church?" said Daphne, consulting her wrist-watch.' Before reaching the end of the first page the newcomer knows that he is amongst top people, free of their company and privy to all their doings. One of them is missing, for excellent reasons. Boy had left *The Courts of Idleness* apparently engaged to Adèle and it would have been too much to lose her as Madrigal Stukely had been lost. To gain time, Adèle is packed home to America for eight episodes, leaving her swain free to continue in his old sad-dog fashion. I suspect Mercer to have borrowed her name from another American dancer of outstanding beauty, the Miss Astaire who was to become Lady Charles Cavendish. Be that as it may, her absence did not seem to affect Boy as the absence of his wife was to inhibit Richard Chandos. He made the most of it.

The book shows more clearly than most that Mercer was, in a sense, a literary Seidlitz powder. In the white packet are the white ankles of Miss Deriot, the brown eyes of Miss Childe and, more properly, the red, red lips of Adèle; Miss Doiran, whose name brought back visions of icy winds, alone is excepted from the catalogue of physical perfections. In the blue packet come the best of Berry's more caustic observations. Not all of them are of the highest quality, for at times he descends to mere facetiousness, especially with shop assistants and others who cannot answer back. The majority, however, have worn wonderfully well.

'There is no room in London. I never remember when there was. But don't you come. The air is purer for your absence, and your silk hats seem to fit me better than my own. My love for Jill is only exceeded by my hatred for you and my contempt for Jonah. I have much more to say, but I have, thank Heaven, something better to do than to communicate with a debauched connection whose pleasure has ever been my pain, and from whom I have learned more vicious ways than I can remember.'

Berry was not always prolix. 'I left a stud within the bath, and heard Jonah find it', is admirable for its brevity.

He thrives upon adversity; 'Twenty paces away was Berry, plodding slowly in our direction, wheeling a tired-looking bicycle. His clothes were thick with dust, his collar was like a piece of wet rag, and on his face there was a look of utter and profound resignation.' His allocution deserves better than mere samples, but there is no room for it all. 'Since I left this morning, woman, I have walked with Death. Oh, more than once. Of course I've walked without him, too. Miles and miles. I never knew there was so much road.' A question from Jonah gets short shrift: 'Foul drain, your venomous bile pollutes the crystal flood of my narration.'

The same man was to write, only a few pages later, of a visit to Oxford and an encounter with an old acquaintance of inferior quality.

'Hullo, Pleydell, old man. How's things? Don't remember me, I suppose. Lewis.' He mentioned the name of the minor college he once adorned. 'You were at Magdalen, weren't you?'

Berry acknowledges this to be so. As for Boy: 'Three minutes later we were exploring my old rooms in Peckwater Quadrangle Christ Church.' University College was not even placed.

There is more blue powder than white in *Berry and Co.* Rosy children and silvery laughter were for the moment at a discount. Berry is well remembered as a result. Many a man could still pass a fairly stiff examination on the Berry stories, though he might find himself unable to persevere to the end with some of the others. The Mercer of the 1915 photograph looks much like Berry ought to have looked; the Mercer of the posed studio photographs, smooth and well-tailored, does not. Although one can easily see him being icy to an intrusive Mr Lewis. Jonah, so far, seems surplus to establishment, a character brought in merely to make up numbers. His main quality is skill with motor-cars: before the war Mercer appears to have had some acquaintance with the famous racing car pioneer S. F. Edge. Possibly something of him rubbed off on to Jonah, whose time was to come.

In this book, more than in most of the others, Mercer shows both sides of his character. There is a story called 'Jonah Obeys His Orders' which demonstrates his ability. All you need to know is that the family has lost its cook, a substitute has been engaged in Paris, and Berry is dispatched to Dover with Boy to meet the new acquisition, Camille François.

> Dover has always worn a war-like mien . . . there is a look of grim efficiency about her heights, an air of masked authority about the windy galleries hung in her cold grey chalk, something of Roman competence about the proud old gatehouse on the Castle Hill. Never in mufti, never in gaudy uniform, Dover is always clad in service dress. A thousand threats have made her porterage a downright office, bluntly performed. And so those four lean years, that whipped the smile from many an English hundred, seem to have passed over the grizzled gate like the east wind, leaving it scatheless.

It is hard to think how this could have been better expressed; all of Dover is in it, combined with the feeling of life slowly resuming its normal tenor after the terrible years.

Boy tells of what he saw there, as they attempted to pick the unknown Camille out of the crowd descending the gangway:

> After fixing my brother-in-law with a freezing stare, his addressee turned as from an offensive odour and invested the

one word she thought fit to employ with an essence of loathing that was terrible to hear. 'Disgusting.'

Similar encounters follow. When all is done, Berry reports to Daphne.

'Pardon, madame,' he said, 'mais vous êtes Camille Franç———. That's your cue. Now you say "Serwine". Just like that. "Serwine." Put all the loathing you can into it—you'll find it can hold quite a lot—and fix me with a glassy eye. Then I blench and break out into a cold sweat. Oh, it's a great game.'

This snippet does less than justice to the whole; not many writers could come up with a phrase like 'whipped the smile from many an English hundred'—a phrase that economically conveys so much—and instantly follow it with such admirable fooling.

There is much of interest about *Berry and Co.*, apart from its content and the fact that it put the name of Dornford Yates on the map. Begin with its dedication—to Valerie, the unfortunate show girl whose fate Bettine might have shared had she not been fortunate enough to encounter William Mercer. It bears the date November 1920 and claims to have been written at Pau.

Many times you have found me at work upon these chapters. Often you have taken ill-written pages of manuscript from my table and, sitting down in a chair, deciphered them for what they were worth. Once or twice, whilst you have read, you have fallen into silvery laughter. Do you wonder that I treasure the sentences which draw forth such music?

It ends with an assurance that her name is not Valerie. 'You will know whom I mean.' We all do. The customers lapped it up. On the outbreak of war in 1939 Berry had been reprinted seventeen times—as near as no matter it had become an annual affair. Even during that war four editions appeared and it has gone on ever since.

Their first appearance in Pau is ill-recorded, but it seems to have come about in this way. Mercer was unhappy in England, partly because the inferior climate was deadly to his rheumatism, and because it was no longer a place in which a gentleman of slender means could live as he should. Many people were of the same mind. General Sir Horace Smith-Dorrien, the man whom Mercer described as being the best soldier of his day, was financially unable to live in his own country—the country that he could claim to have saved had he been that sort of man—as his pension would not run to keeping up a modest establishment and paying the bills due to Harrow School. He settled upon Dinard, as did many other good men. Mercer looked further afield, for the superior climate of the south was needful to him. The Riviera, with its shallow people, had no charms for him. Pau was quite another matter.

Exactly how he hit upon the place is not clear, but it was highly regarded both in England and in America. The Great Duke, possible sometime tenant of Wellesley House and known familiarly to Berry as Arthur, had spent some time there long ago. In the last months of 1813 his army had driven Soult through the passes of the Pyrenees and GHQ had spent an agreeable winter at St Jean de Luz, where the Guards had regularly held their Church Parades on the beach. Arthur, of course, had sent for his fox-hounds and had regularly hunted this most agreeable stretch of country; after the war, many of his officers had returned there and laid the foundations of an English colony. Fred Burnaby of The Blues—the Burnaby who had ridden to Khiva and died at Abu Klea—had visited Pau in the winter of 1868 and found it to be a fashionable watering-place for British and Americans with excellent shooting for snipe and woodcock, a golf course, good hotels and a drag-hunt with an American Master. A French resident, himself an old cavalryman, assured him that Pau was 'le Melton Mowbray de la France'. A member of the Quorn and the Cottesmore took leave to doubt this, but there was undeniably a Hunt.

The date and the number of villas once bearing the names of Southern States suggest that Pau had some popularity amongst ex-Confederates with little appetite for Reconstruction; their grandchildren were no less disaffected to the horrors of Prohibition. Mr Muirhead, never a man to exaggerate, assured readers of his guide that it was frequented 'both on account of its delightful and healthy climate, and for its admirable position as a centre of excursions among the Western Pyrenees. The sunniest months at Pau are December, January and February; and the autumn is usually delightful. The spring and early summer are apt to be rainy, but at all times Pau is an ideal resort for convalescents and nervous patients.'

There were also suitable literary associations. In 1877 Stanley Weyman, who likewise had been a barrister of no great renown, had spent a season thereabouts in company with his friend known as Henry Seton Merriman and had dedicated to him one of his best books, *The Abbess of Vlaye*. The man who had played de Pombal in *Under The Red Robe* would hardly have forgotten this piece of knowledge, common to all who read books as assiduously as he did.

With the ending of the Great War the Anglo-Saxon population increased hand over fist and soon numbered between four and five thousand out of a total of about 35,000. There were notable names amongst them: Haig and Jameson of distilling fame, Drummond Wolff from banking and the newly-married Earl and Countess of Cork. Everything needful to a gentleman's family was at hand, English hotels and tea-shops, preparatory schools, a choice of two churches and an American bank. Villas of good size were to be had at modest rents, servants abounded at the same low rates, and the cost of living was far below that prevailing in England. It can only be supposition, but it is probably safe to deduce that Mercer took his wife and son there for a short period in 1920 in order to make a reconnaissance. The place suited them well. Mercer could write all he wished in a decent climate and there was diversion enough for all of them. It only remained to find the ways and means.

Before Berry appeared in hard covers Mercer was at work on a full-length novel, a much more difficult business than a succession of short stories. Ward Lock had commissioned it, to come out first in the usual way in the *Windsor Magazine* with an instalment every month.

The idea had formed in Mercer's mind of a story beginning with something like his own experiences and then ascending to greater heights. This accorded with his usual habit; autobiography, if honestly written, says 'This happened to me'; Mercer's brand of fiction runs always on the lines of 'This might have happened to me', occasionally 'I wish this had happened to me'. *Anthony Lyveden* began with a stony-broke ex-officer who became a footman; it continued with another, driven mad by his succubus of a country estate. Mercer's taste for the slightly uncanny was developing. He had begun it with the second tale in *Berry and Co.* where Boy falls into a trance in front of a Queen Anne tallboy and sees visions. A brutal husband of the day when the piece was made beats his wife to death with a whip upon suspicion of her having a lover. When

Boy surfaces he finds the whip in a secret drawer. His fascination by old things, especially old wooden things, is pure *Golden Bough*. It would be uncharitable to suggest that it was meant as a warning to Bettine. An entirely pointless ghost bobs up for a moment in *Anthony Lyveden*, presumably because in one particular month his Muse had fallen back baffled.

Before *Anthony Lyveden* had got very far, Cecil John Mercer made his last appearance in this story. His life had been colourless and its last years unhappy, but his manner of leaving it was not commonplace. On a January day in 1921 he walked under a tram on the Embankment; and in St Bartholomew's Hospital a few days later he died. His will was a rather pathetic document, made the previous August and witnessed by a lift-attendant and a chambermaid at Temple Chambers. After a few pitiful legacies of ten pounds here and twenty pounds there, he gave all his estate to his son; Mercer proved the will in the uncommonly short time of fourteen days and sold the tiny practice to a Mr Jones. After paying the legacies he was the richer by some £400, for Cecil John Mercer had run himself dry. Had it not been for a legacy of £230 from his sister Emma who had died in 1914 (she left another £50 to Helen) he would soon have found himself penniless. Though disappointing it was quite a useful sum. Pau now seemed a realizable prospect and Mercer began to look around for a villa. In the entry of Richard's birth in July 1920 the father's occupation is given as barrister-at-law, from which it seems that he had some idea of going back into practice if all else failed. He never used it again. Dornford Yates, a person identifiable with William Mercer only by a privileged few, had become a professional writer.

Back in his study at Elm Tree Road he worked away at the novel and, as he tells, he discovered a new sensation. Short stories had demanded concentration from the first moment until the last and he reckoned six weeks as about par for the course of each of them. The long story, after he had written a few pages, took on its own personality and began to dictate itself. Or so Mercer asserted. *Anthony Lyveden*, however, was not truly a novel, for it was written and published as a series of episodes of varying quality. At the time its author was not a happy man. He does not seem to have had any noticeable affection for his father during his lifetime and Cecil John's manifest disapproval of the marriage, coupled no doubt with assurances that Mother would have taken the same view of the

matter, had been painful; then had come his sudden end, and
the discovery that he was a deal poorer than had been expected.
Add to that the lukewarm reception of the last book by the
reviewers, giving cause to wonder whether he could really
make a living by writing, and it may be imagined that Bettine
had much to do in the way of cheering things up. It has been
suggested that in 1921 Mercer had something not far removed
from a nervous breakdown.

In *Anthony Lyveden* he shows considerable interest in
madness. Colonel Winchester, owner of the Gramarye timber
estate that causes much of the trouble, goes violently off his
head, leaving Lyveden a Power of Attorney to run the place.
Mercer seems to have forgotten his law, for such a Power
would have been valueless on its donor becoming insane.
Lyveden goes very odd in turn, hearing spectral trumpets after
the fashion of *The Courts Of Idleness* and the gun-cum-siren.
The introduction of the ghost is almost insulting to regular
Windsor readers. A judge in his lodgings late at night is trying
to remember where he had come across the name of Lyveden.
To assist him there comes an unidentified phantom that gibbers,
blows its head off, indicates the whereabouts of a letter headed
'Rome', and vanishes from the room and the story. It has
served its purpose. Rome, of course, was all the jog that the
judge's memory needed. Though the description of the scene
could hardly have been bettered it shows a poverty of imagination most unusual in Mercer and suggests him to have been
under great strain. There is not a single peal of silvery laughter
in the entire book. Now and then the author adopts the style of
Bunyan, taking his reader by the hand, addressing him as 'Sir'
and moralizing gently. Could any reader have answered he
might justifiably have said, 'Sir, your hero is a pompous prig.
You let the side down by making the son of a marquis, an Old
Harrovian to boot, behave as an oick. Of your two young
women, one is a humourless, suspicious creature and the other
a trollop *manquée*. You can do better than this.'

There was method in it all. Mercer defied the *Windsor*
tradition that all stories must end in lovers' meetings, though
Hutchinson tried his hardest to make it otherwise. Lyveden,
mad, recovered, and mad again, strides off into the sunset. A
harmless man is left trapped in a forest about to be fired in
order to furnish an unidentifiable body. The heroine, distraught
as is natural, is left with the care of Lyveden's dog, wondering

what to do next. The only possible thing was for Mercer to write a sequel, and this he agreed to do. But not at once. Keep them guessing and they will want it all the more. The dog, incidentally, was the most important of the characters, for Mercer had discovered dogs in a addition to women and, on the whole, liked them better. Nobby, Tester and The Knave were all real. Valerie French and André (so spelt; Mercer's French was shaky in 1921) Strongi'th'arm were not. Having been given also a village called Broadi'th'beam, one looks vainly for the second half of the old jingle, 'Thicki'the'ead', for it is merited. But nobody can fault Mercer's descriptions of scenery; a little florid, perhaps, but better by far than those of any contemporary.

The year 1922 was a happier one and Mercer snapped out of his lugubrious mood. Possibly an unexpected accretion to his treasury had something to do with it. Uncle John Dimsdale, the banker husband of Helen Mercer's sister Mary, died on 23 February at a good age, leaving a good estate. It was proved at £33,000-odd and the bulk of it was left to Mary Dimsdale for life with a third part to pass on her death to William Mercer. Although this put no money into Mercer's pocket for the moment it provided him with an asset upon the security of which he could borrow substantially. Very probably he did, for a thousand or two would have satisfied all his requirements.

Money apart, it was pleasant to know that the old banker had thought so highly of him as to make him a co-trustee with his widow. As much later as 1940, Katharine Scrope, in *Shoal Water* was to tell Jeremy Solon that 'Cardinal only costs a thousand a year to run.' And Cardinal was a castle. A few hundreds would not only keep a villa at Pau for a spell but it would also furnish the means of getting to and from the place with Bettine, Richard, and all Richard's paraphernalia. Mercer bought a small car and learned to drive it.

From this sprang the series that would be made permanent as *Jonah and Co.* No gloomy woods, frantic proprietors, or grisly apparitions. Instead came a merry journey over the long roads of France with all the orphans of White Ladies at the top of their form and all written with the freshness of one who was discovering these things for the first time. Even those with an economical appetite for silvery laughter cannot complain here. Berry is struck down with muscular rheumatism but remains dauntlessly funny; Adèle turns out to be a skilful driver; Jill, the Barrie dream-child—the might-have-been—finds a suitable lover—an Italian duke with English credentials and an estate named after the 8th Mounted Brigade's old Headquarters. Norah Schlegel drew them all beautifully, and any *Windsor* reader still glooming over *Anthony Lyveden* would have been a sad fellow were he not cheered up by the Berries.

The background of the Jonah stories is strictly factual, for the Mercers were installed in Pau for the duration of their writing. The Villa Maryland—pronounced 'Marielond'—in the rue Foster belonged to Mrs Drummond Wolff and was available for letting. It was a big Victorian house of three gables, ornamented in the Basque fashion by small galleries outside the windows of the main bedrooms, with shutters to the windows, sun-blinds over the terrace and two flights of steps leading down from this to a big garden handsomely planted with trees. Mercer was enchanted by it. When, many years later, a new edition of *Adèle and Co.* came out he dedicated the book to the house 'which, with its English garden, made me a home worth having for seventeen years'. There he took into service a maid for Bettine, a bright-eyed local girl named Thérèse Caissa.

Jonah and Co. opens with a valediction to Elm Tree Road. 'Now the farm is gone, and a garage has taken its room. And other changes have come, and others still are coming. So, you see, my lady, it is high time I was gone. This quiet study has seen the making of my books. This—the last it will see—I make bold to offer to you.' Once it was finished (the *Windsor* version came out during 1921 and the book in 1922) Pau became their domicile and London saw Mercer again only as it saw the swallows. The arrangement suited him well. The climate did much for his rheumatism, the nature of his work was such that it could be done anywhere, and they began to explore the country of Bearn and the Pyrenees. It would be hard to find a pleasanter place.

The English colony in Pau was of good quality. If there were some of the new poor amongst them, and there probably were, their comparative poverty did not show. The English Club could have been moved to Pall Mall without anybody noticing and the Hunt was not dressed in ratcatcher. Mercer did not join it, but Geoffrey Stedall was a regular guest and went out with them on a number of occasions.

Another new acquaintance was the manager of the bank at which Mercer opened his account. Arthur Kennard was an interesting man in his own right. In 1907, at the age of twenty, he had gone to seek his fortune in Paris and there he obtained a post with Monro & Co., an American banking firm which claimed to be the oldest house of its kind in Europe. When the war started, Kennard, like the stout fellow he is, left his bank, joined the Army, and served with the ASC in, amongst other places, Macedonia. During the March Retreat of 1918 the manager of Monro's Paris branch, who, as a young man, had gone through the siege of 1870–71, decided that it would be wise to get the bank's money as far away from the capital as possible. The American directors agreed, and they settled upon Pau. Kennard, on demobilization, was offered the chance of taking over the small establishment in the Place de la République and, being in much the same case as Mercer, he jumped at it. The new customer was welcome, as new customers are, and as the staff comprised only a girl and an elderly Frenchman who spoke no English, he transacted most of his business with the manager personally.

Arthur Kennard, like all bank managers in small places, knew everything that went on in Pau. There was then no English bank and practically all the expatriates relied upon Monro & Co. for their cash requirements. Mercer kept only a small account for household purposes but he was regularly about the place in order to cash his cheques. As during his time in the Army, he did not talk much about himself; indeed Mr Kennard was unaware until after Mercer's death that they had both served in the same theatre of the war. He was always inclined to be formal in his address and far from talkative, but Kennard liked him.

From the beginning of their time in Pau the Mercers went little into society. This does not imply misanthropic tendencies on Bill's part for he was a long way from being idle. The book that you can comfortably get through in a few hours takes probably a year of the author's life to prepare, and Mercer was always a slow worker. On top of that, he was still a long way from being a rich man, though the royalties were now coming in at a satisfactory rate. Bettine, one may assume, was fully occupied with the infant Richard, although, being an unusually attractive person, she was in some demand amongst the colonists.

It was neither uxoriousness nor misanthropy that kept Mercer from moving into expatriate company. Armand Praviel, writing at about this time, was rather bitter about the 'city where money abounds' and spoke with some feeling about 'a rich English colony'. Pau, he explained, had trebled in size during the past hundred years and owed much of its prosperity to the English, 'a place which has been chosen for enjoyment by those to whom life has been kind'. There was much truth in this. The English and the Americans were, nearly all of them, well-off; Mercer was just about able to keep up appearances. It was not in his nature to accept hospitality which he could not return on a sufficiently grand scale and until he was in a position to match his wealthier neighbours in the size and quality of his possessions he had no mind to entertain. Later on, perhaps, he might take another view of the matter but for the moment he, Bettine and Richard would content themselves with their own company. Praviel's 'avenues lined with villas that vie with one another in beauty' were pleasant. It remained to be seen whether his aptitude as a writer would be enough to keep them there.

In *Jonah and Co*. Mercer gives the rent of a furnished villa as 12,000 francs, about £400, for a full year. He had the remains of his Army gratuity, the £400 that Cecil John had left, such small sum as *Eastward Ho!* had brought in and a settled expectation of money to come from Ward Lock. His temper had become uncertain, but the book could not have been written by an unhappy man. Berry was at his best in and around Pau. The description of how he sought to break and enter his own house in the absence of a key is amongst the funniest things Mercer ever wrote. 'Oh, and don't say "Work round the gutter", first because it's bad English, and, secondly, because no man born of woman could work round this razor-edged conduit with a hundredweight of drain-pipe round his neck. What I want is a definite instruction which is neither murderous nor futile.' And so on.

He and Bettine set themselves to prove the country of Bearn and they covered a great deal of ground even during the first visit. Mercer is always explicit about geography and you can still follow the journeys he made in the 1920s without much trouble. As it was entirely possible that his stories might come to the notice of people who lived there, in addition to the fact that he was a conscientious craftsman, he took infinite pains over his time and space factors. The tale of how Boy and Piers raced to Bordeaux in order to circumvent the abduction of Jill was not written down, so he says, until he had driven the course half a dozen times.

Biarritz, inevitably, was a place to be visited; the favourite sea-side town of Queen Victoria and King Edward demanded attention. It was subtly different in 1922 from the Biarritz you see now. He also walked around the golf-course at Chiberta, partly for the exercise and the company, but mainly to acquaint himself enough with the game of golf to write convincingly about it. He was not altogether successful. 'With a plop, a golf ball alighted upon the green, trickled a few feet, and stopped a yard from the hole. Presently, another followed it, rolled across the turf, and struggled into the rough . . . Putter in hand, Eulalie walked to her ball—the far one—and turned her back to me. After a little consideration, she holed out.' It may, of course, have been that her mind was on other things and that a benevolent Providence lent loft to her putter. On the whole, Dr Johnson's explanation is the more likely: 'Ignorance, ma'am, pure ignorance.' Solecisms of this kind are not often found in Mercer's work.

There is nothing wrong with the description of boxing. Jonah's demolition job upon an ignoble Spaniard was written right enough by the man who had seen Hopley go to work at Harrow. And there can be no questioning the identity of those excellent hotels, the Grande Monarque at Chartres and the Univers at Tours. Like so many of his countrymen in the years after the war, Mercer had a great affection for France and the French. As it had been with the Bar, this made it all the harder in later years to accept that a change had come over everybody. His flirtation began in 1920 and lasted for twenty years. Oddly enough it did not extend to his command of the language; he never got much beyond School Certificate standard, with credit.

Jonah was as successful as *Berry* had been and the *Windsor* cried out for more. It had to wait. Not only was it too much to ask that, by putting a shilling in the slot and pulling a handle, a new Berry story would drop on to the plate, but there was unfinished business to be cleared up. Between the time that Anthony Lyveden had walked off into the sunset and the moment when some right-minded person put a match to Gramarye, William Mercer underwent a sort of conversion. This was brought about in unlikely fashion, by the chance reading of an article in the *Spectator*; the drift of it was that a man who wrote less well than his talent permitted ought to be ashamed of himself. This Mercer took very much to heart. There had been nothing wrong with the quality of his prose so far, but he took it into his head that it lacked *gravitas*. This is a commodity not commonly reckoned needful or even desirable in the lightweight kind of book that he affected but Mercer determined that thenceforth his work must be heavier.

The first-fruits of this appear in *Valerie French*; for practical purposes it is the second volume of *Anthony Lyveden*, but the style differs from that in the earlier work. For one thing, Mercer decided that he would revive an abandoned form of syntax. He much admired Fowler, not only because he was the greatest living master of language, but also because, in 1914, he had dropped everything at the age of forty-one, got himself into a fighting battalion in France before First Ypres and after that had been removed to the Labour Corps on grounds of age. Banished there, Fowler simply made his own way back to the line, from which he had to be almost forcibly removed before being returned to civil life. In *The King's English*, published in 1906, Fowler had said flatly that 'the systematic use of the colon had died out with the decay of formal periods'. This, to Mercer's mind, was the casting away of a precious heritage and he set himself to put matters right. *Valerie French* is peppered with colons and formal periods. It also introduces Mercer's trademark, the word More, standing alone between periods. Now and then comes a variation. Worse. Whether or not this was an improvement on his old style must be a matter of opinion.

Valerie French is the tale of two young women in love with the same man. It has longueurs during which their complicated states of mind are analysed. Lyveden is an austere character to whom it is impossible to warm; the same might be said of Miss French. She goes into love as people go into shock and comes out of it again on the strength of seeing her man going innocently for a walk with another woman employed in the same house. The character of Sir Andrew Plague, an equally unreal figure, possibly represents something of what Mercer wished himself to have been. He is the greatest lawyer of his day; although he has nothing to say about a freakish will which left a great estate to Lyveden upon the condition that he should be awarded a knighthood or better. The likelihood of a Court upholding a proviso so odd is arguable; in 1920 the practical advice would have been to seek out Mr Maundy Gregory who, as everybody knew, had ways of acquiring for clients any sort of title for an appropriate fee. Plague, a huge man, appears in a magistrates' Court, without a Junior, and is overbearing, rude, not entirely honest and deserving of being turned out with a report to his Benchers in his pocket. He treats his servants, and anybody else who will stand for it, with abuse and violence. All this is because his childhood was unhappy. Mercer admired his creation enough to marry him to a lady called after his own grandmother, Harriet. The other characters are the dotty Colonel Winchester, the neurotic Miss Strongi'th'arm who loves Lyveden, cannot have him and so decides to marry the other, and a dog. Mercer appears to have preferred the dog to any of them and he was probably right. Hutchinson was not enthusiastic. Subsequent readers, though by no means all of them, have shared his view; Mercer was capable of better than this. The seams show too clearly where episodes have been padded out by moralizing and made to fit the space required. Stitched together, they still do not read as a consecutive whole. Cardinal Forest was an old acquaintance, Monsignor George Dixon. It was a pity to waste him, but the Cardinal's part in the business was so slight that he must be regarded as make-weight.

George Dixon deserves a mention, for he appears to have made a considerable impression upon Mercer. One must take it on trust that the name is real; the man certainly was. When the son of a High Anglican mother observes that 'although I am not a Roman Catholic [I feel] that Monseigneur Dixon would have greatly distinguished the English Catholic Church', it is a compliment worth having. Mercer recounts as fact a story about him; it is almost certainly true since there could have been no object in inventing it. A scoundrel sent a telegram in Dixon's name to a rich woman, requesting that she cable him money because he had been robbed. The address given was that of a tobacconist near Waterloo. Dixon lived in Rome ('Pius the Tenth used to call him *Dixon meus*') but by a fluke he was wandering in the neighbourhood of the shop, waiting for his train to Southampton after a home visit, at the time the telegram was sent. The point of the story was that coincidence knows no limits; but it also suggests that Mercer had one priestly friend high in the councils of the Vatican. The coincidence theme (a favourite one with Mercer) was expanded by the fact that the scoundrel suspected of having sent the request turned out to be indistinguishable in appearance from the other scoundrel who had actually sent it.

There is a theory, to which some readers subscribe, that authors tend to grow into the characters they create; another school holds that the characters grow out of the authors.

Which of these applied to Mercer in the early 1920s is an open
question, but there can be little doubt that he identified himself
in some sort with Sir Andrew Plague. Geoffrey Stedall, visiting
Maryland for the hunting, was witness to it. On a non-hunting
morning, whilst making a leisurely toilet, he heard blows and
yells coming from some lower region in the house and felt himself
under the necessity of investigating. He arrived in the breakfast
room, dressing-gowned and unshaven, to see the furious figure
of his host standing with raised fist over the cringing body of one
of the young male servants. At his appearance Mercer cooled
down and explained; on the wall hung a water-colour of great
value to him; time and again he had given orders that the curtains
must at all times be so adjusted that sunlight was never permitted
to fall upon it; his instructions had been disregarded, the picture
was being ruined and, naturally, he had chastised the culprit. In
the household of Sir Andrew Plague such an occurrence would
have been regarded as no more than Pretty Fanny's Way, and
the master would have been rewarded with greater devotion
than ever. The uninstructed, indisciplined French, lacking any
proper tradition of service, took another view of the matter.
Next day a deputation of friends and relations presented itself at
the door demanding reparation. Mercer was obliged to eat a lot
of mud and to dip into his pocket in order to extricate himself.
The story is told that he was hauled in front of a magistrate and
behaved abjectly with a plea of suffering still from shell-shock.
Stedall knows nothing of this and the tale was put about many
years later by Mercer's avowed enemies. All the same Miss
Carson, the governess in *Lower Than Vermin*, would have
taken him sharply to task.

Mercer's fits of temper seem to have begun at about this time.
At the Bar the advocate who is not in control of his emotions had
better find some other employment; in the Army any officer
who strikes a soldier—something almost unheard of—will be
broken without hesitation or sympathy by court martial. In the
old Mercer household any such nasty exhibition would have
been sharply visited by Helen, indulgent though she had always
been to her only child. A sudden falling away of the chains of
discipline affected many ex-servicemen, but most of them soon
got over it. Mercer never did. So long as things went his way he
would be cheerful, amusing and the best of company. Were he
to be crossed, especially by anybody owing allegiance to him in
some form, he would explode like an elderly Poona colonel in a

Punch cartoon. It was not an endearing trait, but it was as much a part of the man as the shape of his ears. An elder sister—Daphne for instance—would have knocked it out of him long ago; so would a subalterns' court martial. A pity for everybody that these advantages had been denied him.

Within limits he could indulge his tempers at Pau, but his visits to London over matters of publishing and the like denied him such a luxury. His friend Ellis Robins ended, for the time being, his Army career as Assistant Provost Marshal in Egypt; from there it was a natural transition to his next job, the secretaryship of the Conservative Club at 74 St James's Street. Mercer became a member, for it was convenient to have a place in London at which to stay; he was, he says, by far the youngest of its inhabitants. It was like the house of a duke, with the duke lying dead upstairs. More than one member had seen a real duke's cortege passing along St James's Street in 1852. It made a useful background for books still unwritten.

Mercer set great store by his possessions and never sat lightly to them. Elm Tree Road had been well furnished with Wall and Mercer and Dornford heirlooms. When his Aunt Emma died in 1929 the great carved desk, made to the order of an eighteenth-century Yates, was transported to Pau along with pastel of Sam in uniform and the brass telescope whipped with yarn that had so often been tucked under the arm of Lieutenant Josiah Dornford; the pictures, the furnishings and above all the books, every article as treasured as any reliquary, were housed and exhibited to best advantage. The Mercers lived well and, as they became richer, they lived expansively. Nothing but the best would serve. Mercer's shirts were of silk and made for him in London, as were his shoes from Lobbs and his suits from Sundon & Co. in Saville Row. Like an earlier Ian Fleming he brings them into his stories but, as advertising was still in its infancy, under faint disguises. Nobb hides nothing; nor does Tendon & Co. The only trade-names permitted needed no puffing; Rolls-Royce motor cars and Cooper's Oxford marmalade. Curiously enough, Mercer never owned a Rolls. He did mention to Arthur Kennard that he had tried one, but found it difficult to drive. As the next best thing, as soon as he could run to something more opulent than his small Ford, he settled on the big open Delage, a marque to which he remained faithful.

On the face of things, Captain Mercer had everything that ought to have fitted him naturally and easily into Pau society.

114

He had been educated as a gentleman, his war record was respectable if not distinguished, he had an admiral in the family and a beautiful wife. Pau was a popular holiday place for the theatrical set, some of whom he knew already. Matheson Lang and his wife were regular visitors; Mrs Patrick Campbell and her pug Moonbeam—detested by all who met him—sometimes took a villa there for the winter. For Mercer her theatrical eminence was almost cancelled out by her friendship for the loathed and despised Bernard Shaw, but they certainly met. Against this, the interests of Pau were sporting rather than dramatic. The Hunt, the Golf Club and a Flying Club the oldest in Europe—it had been started by Orville Wright and continued by Blériot—were the hub of things. Mercer neither hunted, golfed, flew, shot nor fished. These deficiencies naturally made him an object of limited interest to many of the men. His claim to recognition lay in his writings, and it was something that he did not press. His standard of personal behaviour might permit him to thump a careless servant; to stand with his back to the bar in the Cercle Anglais and announce to any possible audience: 'I am Dornford Yates, the quite-famous novelist. You must surely have heard of me,' was quite another. His almost pathological dislike of publicity was entirely genuine and entirely to his credit. It would have been easy enough to spread the news abroad more subtly, but to such things he would not stoop. In all probability he would have been pleased had the recognition come spontaneously, but it never did. As Pau society rarely encountered him in its favourite places it did not go out of its way to seek his company.

Bettine was quite another matter. Her Catholicism was more than skin-deep, she attended Mass punctiliously and regularly made her confession, though her sins must have been venial enough. By this means, and because she possessed great personal charm, spoke good idiomatic French and played an excellent game of tennis, she became popular in her own right with both the women and the men. Unlike her husband she was willing enough to meet the French on their own ground, and they appear to have liked her. This Mercer resented, for his own friends were still limited to such as his bank manager, Mr Carter who kept the gentlemen's outfitters called 'Old England', and Lord and Lady Cork. His leisure time was limited, for writing kept him hard at work. It was his habit to set down everything in careful longhand and then, as each section was completed, to transcribe it slowly and laboriously on his typewriter; then came the correcting, the cutting, the expanding and the re-writing. Mornings were passed in this fashion within the walls of his library and once immured it was well known in the household that the master must on no account be disturbed. The dog of the moment, Sealyham or Alsatian, usually drowsed beside him; dogs were now an important part of his life, and he was seldom seen without one in his company. Should Bettine desire to share the room with him, as she often did, she was welcome enough on the clear understanding that she sat quietly and got on with her knitting or with whatever other female task happened to be engaging her attention. They walked and they drove and they acquired an encyclopaedic knowledge of the Basses Pyrenées. But they did not go much together into society. For a young woman of active habit it became thoroughly boring.

Superficially, there was little of the author about Mercer. His dress and turn-out were always impeccable, his linen without spot and his address formal. The writing of books has the great advantage that it can be carried on with a minimum of intercourse with people other than publishers. Mercer found his own company, together with that of his wife and son, entirely sufficient and he needed no other, except for his dogs. He became a keen and knowledgeable naturalist; the ways of the birds and beasts of Bearn were soon an open book to him and it was by the light of nature that he learned to write of the countryside around him as if he were setting to words the lovely illustrations in the Books of Hours of the Duc de Berri. So far as he was aware, he never met another author; he was quite certain that never in his life did he encounter a reviewer. The *Windsor Magazine* and the books that emanated from it made up his life and, on the whole, he was content with it. All the time, however, there lurked a strong feeling that something was lacking, that something was not quite right somewhere.

Psychologists and psychiatrists he lumped together as charlatans, but a professional opinion of his psyche would make interesting reading. The man who lived at Maryland with the beautiful wife and the dogs was of a piece with the orphans of White Ladies and the rest of his characters in many ways, but there were differences that pronounced themselves stridently. Major Lyveden and Miss French, with their problems of mind and heart do not seem very far away from him, but consider Berry. In many ways, all of them pretty obvious, Mercer the President of the OUDS was still acting out the Berry part. Berry murdering Shakespeare, Berry magistral, Berry reviling the ungodly can all be seen as Mercer incognito. But Berry making observations of a kind at once witty and lavatorial seems the antithesis of the formal and pedantic creator. Mercer in his own person might easily have addressed armed burglars with 'Gentleman seems annoyed. I do hope he hasn't misconstrued anything I've said. D'you think we ought to offer him breakfast? Of course five is rather a lot, but I dare say one of them is a vegetarian, and you can pretend you don't care for haddock. Or they may have some tripe downstairs. You never know. And afterwards we could run them back to Limehouse.' But can you really hear him addressing the meeting on cesspools, vomitoria, slop-pails, dunghills, sewers and drains? Bill Mercer of 1915 would have done it; he might well be saying something of the kind in Stedall's photograph. He probably was.

By 1921, however, he seems to have lost himself inside Captain William Mercer, irascible man of letters. Now and again, however, young Bill peeps out, says what he has to say, and pops back in again. He was never entirely repressible, though on occasions he can be a little wearisome. Blue-based baboons are fundamentally colourful but a little of them goes a long way. The pendulum swung with regularity, from cesspools to bright eyes and red, red lips. The wooing of Jill by Piers, Duke of Padua, is Mercer at his tenderest and agreeably short on the mawkish. There was no blind spot about this. Mercer often makes it clear that he was as aware as any reader that mawkishness existed and that it was not something to be elevated into a vice. Whenever he was guilty of it he sinned with his eyes open. The man capable of drawing from the air all Berry's allocutions could, had he chosen, have kept the habitués of the English Club in paroxysms of laughter and ensured himself popularity as a consummate jester. Mercer chose not to do it. For his own obscure reasons he preferred to be known as the stern, proud man who might, just once in a while, allow himself to unbend. It is hard to avoid the conclusion that he had come to despise his fellow expatriates, a feeling that sometimes marches with what is called in demotic speech an inferiority complex. He had not been much of a success at the Bar; he had been desperately unlucky in his war service, denied the opportunity to distinguish himself and he had been cast into a company with a strong ex-service element. Above all, there was hardly a man he could call a friend. Harrow, Oxford, the Temple and the Army had none of them enriched him with those life-long affectionate relationships that come the way of most people. As no real people existed to whom he could open his heart, he had to invent them.

Encouragement was not lacking, for the *Windsor* readers still clamoured for more. Mercer obliged with another ten stories, to be put together and published in 1924 under the first of his parabolical names, *And Five Were Foolish*. He began, as usual, with a dedication: 'To Richard, whose worst fault is that he is growing up'.

Very possibly he set out to entertain himself in a small way, as well as to instruct his public. Few of them, one imagines, commonly used the word 'appulse' for assault or spelt 'aspodestra' and 'kedjeree' in that fashion. Each tale is given the name of a girl and, in most of them, it is the girl who exhibits the nastier qualities. 'Sarah' begins with another of those freak wills; a testator impishly leaves his large estate to two bright young people upon the condition that they shall marry each other within three months of his death. Though they love, a circumstance the testator had no reason to expect, each for pride's sake affects to be otherwise attached but willing to make the necessary sacrifice in order to obtain material benefits. The gentleman, at the instance of the lady, writes a letter to his imaginary fiancée releasing her from their mutual bonds. The letter comes into the hands of an ill-conditioned servant (female) who threatens action for breach of promise. Galbraith Forsyth, solicitor extraordinary, composes the matter to the satisfaction of all save the villainess. The second, 'Madeleine', is a strange little story apparently brought about by a real experience on the part of Mercer. Madeleine is a village beauty from Ruffec; for no obvious reason she rejects her honest suitors and marries a poisonous brute, the author of the appulse. When he goes off to the war she, on his demand, embroiders the shoulder of his shirts with portions of her chemise. He vanishes, believed killed; she gets a job with an English family and drives with them across France. At a garage the chauffeur, requiring cotton-waste, is fobbed off with a box of 'Essuyages Aseptisés'; what should it contain but, amongst other things, a distinctive piece of shirt imbrued with dried blood, presumably that of the brute. Madeleine marries her decent childhood sweetheart, now blinded. The brute emerges from captivity, visits the new establishment, sees the blind husband and does the decent thing; he goes back to the mistress whose name he had given as next of kin.

'Katharine' is another of Mercer's splendid women cursed with a mean streak. She is married to a VC, and behaves to him with a rudeness that the most amiable of VCs could not tolerate; they agree to live apart, though continuing to love each other. As for the rest, it is only needful to say that Forsyth does it again. 'Spring' introduces the first of the American heroines since Adèle. Her Christian name of Consuelo should have made Willoughby Gray Bagot, Captain late The Blues, to suspect that she was not the underpaid companion she held herself out to be. Possibly the name Vanderbilt meant nothing to him. Anyway, Willoughby Gray Bagot has fallen upon misfortune, sold his stately home to Mr Harp the pork butcher and remained there anonymously in the capacity of Groom of the Chambers. The visitor from Philadelphia is not deceived; affecting a servile station of her own she marries him, buys back the stately home from Mr Harp at ten times his investment—a small matter of £450,000—and presents her new husband with this accomplished fact. It was a ploy to which Mercer was warming; poor but admirable man matched with rich young woman as his own father had once been. Willoughby Gray Bagot found no difficulty in coming to terms with it. 'Presently he picked her up as one picks up a baby child. "I never dreamed", he said slowly, "I never dreamed." ' A sensible man, Willoughby Gray Bagot.

'Elizabeth' is a variant on this theme. Impoverished aristocrat, female, engages herself to marry rich vulgarian. A farewell dinner at the Richelieu with the man she loves, John Richard Shere, Viscount Pembury. The lady being addicted to beer, Pembury furnishes his car with bottle and glass which they jointly consume as their valediction. On the strength of this Pembury is arrested for drunken driving, refuses to divulge the name of his companion and seems in serious trouble. The rich vulgarian improves the occasion by writing to *The Times* that all drunken drivers should go to the treadmill. Elizabeth, learning all this at Castle Charing where both are guests of the Fairies, throws the vulgarian's ring at his feet, his brandy in his face and sets off hot-foot for Lincoln's Inn. Pembury has no money; indeed 'his father had sunk to an annuity and dwelt at a Club', much as Cecil John had done. It does not matter. Forsyth arranges all.

The next story, 'Jo', is much more interesting, for it shows quite another Mercer at work. It is told in the first person; the narrator has no name, though the servants call his wife 'my lady'. Their marriage appears idyllic until the day when Madam does not return home. A pincushion note explains that 'I've got to choose. And I must go to Berwick—Berwick Perowne. I've tried not to—indeed I have. But now I can't fight any more.' The narrator is a tough character, a secret agent by trade, and resolves to make the best of a bad job. When, nearly a year later, Jo comes back to die, with a terrible story of her mistreatment, he takes a sterner resolve. He will have Perowne's life. It is carefully planned, and extremely well written. The men meet as a result of spoof messages at a lonely spot in the Pyrenees. The fight goes sometimes one way, sometimes the other, but it has to end.

He struggled at that, and I bent him back again.

'This won't help her,' he blurted, panting.

'The more's the pity,' said I, 'But it'll help me and it'll make the world cleaner.' Again I bent him back, till his eyes were starting and his back curved like a bow.

'For God's sake, end it,' he whimpered.

'Ask in her name,' said I.

'For . . . her . . . sake.' I broke his back.

Bear this in mind; its relevance will appear presently.

'Jo' was stronger meat than the *Windsor* usually purveyed, but it may well have come from deeper feelings than the sweet-shop stories. In Mercer's philosophy a wife was a possession, and his view of property rights was rigid. Bettine was desirable, Bettine was openly desired by some; a gentle hint might not come amiss. Whether by accident or by design he called the next story 'Athalia', the Christian name that Bettine owned but did not advertise. Apart from being another poor man-rich girl story and containing one of his best descriptions of a drive down the N10 to Biarritz, it is run of the mill work.

Then comes 'Ann'. Here one has to go along with Oscar Wilde; 'only those with hearts of stone can read of the death of Little Nell without collapsing helplessly with laughter', or something like that. The Lady Ann is the daughter of an Earl.

Moved by contemplation of a Morland picture, she decides that she would adore to live in a humble cottage, compassed about by trees and horses. To accomplish this, she marries her father's groom. The groom, slightly baffled, takes the bride straight from the register office to an establishment kept by his aunt at Suet-on-Sea. Once you have the measure of the Yates cypher system it is not difficult to identify this little known watering-place. Suet is hard by Lather: Deal is hard by Walmer. Lather and Walmer sound alike, and both Suet and Deal are four-letter words.

'Sapper' speaks of 'things that it is not good for a white man to see'. So it was with the Lady Ann. Her new friends and relations are abominable almost beyond words; not one of them is granted a single decent instinct, save for fear. She is made to dance on the pier; she is in varying degrees molested; a lighted cigarette is placed in her mouth; stout is forced upon her. 'Yes, We Have No Bananas' is her epithalamium. It was no good fainting; led outside, 'the fresh air revived her immediately'. Deal is notoriously bracing. She was promised food, but had scant appetite.

She could not face that awful parlour again . . . Besides, the meal would be in the nature of a wedding-feast. Its prelusive character would be insisted upon. Jocular references would be made; sly digs administered. It would be hideous—revolting. Ann's flesh crept.

The refection fulfilled every expectation; indeed it did more. Amongst the wedding guests was a Mr Allen, not so much a socialist as a sans-culottes. As all present became disguised in ale, Mr Allen began to speak, a trifle thickly. He spoke of the rich and their deplorable way of life; on learning of Ann's antecedents he warmed to his work. Ann demanded that her lord escort her elsewhere.

'I want to go. It's my wish. I want you to take me away—out of the house—now. Come, please.' . . . She turned to the door. No one said anything at all. The quiet, cold air of authority tied up their tongues. They felt suddenly diminished. A wave of detestable respect had swept them off their feet. Blood had told.

Mr Allen did not long remain diminished and he was having none of that. In a regrettable display of unregulated bolshevism he too came outside, set about the groom and broke his neck. Ann is left crouched in the gutter seeing Morland visions. Finis.

'Eleanor' returns us to the kind of life led by real people. It is an amusing yarn of misunderstanding and misunderstood lovers of the kind now customary. 'Susan', the last of them, shifts the scene to Cannes, to the vast house of vastly wealthy Italians who appear to keep it open for any who may care to drop in. Amongst those who do are the real Duke of Culloden, a spurious Duke of Culloden, an oily, lecherous Frenchman (a type known to Pau), and the unprotected, impecunious Susan. The pseudo-Duke and his ruttish ally corner her in a darkened room. 'Trembling all over, Susan began to edge away from the chair . . . A piercing scream of agony shattered the silence—the sort of scream which is associated with torture—the scream of a human being under the pains of hell.' M. Labotte, with a foreigner's cunning, has crept up on all fours, unconscious of the presence of the Duke who stamps on his hand. Having recently had his appendix removed the Duke is in no case to do more, but it is enough. The flood of fractured English which follows the scream is Mercer at his best; he was very good at that kind of thing. Susan, unaware of her rescuer's identity, has the matter made plain to her by 'a nice-looking man with a merry eye'. Berry is making a brief appearance. The *Windsor Magazine* could never have enough of Berry, but his exploits called for much thought and could not be written to order.

They seem to have liked the book. It was reprinted twice before the year was out and five times more between then and 1939. No mere world war could stop it; apart from a break in 1939 and 1940 it came out again five times under incredible difficulties and remained in print for many years after. Mercer's half-year royalty cheque was becoming handsome.

The cheques still had to be earned, and it was only by a further burst of romance that Mercer could earn them. His enthusiasm for this was wearing thin; it was thirteen years since the first of them, and work that had been worthy enough of a young barrister seeking to supplement very moderate professional earnings was no longer the stuff for which he felt himself best suited. Hutchinson, however, was firm about it. The *Windsor Magazine* readers had insatiable appetites of a certain kind, and it was the business of his writers to pander to it; unless, of course, they no longer wanted to eat. There was an innocence about the stories that made a pleasant contrast to the over heated works of some current favourites.

Mercer obliged with another ten stories, gathered together in 1925 under the title *As Other Men Are*. It was not the last time he would pray in aid of the Gospel according to St Matthew. The dedication, like most of his dedications, shows the way his mind was working. 'To those, alive or dead, with whom I had the honour to serve overseas during the Great War'. He did them proud. His heroes mustered one major, four captains, two ex-officers of rank unspecified and another major and another captain amongst the supporting cast. He was also beginning to interest himself in another market. Five of his heroines are American, one has a twin sister in Philadelphia, and he also brings in a subsidiary character by the peerless name of Mrs Drinkabeer Stoat.

There is a recurrent theme in these stories; he had used it before, but never to anything like the same extent. His characters are now conscious of money, in particular of the consequences of its absence. Again it is the women who have it, and some of them are unable to carry corn. In the very first story Jeremy takes his wife to task for ingesting too many cocktails. Her answer is: 'When you make enough to pay your own washing bills . . .'—'She was worth twenty thousand pounds a year. Finally, she was American . . .' That might explain, but it did not excuse. Jeremy marches out. A reconciliation follows, encouraged by which the lady observes, 'I didn't marry you for that. Well, I don't pay you for that either.' Presumably Bettine followed custom and read the draft, but any silvery laughter would have been a bit forced. Happily, she had nothing like twenty thousand halfpence a year. All comes well in the last pages; it had to, or Arthur Hutchinson would have sent it straight back.

'Simon' is a variation. Both protagonists are hard up, but used to decent living. Simon wins money on a horse race, becomes eligible to marry Patricia (whose mother was American) but uses the winnings to pay off a blackmailer, regrettably domiciled in Crutched Friars, who has got hold of an unwise letter. By way of a change, they marry, live in France, and stay poor. ' "I'm one franc out," murmured Mrs Beaulieu, "Now what did I spend that on?" ' Everybody behaves most creditably.

The third, sub. nom. 'Toby', is set in Pau and tells of the good conduct of Captain Toby Rage and his friend Cicely

Voile whom he has, just possibly, compromised in innocent fashion. 'Oliver' was another for Bettine to digest. Hero and heroine are already married but are becoming bored with each other. Oliver Pauncefote had been through the war, had eighty thousand pounds behind him, and was out to forget. His wife, Philadelphia-born—Bettine's native New York ranked with University College: there were better-class places—had nothing. Oliver loses all by speculating. Jean does not accept this with a becoming philosophy. They remain together, however, and in adversity recover love. No sooner have they done so than a telegram is forwarded from the Hôtel de Rhin in the Place Vendôme, long delayed. All is well; the money is not lost. Never mind why.

'Christopher' takes us into the deep country where the American Audrey is wooed and won by—or woos and wins—Christopher John who is not, after all, his own agent. Mercer could still write an Eclogue when he wanted to. By the time he came to 'Ivan', however, the Muse was becoming jaded; back comes freak-will-and-Forsyth. Nobody seemed to mind. Nor did they complain about 'Hubert', another small comedy of errors written with the old light touch and some amusing passages. 'Titus' produces another grasping American woman. In the first few lines the tone is set. 'Three thousand a year's no earthly use to you.'—'It would be if I had my share.'—'Titus had wooed a lady that loved him heart and soul and had married one that had come to love only herself.' Blanche was not all bad; she apologized a few minutes later. After this bitter start Mercer becomes amusing again, with the adventures of the Cheviots as interior decorators, a task undertaken for the money. Madam emerges as a reformed character and all comes right again. Forsyth surfaces once more for 'Peregrine', whose marriage is not idyllic. 'Peregrine raised his eyes to meet the glint of steel in those of his wife. For a moment he seemed upon the edge of protest: then the cold, level gaze bore down his spirit.' Her strictures upon his behaviour, antecedents and aspect had the same result. The final quarrel, before Peregrine bolts, is Mercer on top of his form; the homilies of dreadful women seem to come naturally from him. In the end Peregrine leaves his wife for a girl improbably called Joan Purchase Atlee; never before had a main figure left his wife, however much she might have deserved it, to set up house with another woman. It could not have happened before 1914, but times had changed.

Luckily for him Peregrine was in a position to pay Forsyth £4,000 a year to be applied as maintenance. The last story, 'Derry', comes near to a genteel form of wife-swapping, but it soon shies away from so middle-class an activity.

There is a harsher tone about most of these stories than in any that had gone before. The happy ending was mandatory and had to be contrived somehow, but there is a hint that the writer was no longer seeing Romance in the old fashion. Some of his women here are harpies; they can be greedy, vinegar-tongued and in every way lacking in that repose that stamps the caste of Vere de Vere. The worst are American by birth. Either it was a deliberate insult to a harmless Bettine or something was going wrong with their marriage. It can hardly have been by accident that he wrote only of chivalrous men—the only male bad characters are very mildly bad—and women as wicked as they dared to be. Possibly he was getting tired of saints; but there is something to think about in the changed attitude.

By the second half of 1925 Mercer was forty, an age at which most men pause to appreciate the situation. He had not done badly for himself; if not rich, he was at least comfortable, with a beautiful home, a beautiful wife and a number of beautiful stories behind him. The question was whether he would be able to keep all these up, and whether his heart was really in it. For fourteen years, apart from those of the war, he had been turning out much the same sort of product; mass production was not a development he admired. The men who were making real money by writing were not all that unlike himself but their work was of a different order. Cyril McNeile, 'Sapper' (who understandably detested his first name, Herman, as much as Mercer did his own), had brought out his *Bulldog Drummond* within weeks of the appearance of *The Courts Of Idleness* and it was making him a fortune; films, successive Drummond stories and even wireless programmes on 2LO made him famous, though his syntax was often faulty, his characters spoke trench-slang, and his mentor was O. Henry (William Sydney Porter). Edgar Wallace was worse still, raking in the money in exchange for very indifferent yarns. John Buchan was about the only contemporary he held in respect and Buchan had ten years' start. Mercer is at pains, later on, to let us know where his real enthusiasm lay. 'What was the best novel written between the wars?'—'That's easy. James Hilton's *Lost Horizon*. About that, to my mind, there is no argument.'

Where his streak of other-worldliness came from it is impossible to say. The Mercers were solid, earthy folk, as were the Yates and the Walls. The Dornfords had a more metaphysical record, for one of their number had studied at Göttingen in the 1790s and achieved some reputation in the higher reaches of philosophy. Perhaps Miss Macnab of Dumfries had fey Highland ancestors. Saki had undoubtedly possessed a similar compartment in his brilliant mind, but that could be blamed on the Munro side. Wherever it came from, a lot of it stuck to William Mercer.

The magic element was not confined to his writings. At some period about this time he acquired a totem of mystic significance, which is introduced into a later book because it was too important to be ignored. His picture-clock now exists only in photographs, for reasons that will appear. On the face of it, the thing is not particularly attractive. It was an ordinary landscape painting of a church in rustic surroudings, the clock in its tower being no picture but a working timepiece. It became at once Mercer's talisman; he talked to it regularly, as Isoult had talked to her tree and as others of his characters were to talk to theirs. Had Maryland caught fire he would have dashed into the flames to save it; both Bettine and Richard had feet of their own. One lobe of Mercer's brain undoubtedly functioned in *Golden Bough* fashion and would make an interesting study for such as understand these deep matters. It certainly displayed itself in his writing.

In point of time, *The Stolen March* came long before *Lost Horizon*—eight years, to be exact—and it was Mercer's own creation. It is hard to believe that Arthur Hutchinson would have taken it as a serial had he been let into the secret of how the tale would unfold. Mercer always claimed that he was unable to write a synopsis of his novels as he had no idea of where the opening situation would lead him; on this occasion it was probably convenient. *Windsor* readers craved Romance, not Fantasy. In the event they got both. The story begins credibly enough and gives rise to no suspicion. In the first three instalments we are brought back into the company of old friends, Simon and Patricia Beaulieu (in 'Simon', *As Other Men Are*); the latter we left in Chartres trying to balance her accounts after giving a franc to a beggar-boy. They were hard up enough then, but worse is to come. Simon falls seriously ill; Patricia, in patrician fashion, sells her rings to pay the doctor. He, not to be outdone, prescribes fresh air, preferably mountainous, and gentle exercise; a friend of his will furnish the means with the loan of a caravan, 'Its squire, a steam-car, not only drew it along the roads, but found it in light and heat, filled its cistern from streams, cooled its larder and kept it free from dust.' Perhaps in writing this Mercer's mind went back to one of the most famous sights of Salonika. The French, desirous of keeping down speeds of motor lorries on dust roads, erected there a large sign bearing the command 'Stokers! Slacken!' A good literal translation of 'chauffeur', and a chauffeur went with the steam-car.

In this earthly paradise the Beaulieus meet a girl, known to us but not to them. Eulalie, the putter expert, is on the run from her criminal associates and her car breaks down at a convenient point. The three find each other congenial, Simon pays a quick visit to Paris in order to put their guest's business affairs on a sound footing and, at The Red Nose, he encounters again his own old blackmailer, late of Crutched Friars. Having put him in his place, Simon returns, Eulalie joins up with them and the party continues travelling south from Marmande in search of Etchechuria, the unknown country with the Basque-sounding name. Here the Mercer up-dating system breaks down. The blackmailer's receipt bears the date, in my copy, 'June 12, 1926'. On Simon's return we are told that 'they would remind one another that it was 1930'. One cannot blame the steam-car, since he had made the journey by train. Because a male partner for Eulalie is imperative, Mercer conjures one up. Patricia, in a lonely place, is accosted by another of those greasy Frenchmen bent upon an audacious rape. Pomfret Tudor, an eminent architectural archaeologist, broke and touring France to gather material for his book, is on the spot. He demolishes Porus Bureau not quite as neatly as Jonah would have done it, but efficiently enough. As he explains, his veteran car is in the river, driven there by himself in a fury after its repeated failure to perform its office. There seems no obstacle to his accompanying the party and he is taken on the strength. Happily he and Eulalie think well of each other; had it been otherwise matters would have fallen out differently. Episode three ends with the four young people more or less benighted in a Pyrenean chaos, leading a pair of mules after the fashion of Modestine in the Cevennes. A pleasant story, and the reader is naturally eager to know what happens to them. Episode Four soon shows him; Norah Schlegel draws the party beautifully.

The men wear hats, collars and ties and are neatly turned out all over; the girls are dressed more for Hay Hill than the Rhune, their only concession to roughing it being their light walking-sticks. Little do they know what awaits them.

Their worries begin when one of the mules addresses them in Oxford English; they are compounded when the mules disappear and are replaced by an animated illustration from the Luttrell Psalter, Gog by name, who explains that he is the mules. Thenceforward nightmare takes over. For a time the characters are harmless nursery rhyme characters, but they develop a habit of turning murderous for no obvious reason. Fortuitously a passing priest turns up and marries Pomfret and Eulalie in accordance with the *lex loci contractus*, or so one hopes; this was very convenient, and they are not subjected to the indignities heaped upon Ann.

There seems no need to dwell upon the content of the story, for it is there for the reading. 'Saki's' comic kings are present, along with the cruel streak he showed in tales like 'The Music On The Hill'; there is a dash of Hans Christian Andersen, a bigger one of the Brothers Grimm, something of Edgar Allen Poe, and a measure of Aesop. Mercer's dedication speaks of *As You Like It* and nursery rhymes, each of which is laid under contribution. Whatever you make of the tale, it cannot be denied that it contains some of his best pastoral writing, and Pomfret Tudor, on the top of his form, is very funny indeed. Consider this by way of a sample. Under discussion is a malignant dwarf, Sunspot by name.

> 'But can't something be done?', said Pomfret. 'Can't someone drop Sunspot a hint—in the shape of a thick ear or a kidney punch?'
> 'We've thought of that', said the Mayor uneasily, 'but he hasn't got any ears'.
> 'Well, he must have some kidneys,' said Pomfret. 'If he hadn't got any kidneys, he wouldn't work'.

Mercer loved it: '"My favourite", said Jill, "It always was."—"But a lot of people didn't like it, you know."' Numbered amongst these was Arthur Hutchinson. *The Stolen March* took up all Mercer's space in the *Windsor* for the first half of 1926, but in the numbers for the second half the name of Dornford Yates does not appear. It seems that Mercer tried his hand at a sequel, but gave it up as a bad job after fifty pages.

This, his first near-failure, did nothing for Mercer's temper. His status in Pau was an odd one. His background was not too high to make it impossible to hob-nob with the likes of Mr Carter of Old England nor too inconsiderable to prevent the Corks from inviting him to dinner. He joined the Pau branch of the British Legion and was a dutiful member, but still, as against society in general, he was on the outside looking in. To be an author was not a claim to recognition, but neither did it lower a man in the eyes of the colóny. Buchan or Sapper would have been popular members of the Club; it is easy to imagine either of them standing before a winter fire, dinner-jacketed of course, and holding forth to a highly-entertained audience. A few years later Mercer, the writer of first-rate thrillers, could have done it equally well, but Mercer, the writer of light romantic stuff mostly for women, could not. He continued to distance himself and he did not add to his reputation as a clubbable man. Rather the reverse. Mr Kennard remembers an ugly scene in Monro's Bank. Mercer, it seems, came in to cash his usual cheque and was served by a new clerk who 'shovelled out the money as if he were shovelling coal'. Mercer, who never could stand an affront to his dignity, lost his temper and raised his voice enough to bring the Manager out of his office. Mr Kennard apologized on behalf of the Bank, addressed the young man as he had never been addressed before, and calmed things down. Mercer had the right of it, but the feeling was that he had been needlessly high-handed. No doubt the story got round, as such stories do, and improved with the telling.

It was not only bank clerks who were the objects of his wrath. Hutchinson was punished by being given only one story during the first half of 1927. It was called 'Court Cards', appears in no book, and was not one of Mercer's best. An hotel in the south of France is destroyed by fire. Mr Lacey, whose Rolls has escaped damage, is confronted by a Miss Landfall who has lost all her belongings, including her Renault, is without means, and desires to be returned to the home she shares with her brothers near Rouen. Mr Lacey—he is called 'I' and his Christian name is unrevealed—takes her there, dallying briefly in Blois. On arrival in Rouen he drops her at the Hôtel de la Poste and is bidden never to attempt to find her again. He does, of course, and she and her brothers turn out to be smugglers. The brothers are packed off to Rhodesia and Mr Lacey marries their sister.

The fact of the matter was that Mercer had become thoroughly bored with Romance and wanted to write something worthier of a real author. In his mind was the possibility of a thriller, something on the lines of *Bulldog Drummond* or *The Thirty-Nine Steps*, but set in a romantic place. Jonah was seriously under-employed and his talents could be put to use. Not only would there be no magic in the book but, more important still, there would be no women. The pattern already existed, in a book that Mercer greatly admired, *Treasure Island*. *Blind Corner* owes much to Stevenson. It is told in the first person; when that becomes impossible for narrative, another character will take over. There is a robber's treasure and the equivalent of a map. It is hidden not on an island, but in a chamber at the bottom of a great well. Wells are sinister things, about the most frightening of all man's works, and Mercer had been familiar with the concept since childhood. The Great Well of Dover Castle is one of the most famous in the world. There must be villains, but, to a man who had seen Stinie Morrison, the Reubens and Crippen, villains were commonplace.

While *The Stolen March* was baffling and irritating *Windsor* people, between June 1925 and May 1926, Mercer was at work on his *magnum opus*. Hutchinson did not want it, and said so. Ward Lock shared this lack of enthusiasm; cobblers should stick to their lasts. Hodder & Stoughton had published the Bulldog Drummond books and had plainly done very well for Hugh's creator. Would they care to take on *Blind Corner*? They would. This was very satisfactory. 'The author who writes what his public wants him to write, because his public wants him to write it, is doomed,' Mercer once wrote complacently. By then, of course, he was already rich.

The change of style made a great deal of difference to Mercer, but it made none for Bettine. Richard was growing up, the work was bringing in enough money for her to make occasional trips to her family in America with him, but life in general was boring. She and her husband went little into society and he did not encourage her to make friends of her own. On the threshold of middle age, but still as beautiful as ever, she was confined to the curtilage of Maryland and though in all things she behaved as a dutiful wife, Bettine was not happy. Her only confidante was her maid Thérèse, for Mercer was anything but a complaisant husband. It would hardly be a misuse of words to say that he resented any favour shown to his wife and was becoming almost morbidly jealous of her popularity. Many people hesitated to ask Bettine to their homes if the price had to be the attendance of her husband also. Not that he was ill-conducted; rather it was that the effortless superiority seemed to call for a little too much effort. He was a shade too glossy and a bit too consciously literary for a largely sporting community. With the French he made no serious effort to get on. More than twenty years later he was writing to Mr Carter that 'I can get along in French but do not know a great many French words.' Bettine, according to Thérèse, spoke the language very well. Pau was certainly prepared to take Mercer in, and it was by his own desire that his life took an eremitical form. Mr Yates enjoyed a wide reputation for being one of the nicest men of his time. Captain Mercer, although he insisted that the boy Richard kiss his mother's hand daily, did not. Pau reckoned him rather over-pleased with himself for easy intercourse.

Much, perhaps too much, has been made of this less attractive side of Mercer's character and it may be worth comparing him with two of his most famous contemporaries. Gerard Fairlie knew both 'Sapper' and P. G. Wodehouse well and wrote his impressions of them. 'Sapper' 'loved gay company, stoups of ale, all men's sports, the short ones before and after meals, smoking, good talk, robust stories, and all pretty girls.' Very different from Mercer at first glance, but Fairlie goes on to say that his hero too could be pompous. 'He did have these fits at times when he did or said something so startlingly out of character that his friends were completely at a loss to understand the impulse.' He also, though with plain reluctance, speaks of 'conceit'. As to Wodehouse, he was 'not a particularly funny man to meet . . . he is curiously detached and impersonal, and I believe that he lives chiefly in a world of his own imagination, on which events happening all round him make little impact'. Possibly these things are the common occupational disease of successful authors. As against the rest of his kind William Mercer was not all that far removed from being as other men were.

7

Richard Chandos and Co.

Blind Corner took up a year of Mercer's life, but it was time
well spent. As his new publishers were also the publishers
of the Bulldog Drummond books it was necessary for him to
take care over the nature of his hero. Jonathan Mansel had to
be developed, but he must not become a carbon copy. The
two famous characters began with a lot in common. Each had
left the Army as Captain and with a DSO. As both McNeile
and Mercer knew, this was a decoration whose value could
be measured by relation to its owner's rank; for field officers
and upwards it was little more than a service stripe but
for captains and below it ranked only just short of a VC.
Drummond lived in Half Moon Street and drove a Bentley;
Mansel had his quarters in Cleveland Row (possibly the
next tenant was General de Gaulle) and owned a Rolls.
Both excelled in a rough-house; Drummond could see off a
gorilla or a Thing whilst Jonah avoided fisticuffs for fear of
killing his man by a piece of carelessness. Though he never
fought with other than humans, Mansel made up for it by
once knocking out a woman, the Duchess of Varvic. It was, of
course, done for the best of motives, in order to simulate a
car smash and thus withdraw her from the homicidal Duke.
Had some earlier Mercer heroes done something of the kind
to their wives—not with a fist but by means of a long-handled
hairbrush judiciously and judicially applied—their lives
might have been happier. Both men were expert shots and
possessed a considerable armoury. Jonah's way of life was the
obscurer, for the secret locker in his Rolls must have been
capacious. 'Each of the two open windows was framing a rifle
barrel,' we are told early on; two rifles and several pistols
take up quite a lot of space. Drummond only kept a couple

of automatics and a water-pistol, the usual equipment of a gentleman.

There the similarity ended. Drummond was a hearty, more often than not dressed in ancient tweeds, a flannel shirt and a Loamshire tie. Mansel was always so carefully dressed that one could hardly appear before him without nervously making sure that one's own linen had no spot or stain. Drummond spoke the tongue of a thousand officers' Messes; Mansel's was the English of one of the better senior common rooms. When Mansel and his party took lodgings at a remote Austrian inn they were treated like royalty and kept their distance: Drummond would have called for beer, and before the night was out russet-cheeked foresters in Lincoln green would have been banging their pots on the table and bawling out a rude version of 'The Frothblowers' Anthem'. It is not all that surprising, for 'Sapper' was amusing himself by extending the personality of his old friend Gerard Fairlie, late of the Scots Guards, while Mercer had to draw his champion entirely by the light of nature. Good regimental officers were thicker on the ground in the 1920s than *preux chevaliers*. All the same, Mercer was getting better. Mansel may not be as recognizable as Drummond, but he was more than the lay-figure called Anthony Lyveden. In Berry's company Jonah could be very funny indeed, but there is not a smile to be raised from one end of *Blind Corner* to the other.

In part this was due to Mercer's choice of a second lead. Richard William Chandos explains himself in his very name. Richard and William, the two generations of Mercers, prefixed to Sir John Chandos, the flower of Plantagenet chivalry, could hardly be a comical dog. At twenty-two he had been too young for the war and was fair game for Mansel's demand that in all things he and his friend Hanbury should do as he told them. 'You see, I am older.' Exactly the phrase used by Second Lieutenant William Mercer that had so annoyed Second Lieutenant Stedall a decade earlier.

The story starts as it means to go on. Chandos, sent down from Oxford for beating up some communists in Drummond fashion, is making a leisurely journey by car back to London after passing five weeks in Biarritz with the unexciting prospect ahead of going into his uncle's business as 'a merchant of consequence in the City of London'. Does this sound familiar? Outside Chartres he sees a murder, comforts the victim and

133

takes over his dog. At their London Club, Mansel walks off absent-mindedly in the younger man's greatcoat. As Chandos is later described as a giant, Jonah was either uncommonly absorbed in his thoughts or bigger than Mr Wilmshurst had realized. In the pocket is the dog's collar; in the collar the well-digger's statement, telling of treasure. Mansel makes preparations for the party to leave for Austria. 'I never in my life saw him hurry or use the telephone.' Jonathan Mansel was compounded not only of S. F. Edge and Hopley, but also something of Drummond and Squire Trelawney. There was a tincture of Mercer's old master N. K. Stephen, of whom he said the same thing and to whom he dedicated the book.

After a brush on the road with 'Rose' Noble and his rout, the party arrives at Wagensburg. The bad men already have an option to purchase the freehold of the place; Mansel persuades the agent to grant him a lease during the currency of the option. The stratagem seems of doubtful legality but nobody bothers about that. The next move demonstrates the difference of mentality between Mansel and Drummond. That the villains would come to the well was certain. Hugh would have laid up patiently for them, as he had laid up for Germans around Ginchy brickstacks, and bagged them on arrival. Ellis and 'Rose' Noble would have been neutralized, the rest driven to a remote place, debagged and enlarged with kicks administered to their hinder ends. Then the treasure could have been got at leisure. The trouble would have been that the story must end on about page 100. Mansel is harder on himself and his men but kinder to his reader. After a successful ambush, during which he knocks 'Rose' Noble out, he merely dismisses them with a warning and the certainty of future mischief.

This was wisdom, for we are given as a result the best adventure story of the inter-war years. Chandos bumbles into enemy hands and is freed by Mansel just as his back is being roasted against a car radiator. Within the castle they discover an oubliette and are constrained to reach the treasure chamber in mole fashion. The description of their labours to achieve this is fine writing indeed and marks a new departure in Mercer's style. Up to this point all his work had been of a rather trivial kind, but the second part of *Blind Corner* is literature. The fight in the dark, between Chandos and 'Rose' Noble in a subterranean chamber, is exciting; the tension built up during the tunnelling operation even more so.

For the pace was too hot to last: we all knew that: and unless we could win very soon we were playing a losing game. Yet we went steadily on, like men in a dream, losing all count of time and confusing Night with Day. Indeed, the demands of the battle so possessed our senses that, used in some other direction, these were beginning to fail. We shouted, one to another, when a whisper could have been heard: the hand that could still ply a hammer, could not be trusted to raise a glass to the lips: and if ever I glanced at my wrist-watch, this seemed a great way off.

Anybody who has ever dug a trench against time will understand what he means. Nor does the convoluted prose detract from the story: it is, indeed, curiously effective. Hope is deferred, tunnels are cut with terrible effort and have to be abandoned. The roof falls in behind them. At last, at the limit of their strength, the *moment critique* arrives.

The noise was distinct now—a thin regular murmur, as if someone was whetting a chisel upon a hone. What it was I could not imagine, and was just beginning to think that our calculations had led us to the top of the well, when Mansel let out a sob and caught us each by an arm. 'My God, I've got it,' he cried, 'That's the chamber ahead. AND THEY'RE FILING THE BARS'.

A little later Chandos appreciates the situation.

We were entombed alive: this, by our own act, with the treasure under our hand, in the knowledge of an attack upon one man and a dog, who would count in vain upon our succour. Had we had the tools, we had no longer the strength to hew our way back: indeed, to judge from the sound, it seemed likely that ten or more yards of our tunnel had fallen in. Yet, could we have performed this unthinkable task, it would only have been to fall into the enemy's hands. And the other way out was barred: and beyond the bars was the shaft, the mouth of which would be sealed in less than an hour: and beyond the shaft was the well, some ninety feet deep.

At this point we must leave *Blind Corner* and turn to *As Berry And I Were Saying*.

'No woman in it,' said Berry, 'The best thing you ever did. Not that that's saying much.'

'Be quiet,' said Jill.

'At the end of the penultimate chapter, the faithful party is stuck. Stuck good and proper. Am I right?'

'Yes', said Berry, 'I suppose you might call it stuck. They're only entombed alive. Ten yards or so of their tunnel have fallen in, and they have no shovels or picks: the other way out is barred—by four bars which they cannot move: beyond the bars is a passage which leads to the bottom of a well, in which the water is rising very fast: and the well is ninety feet deep. And you call it being "stuck".'

'Well, I wrote the last words of that chapter late one night. When I read them through the next morning, I almost lost my nerve. I remember saying aloud, "My God, I've done it now." For I could not see how any men could emerge from such a predicament. Then I calmed down. "Well," I said to myself, "the book has brought me so far: the only thing I can do is go straight on." And so I did. And the book brought them out all right without any fuss. And *The Times* said, "The escape from the well is story-telling of a high order".'

Blind Corner introduced Mercer to a wider public, but the change of publisher brought its troubles.

I was never sent any slip proofs, as of course I should have been. When I was reading the page proof, I found that the well-digger's statement, which I had marked to be printed in italic, had been printed in type so small that it could hardly be read. Now, as the whole tale was founded on that statement, it was of great importance that it should be at least as easy to read as the rest of the text. Well, it was up to the printers, for I, of course, declined to pass the proof. It meant rearranging about forty pages. But it had to be done.

What exactly Mercer said is unrecorded, but it is not too difficult to make some sort of a guess. Publishers do not find such things endearing.

Blind Corner was well reviewed and made his reputation amongst people who would not have cared greatly for such as 'Ann'. Wisely, he kept 'Rose' Noble unslaughtered: he was bound to come in useful again.

Authors enjoy few natural advantages over other men but they have one asset that is shared with no other vocation. The author, so long as he keeps to the trade of writing fiction, can build a private world entirely to his liking and inhabited only by the kind of people he favours. Once in a while the builder withdraws completely into his dream country but in such cases he usually ends by being quietly taken from it by men in white coats. The great majority prefer to use their creations as week-end cottages to which they can repair whenever the real world seems unattractive. Thus it was with Mercer. Long before Bettine had entered his life it had been his habit to become Boy Pleydell of White Ladies whenever the fancy took him. He had been an amalgam of all Pleydells and Mansels, driving through France in a large car, as familiar with Rouen, Dieppe, Chartres, Angoulême, Tours and Poitiers as William Mercer had once been with Clerkenwell and the Temple. Now that he had been metamorphosed into them as the squire of Villa Maryland at Pau he was no longer enjoying himself. First was the matter of his books. The earlier ones had done well; it was not only in the *Windsor Magazine* that the name of Dornford Yates had appeared, for Hutchinson had sold some of the stories to American periodicals and they had paid handsomely for them. It was going to be a hard decision, whether to turn aside from all this in order to become a thriller writer. It was perfectly true that *Blind Corner* had made his name and had given Arthur Hutchinson a sharp reminder that editors were not the commanding figures they believed themselves to be; it was equally true that another school of thought existed.

Mercer had what may seem to many a blind spot about his writings. When Berry observes that ' "Ann" is the very best short story you ever wrote', he is speaking with the voice of Ann's creator. It is hard to believe that a sensible man, blessed with a huge and cultivated sense of humour, could take 'Ann' seriously, but that Mercer did. His quarrel with Hutchinson, if quarrel it can be called, was over and he was willing to put machismo aside for a season and go back. The fact that 'I got stacks of letters saying "Anybody can do stuff like *Blind Corner*, but nobody else can do your light stuff. Please stick to your last" ' may have had something to do with it. Mercer always preferred to be the cock on top of the tiniest dung-hill to being one slightly below the summit of a bigger one. Competition of any kind always irked him; so long as 'Sapper', Buchan and Edgar Wallace were about he would never top the big one; better to dominate the smaller. In the autobiography he goes on to say that 'I write three more Chandos books before throwing back.' This is mere bravado, pointing the fact that nobody was going to tell him what he ought to write. In point of fact, he wrote another series of *Windsor* stories, published between June 1927 and May 1928. They came out in book form under the name of *Maiden Stakes*.

'Every one of your people is true to life. Dead true. And those who say they aren't declare their ignorance. Take Ewart in *Maiden Stakes*—I've met the man,' observes Berry, adding later, 'You saw the Spanish Grand Prix?'

'Oh yes, you've got to see it to do a tale like *Maiden Stakes*. But that account is dead accurate. In fact I saw the race twice—once before I wrote the tale and once a few years later; and I remember thinking I wouldn't have changed a word. And I saw it from the point I described, the point at which Gyneth was standing, watching the cars go by . . . I went twice to San Sebastian to get that picture right. It wasn't so easy as it looked. And I did once see Zero turn up seven times in ten spins. At Madeira, I think. I was on it the last four times and we broke the Bank.'

Presumably this is William Mercer and not Boy Pleydell speaking.

The next line is certainly Mercer. Asked by Daphne why so many writers report the sordid side, he explains.

'I can't imagine. Sometimes they do it very well. And reviewers seem to love it. The more sordid the tale, the higher their commendation. I could have done it, of course. I've seen the sordid side again and again. But I can see no object in presenting it in fiction. Life's sad and hard enough, without adding some sordid picture, to wring men's hearts.'

For the moment he seemed to have forgotten 'Ann'.

Though sordid was hardly the word for it, it seems plain that by 1929 the Mercers' marriage was heading for the rocks. Bettine, with all her excellent qualities, had never been the right wife for a husband of Mercer's attributes. Richard had been sent away to his preparatory school at Summer Fields, near Oxford, where the Eccles-Williams were Mercer's long-standing friends. Lacking even him, Bettine's life imperceptibly moved from mere boredom to something more like bondage. Though nearly forty she was as lovely as ever and resented the restrictions that Mercer was now imposing upon her freedom of movement. For the first twenty-nine years of her life Bettine had had to fend for herself and she felt no inclination to be anybody's doormat. It is beyond argument that they quarrelled, but they had the good sense and good taste to keep such scenes behind closed doors. Both were becoming miserably unhappy, but they soldiered on. Richard, for his part, was enjoying himself hugely. Many years later he was to write that the years at Summer Fields were the happiest of his life.

His father could at least take himself off to his study, shut the door and translate himself into that other world. *Maiden Stakes* lacked Norah Schlegel for an illustrator, but Lindsay Cable made an adequate substitute. When he observed that he knew all his characters, Mercer was speaking sober truth. Look at the illustrations and, unless you are at least well into your fifties, you may well wonder whether such beautiful people ever really existed. Those of us who were about at the time know that they did. In the good hotels, at the theatre and in first-class carriages you could see them at any time, the survivors of the pre-1914 world now passing into middle age. The clipped moustaches, lean faces and patrician air of the men; the neatly bobbed, flat-chested and low-waisted women, meticulously turned out in every detail by their maids, were England, the kind of English jealously admired by foreigners and objects of emulation by their own inferiors. There was, without doubt, a pre-war face; you seldom see it now, for the two wars have slaughtered much of our best stock and for a couple of generations we have been breeding largely from poorer stuff. This may be hard to accept, but those who were there know it to be true. The English gentleman and the English lady were, not so very long ago, the admired of the world; the expression 'word of an Englishman' would now invite derision, but it did not come into use for nothing. Only in Spain did the grandee tradition linger on, and Spain was going through hard times. A bloody colonial war, brought to the world's notice by the defeat of a Spanish army by Abd-el-Krim in 1923, was shaking the foundations of the throne; it was making a name for a young colonel called Francisco Franco, but the world did not yet know that. Meanwhile San Sebastian beckoned to the rich, the Spanish Grand Prix was one of the great events of the year and there was much money about. Nor were its possessors stingy with it, as their outward appearance displayed.

Before *Blind Corner* was in the bookshops Mercer was back

on his treadmill, turning out yet again the kind of story that everybody reckoned him to do so much better than anybody else. His imagination was flagging and his private unhappiness did little to stimulate it. The first story of the new batch appeared in the *Windsor* issue for June 1927. As it was called 'St. Jeames' you can guess its content without much effort. John Rodney Shere loses all his money and takes service as butler with the old father of the girl he had met at a dance in Arlington Street. Her manner of setting down an over-ambitious fellow-guest had captivated him.

> 'You intolerable outsider', said Estelle. 'Because, thanks to the War, you are admitted to this house, can you see no difference between yourself and me? At a dance like this the food and the band are hired, but not the women. Be good enough to let me pass.'

The details you can fill in for yourself. The illustrations are excellent. The next two come nearer home. William Red Spenser, a gentleman brought to necessity, lives in a small croft in the Pyrenees, where he writes for his bread. Friends of his own kind in Biarritz introduce to him a young woman of surpassing wealth and beauty but possessing also a serviceable talent. William Red Spenser's existence is threatened by drought: Miss Longwood is a competent amateur water-diviner; thus all marches. The rich woman and the poor man once more combine, along with several dogs.

'Bricks Without Straw' came out early in 1928; if it was still the custom for Bettine to read the much-amended first drafts of her husband's stories she would have found little cause for silvery laughter in this one. It develops an old theme; women when they are good are very good indeed, but when they are bad they are horrid. The beginning is ominous.

> Nadège Lambert, spinster, tilted her chin. 'Don't be absurd,' she said shortly. 'I agreed to marry you, not to ignore the existence of everyone else.'

Faced by mild correction, she continues:

> 'I'm afraid you're out of date,' said the lady. She raised her beautiful eyebrows to point the sneer. 'A woman's time is her own. It wasn't once: she had to give it up right and left: the process was called "devotion".'

Later still:

> 'A girl believes in amusement: it's the article of her faith: but
> she doesn't marry for amusement, unless she's a fool. She
> takes the best man she can get that won't let her down.'

And so on, until:

> 'Our marriage will be convenient: your name is quite a good
> one, and I can put up the wealth. Try to dig any deeper, my
> friend, and, I warn you, you'll ring the bell.' Dominick
> looked away. 'You may take it as rung,' he said quietly.

Miss Lambert was, of course, not wholly out of the top drawer.
Her father was all right. ' "Poor old Lambert. We found together
at Harrow in '76," ' Sir John Medmenham observed to Forsyth
when telling him how he had cut his son off without even a
shilling upon learning of the broken engagement. Lambert,
however, was dead. Mrs Lambert lived in Eaton Square but as
her father had been born in Wapping she could not know how to
behave. She, too, turns her daughter out. Nadège, a name oddly
like Adèle, turns her only accomplishment to a useful purpose.
She becomes a chorus girl and has a terrible time of it. She pawns
her umbrella for half a crown. 'She felt for the first time the
definite stab of Fear. Other stripes she had suffered again and
again: Misery, Want, Horror had all laid on.' That taught her.
Dominick Medmenham—any connection with the Hell Fire
Club or Buchan's 1924 character Dominic Medina was purely
coincidental—did better. He took to driving a taxi, and picked
her up at the stage door just as she was down to coppers.
Consciously or unconsciously, Mercer seemed to be giving a
warning. At their first meeting Bettine had been a chorus girl
and rather elderly for the job. Ten years later she would not
want to return to the old trade. It would be prudent in her to
accommodate herself a little more towards the high-minded
husband she might have been neglecting.

Having made his point, Mercer moved on to a harmless little
story called 'Force Majeure'. Terence Ammiral writes books
that some might call whimsical and others, using a favourite
Yates word, soppy. He takes a camping holiday in the Pyrenees,
something his creator does not seem to have done. 'The tent
was a small marquee, divided in two by a curtain of soft, grey
rep. The walls and roof were lined with the same material, and
an aged Persian carpet covered the floor.' Mercer had seen

marquees often enough, but they had been erected by per-
spiring fatigue-parties lashed on by a NCO. To put one up
single-handed calls to mind that traditional figure, the one-
armed paper-hanger, with fleas. Still, as 'a candle-lantern was
shedding a decent light', it cannot have been very big, as
marquees go. To it comes a rich American girl, in flight from an
arranged marriage with a Frenchman 'who looked like a third-
class waiter'. Ammiral was all that he should have been, 'gentle,
scrupulous to a hair. His guest was, of course, as safe in his
keeping as if she had lain in a hospice governed by nuns.' A
more seemly marriage is brought about. Miss Carey, once
again, was 'very rich'. Ammiral enjoyed only a modified success
in his trade; his whimsical book, *The Bow In The Clouds* (cf.
The Stolen March) was known to Miss Carey, who spoke of it.
Ammiral honestly admits that 'it hardly sold'. When the lady
assures him that 'I love the bit where the maiden helps the
shepherd to write his love-letter and all the time it's going to be
to her', the reader begins to understand why.

'Vanity of Vanities' will go into four words. Freak-will-and-
Forsyth. The *Windsor* readership was either short in its memory
or very forgiving. Mercer may have had a conscience about it,
for the next story breaks new ground. 'Service' takes us into the
upper reaches of the used-car business and is one of the very few
short stories, other than Berry's, that can be called funny. The
narrator had rowed for Oxford and thus possessed scruples.
After all, when two car salesmen had been up at Magdalen when
the purchaser's brother was up at the House it is not seemly to
drive too hard a bargain. We go back to the old ground, south of
Marmande, and the tale is one of Mercer's best; original and
amusing; one can take for granted that it is well-written. For 'In
Evidence' he goes back to the Bar and solemnity. A lady gets
into bad, theatrical company. There is a car smash. The friends
conduct themselves ill towards the gentlewoman whose car they
have damaged by the drunken driving of one of them. In the
lawsuit that follows the heroine finds herself cross-examined by
the young barrister whom she has met and by whom she is
attracted. In the box she undergoes a moral crisis. Should she be
faithful to her now condemned friends, or tell the truth and let
them down? I shall not tell you the answer.

Captain Adam Boleyn in 'Childish Things' makes his own
position quite clear. 'I was shot through the brain during the
war.' The cure for this, the surgeon tells him, is to marry. The

story is of how this was achieved. All Mercer's ex-officers are acquainted with each other and often have walking-on parts in each others' plays. Toby and Cicely Rage, of 'Toby', invite Boleyn to visit them at Biarritz. Having accepted, he can hardly refuse to find room in his car for a young woman and her dog, whose addiction to rolling in manure is concealed from him until too late. At Angoulême, Boleyn goes down with malaria, a condition with which Mercer was demonstrably familiar. In order to minister to him in an hotel, Miss Sentinel affects to be his wife, going even to the length of buying her own ring. Only when they get to Biarritz does Boleyn learn that she is not merely rich—as he knew her to be American he had probably guessed that—but very rich indeed and famous into the bargain. Once they were married Boleyn would have had plenty of friends in the same boat to whom he could turn for advice. Three regular gambits are used in the story, none of them for the last time. Moderately poor ex-officer meets rich American girl: a pretended marriage that had later to be legitimated: the soldier with the head wound. Dogs, the hotels of Chartres and Angoulême and the car journey to Biarritz come up as regularly as colons and need no mention.

Maiden Stakes itself is one of the best things of its kind. It all turns on the Spanish Grand Prix. Roderick St Loe is reminded sadly by his employer, Ewart, that 'You were too young for the war', but that was not his fault. He is hard up, his only accomplishment is that of being an uncommonly good driver, and he wants to marry his Gyneth. Just this once, the lady has no money either. When his gladiator drops out, Ewart offers St Loe the chance of a lifetime. Will he drive the Lapage—not Delage but as near as no matter—in the race? If he wins, his fortune is made.

He saw a Madrid apartment, with tall curtained windows and the play of a great log fire on the sober walls: he saw Seville at Easter and the blue of the Mediterranean in Malaga Bay: he saw the great pile at Burgos and the long Atlantic rollers, nosing the sands of San Sebastian under the August sun. Against each one of these backgrounds he saw Gyneth— Gyneth lapped in the comfort of the stately flat, Gyneth in the sunshine of Malaga, Gyneth at San Sebastian, with her precious lips parted and the brilliant water leaping around her slim, brown legs.

143

There is a snag, of course. Gyneth is one of the family—she
had left the Boleyns to stay with the Paduas and had gone
thence to the Rages—but she disapproved Roderick risking his
life. A degree of *pia fraus* became necessary; the lady convinces
herself that he is up to something and breaks the engagement.
Only on the evening before the race does she learn the truth; as
soon as this has penetrated, Gyneth behaves very properly.
'Please give Toby my ring. I shall be there to-morrow and I
want to have it on. God speed and save you, my darling.
YOUR FUTURE WIFE.' After that, what could possibly go
wrong? The account of the race is first-rate. Mercer plainly
enjoyed writing of fast cars tearing along the empty roads of
Europe in the 1920s and he did it very well indeed. There is no
object in extracting a sample; if you have not read it before you
could do worse than read it now. Like his others, the book has
been reprinted over and over again.

The last four of the *Maiden Stakes* yarns came out in
magazine form long after the book had been published.
Amongst them comes, most unexpectedly, a Berry story. It
appears in the book under the same name as it was to bear in the
Windsor Magazine for April 1929, 'Letters Patent', but the
magazine version is the longer. The tale begins with the family
critically examining Boy's new book, the identity of which will
soon become plain.

'Oh, he mustn't die', said Adèle, 'don't make him die.'

'Of course he must die', said Berry, 'in great agony. I'll
help you with that bit.'

'I'm not sure I oughtn't to,' said Jonah, 'Besides, I rather
fancy that chapel. Make a magnificent tomb.'

Later: 'As juvenile lead and home-wrecker, I think I've the
right to be told whether my *grande passion* is extinguished by
the waters of death.'

The manner in which the family discuss the end of the story
shows the second Mercer, a man ready and willing to deride his
own work. Adèle continues to demand to know the ending.

'Remember I'm madly in love. If Jonah were to die . . .'

I looked up into her eyes. 'It's all right,' I said weakly,
'He—he doesn't die.'

The statement was afforded a mixed reception . . . 'Of
course you've ruined it,' said Berry. 'Justice demands a

victim. There's the ram all ready, caught by his corns—horns, and you ignore him. Besides, it's fantastic. He's an ounce of lead inside him and a cold on his chest. Does Adèle suck the wound?'

'Price seven and sixpence', said I.

This is all most interesting. Mercer is deliberately and publicly guying a serious piece of his own work only a few months after it had appeared in print. Had anybody else said half as much, he would have been ripe for murder. Yet he is able to mock the book in full view of his readers and is ready to share in the joke against himself. *Perishable Goods* is not funny; there is no smile in it from beginning to end, though it contains every crime in the calendar and a heart-rending finale; every word is written with a deadly seriousness of purpose but he can still hold it up to ridicule. A complicated man, Captain Mercer.

The rest of the story is of little importance. Boy receives a letter from Mr E. D. Geoffray, complaining about the tone of the new book. They go to Ascot where Berry lunches in the tent of the Marlborough. On their return they press Boy to alter the end of the story; he writes 'with many misgivings' to the publishers. 'To judge from the reception of my book, there seems to be a considerable consensus of opinion that the love-interest does not command sufficient sympathy. With your permission, therefore, I propose to revise this passage and to let you have the new version in time for it to appear in the second edition of the book.' When they go back to Ascot, Boy spots the name of a horse, Edge of Fray; E. D. Geoffray. He cleans up four hundred pounds, and spends it on a ring for Adèle.

Now consider the time at which this was written. Relations between Mercer and his wife were getting steadily worse. Stories were going about Pau of his shutting the windows whenever she sang, in order to keep out any possible listeners. When she wished to see anybody at the Club she was ordered to speak to them from the car, lowering the window in the least possible degree. Such a honey-pot as Bettine inevitably attracted flies, and flies there were in plenty. It was not so much amongst the English or the American members of the community that word got around but amongst the more ambitious of the Frenchmen. The Auguste Labottes and Porus Bureaux stroked their moustaches and set their minds to work. The beautiful

Mrs Mercer was not, it seemed, appreciated by her stuck-up husband. Well then, it would be almost a duty, as well as a pleasure, to comfort her. Bettine's only confidante was her maid, Thérèse and Thérèse had her lady's measure. Many years later she was to explain that Bettine was 'très stupide'. Possibly Thérèse was right; she had every opportunity of knowing, though Josephine, Bettine's sister, took a different view.

Mercer retreated into his study and his private world. After having written half a hundred romantic tales he was in no mood to keep up the supply for ever, although he valued them more highly as literature than ever he did the adventure stories. *Blind Corner* had made a name for him amongst a wider public than he had so far enjoyed and the characters in it were ready and waiting for further exploits. To such he addressed himself.

It was probably no accident that he had left the last book with the villains still living and rancorous. The next must tell of how 'Rose' Noble sought vengeance, and that it did. The plot of *Blind Corner* had derived from Stevenson, but Mercer had never lost sight of the old master. Anthony Hope had ended *The Prisoner of Zenda* with a flashback, the hero mulling over his own escapade. The last pages of *Blind Corner* were on the same lines, and Mercer took the idea for his trademark. Hope— yet another lawyer turned author—had given the pattern on which a sequel should be constructed. *Perishable Goods* is *The Prisoner of Zenda*, with variations. The Kings and Queens, of course, had to be laid aside, save for Chandos's description of Jonathan Mansel: 'there was a natural royalty about him such as, I think, few monarchs have been able to boast'. The kidnap victim is Adèle, and unbeknown to anybody she and Jonah love each other in a decorous way. It is not necessary to be tiresome and inquire how 'Rose' Noble came to learn of this; suffice it that he did, and that he stole first Adèle's letters and then Adèle.

The story opens with the words 'It was in October 1926', but it might have been written last week and still reads as well as when it first came out. There are details that stir ancient memories, things like carnets and triptyques for the Rolls and the sending ahead of a servant to prepare a dump of petrol tins, but that is all. With the advantage of knowing what lay ahead for Mercer himself, it is not hard to invite attention to certain passages. Of Mansel it is written that 'Full measure he gave in all things, though it were to his own beggary; and that he would palter where a girl's heart was concerned was unimaginable.' When the avengers reach Carinthia—for that, of course, is the backcloth again—they find the Pleydells, all save Jill who is, presumably, coping with children and guests at Irikli. Of Boy, Chandos observes, 'the thick dark hair I remembered was white as snow'. Remember this phrase; you will encounter it again.

Boy is *hors de combat* after a riding accident. Berry is relegated to the duties of connecting file. Jonah, Chandos and the others take up the trail, which eventually leads them to a castle seemingly designed by some forebear of Ludwig II, with a disappearing table modelled on that at Linderhof. The story is excellent, a thoroughly professional piece of work. If you know it already you will not thank me for a brief paraphrase; if you have not yet read it then the omission should be repaired as quickly as possible. A little underlining, however, can do no harm.

Mercer has left it on record that he saw himself as a compound of the men of White Ladies. For the duration of this book he is Jonathan Mansel, a quiet man, but capable of anything when under pressure. Consider this scene. Jute, a bad man, has fallen into his hands; after 'a beastly light slid into his bloodshot eyes', he announces that he has something in his pocket, as indeed he has. Adèle's blouse. Mansel calls the servants. 'He is trying to win by taking Mrs Pleydell's clothes from her back and advertising that outrage to make me throw in my hand. I do not think that a man who does that is fit to live.' Mansel sends the younger men away and, aided by the servants, executes Jute by hanging. It was inexpertly done, for 'timber hitch on the wood, slip-knot the other end' is not the way to hang a man. No wonder the job took two hours. Mercer's angels could be as ruthless as his demons at need. It was not a quality that he despised. The book ends as *Rupert of Hentzau* had ended. Mansel and Adèle had their idyll; as Adèle herself put it, 'Nature and Fortune have driven us into this Eden, and I don't think we should be human if we didn't help each other to pick the flowers.' Then an overlooked ruffian shoots Mansel—puts Berry's ounce of lead into him. Chandos, like Bernenstein, attends to him. 'Before Casemate could turn, I had knocked him flat on his face and was kneeling upon his back. Then I took my knife and drove it into his spine.' A day would come when Mercer was to feel like doing the same thing himself.

Perishable Goods first came out in July 1928 and the critics received it warmly. The price, incidentally, was not seven and six but a mere three and six. It sold many thousands of copies and continued to be reprinted until recently. The printing history of the two books published nearly simultaneously tells of the view held by the buyers. *Perishable Goods* was reprinted three times in the month of its publication, twice more before 1928 was out and twice again during each of the following years. *Maiden Stakes* had to wait until 1931 before it went back to the printers for the second time. Mercer was not slow to see the way the wind was blowing. The light romantic stuff of 1911 onwards had nearly had its day. Berry was ageless but, for the rest, he laid it aside save for a few magazine pieces in the years to come. Henceforth Chandos would be his man.

Far away from Pau, things were happening that are now more obvious than they seemed at the time. The Wall Street crash brought down Monro's Bank and dragged down the highly successful Pau branch with it. Lloyds took it over and had the wisdom to retain Mr Kennard as manager. Ellis Robins gave up his post as secretary to the Conservative Club and followed the example of the delinquent Landfall brothers by going to seek his fortune in Southern Rhodesia. The American contingent of the expatriate community suffered its share of casualties and new authors found it harder than ever to find publishers. For Mercer it made little difference. A public living a grey life cried out for more romance of the Rolls-and-castle-in-Carinthia kind and he had no difficulty in satisfying it. There was a lot of mileage left in Anthony Hope and he worked hard to bring the good Victorian stories up to date.

Since he was a slow worker it must have been that Mercer toiled exceedingly hard over *Blood Royal*, for it came out exactly a year after *Perishable Goods*, in July 1929. Mansel does not appear. It may have been that his wound still troubled him, but more probably he was under something of a cloud in consequence of his recent carryings-on with Adèle. Such things had to be taken seriously half a century ago. Chandos is promoted to juvenile lead, the Rudolf Rassendyll part, and his faithful accomplice George Hanbury moves up in the batting order.

Blood Royal retains the old *Treasure Island* formula by being recounted in the first person. Chandos, of course, is the narrator. He and Hanbury, rich now and bored by minding their acres and hunting five days a week, decide to go fishing in Carinthia. Mindful of their last visit, they set themselves to learn German, being instructed by a mysterious gentleman who had obviously known better days. The Rolls is waylaid during a storm; 'so savage was the rage of the wind that I expected every moment our hood to be carried away'. It was all a mistake. Duke Paul of Riechtenburg, a character even less delicious than Prince Rudolf, is being abducted by Major Grieg of the household of the aspiring Duke Johann, and his captors have stopped the wrong car. It turns out that the Prince is moribund, that Duke Paul is the rightful heir and that he is being removed in order that Duke Johann may be proclaimed prince in his stead. Duke Paul has the unmerited good fortune to be betrothed to the Grand Duchess Leonie, a haughty maid living in a castle and daughter to an English mother. Chandos falls exuberantly in love with her but, as a *preux chevalier*, agrees to do all that is needful to have her odious fiancé restored to his rightful place. The tutor turns out to be a gentleman of high degree, Baron Sully, Lord President of the Council no less, who had been banished by the Prince after a quarrel but now recalled to duty.

Mercer's talent for this kind of story was immense. The pace never flags, the reader is constantly kept on the edge of his chair and the quality of its language is, as always, admirable. It is perfectly true that Mercer wrote after a fashion of his own and there is no other writer of the time with whose style he can be compared. It is almost archaic in places, designedly so, and gives all the time the feeling that one is not just reading a rollicking good yarn but is having a piece of contemporary history recounted by one who was there. His touch is heavy, as he intended it to be. When Stanley Weyman (who died whilst the book was being written) was taken to task for doing something of the same kind, in writing of another Sully, he replied that 'the prolix sentences were meant to convey the stately leisure of one who, whether he dictated letters from the Arsenal of France, or lay beleaguered by a sudden *émeute* in some village inn, never forgot that his nod was life, and his word was ruin.' Mercer could have answered after the same fashion. Chandos was a heavy, solemn young man and the cadences of his descriptions of places and fierce happenings are put in language that would have come naturally to him. Weyman has also something useful and to the point on the subject of writing about far away places and events. *Under The Red Robe* was written 'in a little more than three months, spent, for the most part, on board a house-boat in the quieter reaches of the Upper Thames'. Rich imagination is as useful as encyclopaedic knowledge on such occasions, and far less tiring. If Bearn of 'the brawling streams and beech groves' could be recalled to him by 'the hanging woods above Basildon and Wittenham Clump against an evening sky', so could the castles and mountains around Pau do duty for those of Riechtenburg. As Lamartine had said, 'the land view at Pau is like the sea-view at Naples, the finest in the world'.

The virtue of *Blood Royal* lies in the fact that the plot, while hardly probable, never trespasses beyond the boundary of the possible. In a Europe that still knew nothing of Hitler there yet remained a few small kingdoms and principalities in which such things might just conceivably happen. Chandos, as a companion in common life, would have seemed muscle-bound and boring; as a gentleman of England at large and unattached he becomes a formidable figure. Some aspects of him are, perhaps, Mercer's dream of what he himself would have wished to be. Immitigable to the impertinent; Bettine was to write in her diary years afterwards that Bill 'enjoys hurting [people] and sending them off with "a flea in their ear"'. Terrible in a rough-house, as Mercer could be; preternaturally cunning and resourceful at outwitting enemies; formal to the point of pedantry in his address to all comers. The 1926 photograph that adorned the back of the dust-jackets for so many years was believed by many people to be an artist's idea of Chandos. It was, in fact, Mercer himself, looking as proud and stern as any hidalgo who ever came out of Old Castile.

The reviewers were as enthusiastic about *Blood Royal* as they had been over the two earlier Chandos books and it was clear that Mercer had struck a rich vein. He decided to try his luck with the story in America. The *Saturday Evening Post* was willing to run it as a serial, but only upon the condition that Chandos became an American citizen for the duration. Mercer, now well enough off to be discriminating, flatly refused. He had hopes of Hollywood, but no business resulted and he made no serious effort to press it upon the film people.

Mercer had an attitude towards publicity that was all his own. It was based upon the indisputable fact that gentlemen do not show off, least of all in public. He would never have had the smallest objection to being awarded the palm—indeed he had a strong streak of ambition in his nature—but the dust of the arena was abhorrent to him. He had no objection to a photograph of Dornford Yates appearing on covers; at least it showed the unknown author to be no jumped-up plebeian; but intrusion into his privacy was not to be permitted. No literary lunches; no launching parties; not even membership of the uncouth occupational bodies to which authors commonly subscribe. The Garbo touch was effective in making him a figure of high mystery; it also did no harm to his sales.

Blood Royal is strong on sheer adventure but weak on romance; the moth-and-star courtship of a Grand Duchess by a man who, but for the spoiling of his solitary picnic outside Chartres by Ellis, might have gone into trade, is carried out with the utmost decorum. This time the likes of Mr E. D. Geoffray would have no suggestions of sin, adultery, fornication and threatened rape to spoil their wholesome reading. Nor is there any killing. Chandos half-kills Major Grieg and one or two others amongst the clowns and Augustes, but his game-book still contains only Casemate (stabbed). As he leaves the pages of the book equipped with a rich wife, whose fortune, added to his own, made the pair rich indeed, one might have expected that Chandos had outlived his usefulness. Captain Mercer took a different view.

Blood Royal was reprinted four times within its first six months. This was rather less than its predecessor, but it may well have been that larger numbers were turned out. The records went in the war. It is fairly certain that the slump hit book buyers as hard as other people, but the figures were still more than satisfactory; in the days of Boots, Smiths, and other great circulating libraries a popular novel was assured of a multitude of readers and Dornford Yates was now an important name amongst authors.

Mercer went straight back to his great desk and worked away at a sequel, *Fire Below*. Once again he took his pick and shovel into the old quarry. *The Prisoner of Zenda* had left Mr Rassendyll exiled from Ruritania, with the woman he loved married to another man. His enemies employed a stratagem based upon that love to lure him back into the country and thus to furnish a plot for *Rupert of Hentzau*. So excellent a precedent should not be wasted. The Grand Duchess being already his wife, Chandos could hardly be enticed in quite the same fashion, but all was not lost. A female friend, lately widowed, has been left behind, and a forged telegram from her serves as a sufficient bait; to round things off, George Hanbury reveals an unsuspected passion for the lady and the party sets off once more into forbidden territory in order to enlarge her. How they return, are compelled to quit the country leaving her hostage, come back again and carry her off makes up the tale. In no way does it fall below the others. Chandos adds another name to the roll begun with Casemate by hurling the wicked Major Grieg from a cliff into a torrent, this time with a lethal result. He also demonstrates the Puritan—one is hard put to avoiding the word priggish—side of his creator. A pretty country girl who loves him asks for a kiss. Instead of this, she gets a pompous lecture on marital fidelity, much to her chagrin. Hugh Drummond would have kissed the girl heartily, though not in a nasty way, and, had he remembered it, might have mentioned the fact to Phyllis at some convenient opportunity. Neither Hannay nor Leithen would have been offered the chance. But what can you expect from a man who, after all their adventures, still addresses his friends by surname? It is, of course, entirely possible that the homily was really addressed to Bettine, compassed about with many admirers as she was.

Fire Below owes something to Mercer's favourite composer as well as to Anthony Hope. In *Blood Royal* The Grand Duchess accompanies Duke Paul to a gala performance of *Tosca*, Richard Chandos being somewhere in the audience. The police chief Scarpia was paralleled by Major Grieg. Like Tosca, the Countess Dresden is given a chance between submission to her captor or the imprisonment and probable murder of her lover. Then comes a difference in degree. Floria Tosca promptly knifes the scoundrel; Marya Dresden goes through a form of marriage with him. Whether or not this was limited to a paper transaction is kept unrevealed, in the same way as the reader is left to guess what really happened between Adèle and Jonathan Mansel. The climax is much the same, though it is Scarpia and not Tosca who goes over the edge. Should Mercer's work ever be set to music it ought to be Puccini who furnishes it for the Chandos books; White Ladies demand Elgar. *Fire Below* is the name of a sea shanty, but it is the stuff of a grand opera.

The book emerged from printers and binders in June 1930 and was snapped up as eagerly as the others had been. Shortly after its appearance another event secured Mercer's fortune.

On 4 September his aunt Mary, daughter to Admiral Sam and widow of John Dimsdale, died in London leaving estate to the tune of nearly £25,000. Of this Mercer received a cash legacy of about £800 and a life interest in the residue. A substantial gift went also to the Nuns of St Mary's Convent at Chiswick. Convents seem to have been a subject of family interest, and crop up from time to time in the books.

This windfall, together with increasing royalties, made Mercer more than comfortably off. He had always rather fancied himself as a judge of old furniture, of silver and of precious stones, probably with some justice. His standing as a connoisseur of brandy, by which he set store, is more open to question. A man who asserts, as Mercer often did, that a good brandy should burn your throat cannot complain at raised eyebrows. The contents of Villa Maryland increased in number and sumptuousness.

None of these considerations diminished his appetite for work. The Chandos books had made the name of Dornford Yates widely known, had brought in a pleasing amount of money and had broadened his experience as a writer of contemporary novels. The fact remained that he was still more Boy Pleydell than Richard Chandos, that his heart was more than ever at White Ladies, with distance lending enchantment, and people were demanding to know what had become of Berry. 'Letters Patent' had made some effort to explain that *Perishable Goods* had really been just a leg-pull and Jonah, Adèle, Boy and the rest were in truth as united and comradely as ever. It was stretching credulity too far to furnish Chandos with a new adventure every summer and it was high time that the old faithfuls were resurrected. To this operation Mercer turned his mind.

It was the unhappiest period of his life, for his marriage was now firmly on the rocks. To seek out the reasons and to apportion blame is as profitless as impertinent. For a long time now Mercer had been working very hard and his wife, with some reason, felt herself both neglected and ill used. Her sister Josephine, who detested Mercer, has asserted that Bettine was 'very entertaining, talented and intelligent', a view not shared by Thérèse. She goes on to tell that 'my sister had many admirers as most attractive ladies'. This Mercer would not tolerate; on parade they behaved as civilized people do, but once dismissed their private quarrels seem to have become bitter. For his part, Mercer had no friend with whom he could talk freely and, in any event, mental undressing was against his nature. The picture-clock made a poor substitute, but it was his only confidant.

He was away from Pau a good deal, for journeys to London were necessary, partly in order to keep in touch with Richard and also for publishing reasons. Ward Lock were happy to see him. No Dornford Yates story had enlivened the *Windsor Magazine* since early in 1929 and the firm was glad enough to agree to publish another one as soon as it could be finished. Mercer took to flying, for Imperial Airways were running thrice daily services between Le Bourget and Croydon. The return fare was eleven guineas, the time taken two hours and fifty minutes. In Paris he usually stayed at the Hôtel du Rhin in the Place Vendôme; in London at the Conservative Club. He also discovered an excellent hotel, convenient for visits to Oxford, at Great Fosters in Egham, a place by which he was so taken that he later put it into a short story under the name of Cock Feathers. From time to time he visited former haunts, the Old Bailey and the Law Courts; the new generation of counsel were not of the former quality. In *B-Berry and I Look Back* he tells of Patrick Hastings. 'He was not in the same street. Such was his reputation between the wars that I made a point of going to hear him in a cause célèbre . . . I believe he was very successful; but, quite honestly, he simply didn't compare with Marshall Hall.' He seems to have witnessed the trial of Brown and Kennedy for the murder of PC Gutteridge, for he made it the subject of one of the last *Windsor* stories in 1937. One thing he did not see was a female barrister; his opinion of their probable serviceability is on record. The actuality would hardly have altered it. Had anyone told him that a day would come when women, dressed as gentlemen of Queen Anne's day, would sit upon the Bench, or that a gentleman of Asiatic antecedents not wigged but hatted after the fashion of his people would appear at an elevation only a little lower, he would have fled the country for good. Either that or damned the prophet for a liar.

Back in Pau, Mercer returned to his study and his dog in order to begin work on a book which contains many of the funniest passages he ever wrote. Not Puccini this time; more the Prologue to *I Pagliacci*. His health was not good, his private life was a wreck, his personal popularity minimal. Once the study door closed behind him, these things fell away and William Mercer translated himself into Boy Pleydell again.

8

'Of Making Many Books'

'After the first four Chandos books, you wrote *Adèle and Co.*'
'To my mind', said Berry, 'taking it by and large, you've never bettered that book'.
'I shall always think it's the best of the Berry books'.
'Better', said Daphne, 'than *The House That Berry Built*?'
'That's my belief'.

It is also the belief of many of the most dedicated readers. *Adèle and Co.* contains all the things that Mercer did best. Unlike the earlier Berries, it reads as a connected whole and it includes both crime, criminals and some of the funniest writing in the English language. The story deserves more than a passing mention. At the beginning, the family is found drugged in a room overlooking the Place Vendôme and thus, by inference in the Hôtel du Rhin. Let the description of Berry's plight serve for all of them.

Against her—Adèle—reclined Berry Pleydell, my brother-in-law. His head lolled upon her shoulder, his body was supported by hers, and his arms and legs were sprawling like those of a sawdust doll. I regret to record that he looked especially shameless and more than anyone present sounded the Roman note.

All their jewels have gone: 'my sister's emerald bracelets that came from Prague, her diamond and emerald necklace and diamond rings: the Duchess of Padua's pearls— historic gems which appear in a portrait by Velasquez that hangs at Rome;' and others. Jonah, characteristically, has his wits still about him and soon concludes that the villain is their similarly drugged companion, Casca de Palk.

155

With Jonah of the company it is plain that the outrage must be dealt with by their own resources; a visit to his unsavoury friends at the Wet Flag in Rouen (where an Old Harrovian makes the band play the Eton Boating Song) furnishes the necessary lead. It also produces the immortal phrase 'I think Sweaty knows them cuffs.' Simple adjectives suggesting an imperfect toilet are commonly used amongst the lower orders. Sweaty, Lousy, Mangey and even Goat all imply hygienic defects.

The trail leads them to Tours and a house that demands inspection. Berry and Boy, visiting it by night, discover an alley-way at the rear inhabited only by animal life. As Berry is speaking of 'the crisp brush of garbage about my insteps', there comes an interruption.

The insolent growl of a cat cut short the memory. 'Oh, I beg your pardon. I fear that was your sardine. I do hope I haven't hurt it. There's a nest of putrid tomatoes a yard or two back, if that's any use to you. No? Oh, I'm sorry about that. You couldn't come a little closer, could you? No, I thought not, you craven. Never mind. Here's a little present from Uncle Rex.' An empty can met the base of the wall with great savagery, and four or five cats took flight.

A few moments later:

The contents of a slop-pail pitched directly before us three feet from where we stood. To say that we were bespattered is half the truth. When about five gallons of fluid are discharged from a height of forty feet on to a cobbled pavement, the fountain induced is bold and generous. A venomous wave of muck thrashed us from head to foot.

There was a dreadful silence. Then the window above us was violently shut.

'Can I go home now?' said Berry. 'I mean, I don't want to miss anything, but if that's the end. . . .'

The chase takes them over all the familiar parts of France. It brings in characters some of whom are due to live another day and others, notably Jill's babies, whose days are to be short. The climax comes at Eaux Bonnes and it is plain that Mercer had examined the ground thereabouts in considerable detail. Whether he knew what was coming or not can only be guess-work, but the book is Adèle valediction. She never appears again.

After *Adèle and Co.* there comes a long gap in Mercer's work. The oddest thing about it all is that he wrote this, the most joyous and uproarious book of them all, at a time when his life was at its most miserable. By 1931, when it was first published, the Mercers' marriage had passed the point of no return. It is not a subject about which one can write dogmatically, and this for several reasons. In the first place, whilst Bettine has left some account of her view of the matter, Mercer left none. Anybody with experience of the Divorce Court knows it to be the forum in which more hard lying has taken place than in any other, and it is by no means always deliberate. Husbands and wives, once they have finally taken against each other, are the worst possible judges of each other's quality and motives. A proof of evidence that, on its face value, seems to show an unanswerable case often looks very different after its maker has been strictly cross-examined. Bettine's version of how the wreck came about was never so tested. This does not mean that she was being consciously untruthful; the simple fact is that the two stories were never laid side by side for comparison.

Some facts are solid; some assertions are made by people whose own conduct would not bear close examination and some of these are still living. By about 1929 the marriage had become a façade. The things that were common knowledge in Pau, and the deductions to be drawn from Mercer's letters to Thérèse at the end of 1931, add up to a fairly coherent story, but it is not possible, relying on the memories of people now of great age, to assemble them in chronological order with any certainty of being right. Bettine was under siege from a Frenchman named Marie-Valéry Ollivier, who was rich and notorious as a chaser of women. She asserts that she entreated Mercer to rid her of him, but that he declined to act. This may well be true. Hugh Drummond would have sought out the miscreant and informed him genially that if ever his face was seen around the home again he would have his spine kicked through his hat. Mercer, a more precise man, would have drawn the line at saying, in effect, 'Keep away from my wife; I cannot be confident of her virtue if pressed too hard.' He was not, however, in the least complaisant. Mr Kennard has told the writer of how Mercer dealt with the matter, but understandably cannot put a date to it. One day he came into the bank and, after transacting his business there, he observed, 'By the way,

have you heard the news?'—'What news?' 'You'll soon know':
this with a grin. Next day it was all over Pau, how Mercer had
fallen on some Frenchman on the steps of the English Club,
thrashed him with a crop and broken his arm, to repeated cries
of '*Sale Juif*'. It seems reasonable to identify him as M. Ollivier.

Whether Bettine had already returned to her family in New
York at the time or whether she left soon afterwards is uncertain, but leave she did. Mercer made a confidante of Thérèse,
writing to her regularly during his visits to Paris and London at
the end of the year. Thérèse in turn kept up a correspondence
with Bettine and it seems fairly plain that much of what she
wrote was at Mercer's dictation. So matters might have drifted
on, had not fate taken a hand in the game. In the spring of 1932,
Mercer, low in health and spirits, signed on for a cruise to
Madeira in the *Arandora Star*. Amongst the passengers was a
young woman of twenty-six named Doreen Elizabeth Lucy
Bowie, the daughter of a London solicitor, who was also
travelling for reasons of health; she had the misfortune to be
afflicted with the disease then commonly called infantile
paralysis and had difficulty in walking. Mercer was captivated;
here was an English girl of his own kind, the incarnation of the
imaginary Jill. Miss Bowie, for her part, was attracted to this
distinguished-looking man whose company and conversation
she greatly enjoyed; when *Arandora Star* berthed at San
Sebastian he seized the opportunity of taking her to Pau in
order that she might see his beautiful home. The chance meeting
made his predicament even worse than it had been. More than
anything in the world Mercer now wanted to rid himself of
Bettine and to marry a girl who might have been designed to fit
into his dream world of White Ladies and all that it represented.

By June 1932 he was back in the empty Villa Maryland.
Thérèse, it seems fair to assume, had told him her tale of a
surreptitious visit by M. Ollivier and of a rumpled bed. It is not
possible to vouch for its truth or falsity, but it was certainly
presented to him in that fashion. On 7 June 1932 he sat down
to write a long letter to Bettine in America. It is a curious
document, too long to be set out in full, and it suggests a
confused mind at work on it. Mercer, of course, was a trained
lawyer. Divorce had not been his subject, but he knew enough
about it to realize that a letter written by a prospective petitioner
to a prospective respondent would almost certainly be read out
some day in open Court. Had he intended to produce a

document in support of an allegation of adultery, the sense of it would have been something like 'Since you admitted to me on such-and-such a day that you had been to bed with M. Ollivier it becomes impossible that our marriage continue, but I will be as generous to you as I can.' Her answer, admission or denial, would have been useful in the proceedings. Mercer wrote nothing of the kind. He thanks 'My dear Bet' for her cable reporting her safe arrival in America, tells of his trip—'I am very burned and awfully well mentally as well as physically. I must say the cruise was the very thing I needed and I am a man again'—says that the people on board had been very nice to him—'though I don't know that you would have found them very amusing, they were the sort of people that I can get on with'—and speaks of Madeira. He assures her that Richard is well and happy 'and asks for a mouth organ'. Then he comes to the point. 'My dear, I have been so blind, but now I can see. Our dream crashed at least two years ago . . . And I fought like a madman—or spoiled child—to mend what was unmendable . . . We ought to have parted before, of course, long ago. That we didn't was my fault.' He thanks her for ten happy years, observes that he hopes she will stay on in America 'and take some decent, honest man—you'll have so many suitors—who will make you really happy again'. A strange thing to say to a Catholic, but there it is. He goes on to say that though they must never meet again she can always count on him for help, and ends with a flowery compliment. It might have been a genuine expression of mixed-up feelings: it could have been plain humbug. The fact that its sound to a judge would have done his cause no good—there is no hint of accusation of any matrimonial offence in it—tends to suggest that it was what it seemed to be. Muddled, distraught, but genuine. There is that cryptic sentence 'I am a man again'. Years later, Bettine was to write in her diary, 'The only thing in him that can be touched is his sex and his pride'. It may add up to something: equally it may not. It is useless to worry at it.

In July Bettine received another letter, this time from Thérèse. The terminology suggests that the true author had a greater command of language than is usual amongst servants. The drift of it is that Bettine would serve her own interests best by letting Mercer have what he wanted and trust to his generosity. It contains a most curious passage. In translation it reads that Monsieur does not regard himself as insulted because he does not regard this man as a man but as a monkey. Mercer certainly ranked M. Ollivier as both socially and aesthetically below Guy the Gorilla but it is an odd thing to say. Perhaps blue-based baboons were in his mind, Ollivier counting as one. Thérèse adds affectingly that 'Monsieur's hair has gone very white', as Boy's had done on a similar occasion. The words following, 'et les miens commencent', suggest themselves as Thérèse's own.

The testimony of a visitor suggests that Mercer, as a grass-widower, took on a new lease of life. Oddly enough, and unknown to either, there was a link of sorts between them. Guy Tassell was a highly-respected East Kent solicitor, a member of one of the oldest firms in the county; in 1911 he had drawn up the will of Robert Mercer of Rodmersham Hall, possibly a distant relation to Bill, who had died in 1917 leaving estate to the value of a quarter of a million pounds and a son named Bertram. Mr Tassell, as well as being Robert Mercer's trustee, was father to a daughter with a name known in golfing circles and a visitor to the Chiberta links since 1930. Miss Tassell, at twenty-one, was well-read in Yates lore and in August 1932, at about the moment when Bettine was digesting the letter, she received an invitation to visit the great man at Maryland. This in itself was a new departure, for Major Stedall tells that under the old regime guests at Maryland had been few. Joan Tassell passed two enjoyable hours 'in the study where he wrote, looking out at the superb view of the Pyrenees', for Mercer was in an excellent humour and his hair as dark as ever; he positively enjoyed being taken to task over the business of Eulalie and the putter and his guest took her leave carrying an autographed copy of *And Five Were Foolish*, still on her bookshelves. No word was spoken about the absent mistress of the Villa nor was there a hint in the conversation to suggest that anything was amiss. The secret was well kept. Even Mr Kennard knew nothing about the pending proceedings until they were over.

In spite of all these distractions the work had gone on, the study still providing an escape from reality. *Safe Custody*, first published in 1932, shows how much was still left to be extracted from the old quarry. A castle in Carinthia—its description once more suggests Hochosterwitz, near Klagenfurt—a treasure of priceless gems deposited by the Borgia Pope Alexander VI, Rolls-Royces, battle, murder and very sudden death by original means. No Chandos this time, but adequate one-off substitutes. By all the rules his public ought to have become disenchanted by now with such well-worn stuff, but it cannot be denied that *Safe Custody* came as fresh as any of the others. Mercer must have been feeling homesick when he wrote it, for it bears the dedication 'To the finest city in the world incomparable LONDON TOWN'. It was acclaimed by the critics in the way now to be expected and the printers were put to work once more before the year was out.

Some account now seems inescapable of the workings of the Divorce Court in the 1930s. To begin with, the Court in England could only act when the matrimonial domicile—in plain language, the permanent home of the husband—was within that country. Next, it was for the injured party to prepare his or her petition, a formal document setting out such things as the date and place of the wedding, the birth of children and the matrimonial offence upon which the Court was asked to dissolve the marriage. In addition to this it had to contain a declaration that it was not presented in collusion with the respondent. To the truth of all these matters the petitioner was obliged to swear an oath. Collusion, a private deal between the parties made behind the Judge's back, was an absolute bar to the getting of a decree and any lawyer who might be party to it would be in serious trouble. It went on regularly, as every-body knew, for the obvious reason that it was impossible to stop it. Nevertheless, if a husband-petitioner struck a bargain with his wife he must be prepared to perjure himself in order to give effect to it. Most consciences seem to have been elastic enough to face the prospect bravely. The petition then had to be served personally upon the respondent and any adulterer named in it. The process server was himself required to swear that he had done this before the suit could be entered in the list. Mercer was taking no chances with Ollivier; he was of the party that ambushed him for the purpose. Bettine's sister asserts that he lured his wife to London by cabling that Richard was in hospital for an operation on his eye, and caused the petition to be handed to her in the street. It is hard to see what he stood to gain by this; it would have been easy enough to have had the document served on her in America, for Bettine was no absconding debtor.

I am told by several people that Mercer made it his business to travel to France and to lurk in the bushes whilst his process server handed the petition to the co-respondent. This is quoted as evidence of spiteful behaviour, but a more charitable, and more likely, explanation is possible. Leave had been given for the papers to be served out of the jurisdiction. The server would have had to satisfy the Court that his task had been regularly accomplished; should he fail in this it would have been necessary to start all over again. Mercer knew Ollivier by sight and was anxious to make certain that all was properly carried out; possibly he derived some grim satisfaction from seeing the thing done, but that is hardly likely to have been his first consideration. The feelings of M. Ollivier are nowhere recorded. Very possibly he felt flattered by the allegation that he had had his will of the beautiful Bettine. He certainly took no part in the proceedings, and for the rest of his life he would be able to produce documentary evidence that a Court had found his efforts not to have been denied the success they deserved. It would be no surprise to learn that the decree found a place amongst his most treasured possessions.

Once the petition had been served, the respondent had to decide whether or not to defend, which is done by filing an Answer. Bettine, who always flatly denied adultery, says that she was seriously considering doing this when a message arrived from Mercer offering her £500 a year as the price of taking no part in the suit. In the nature of things neither proof nor disproof is possible, for the utmost secrecy would have had to be kept. Bettine, who does not appear to have sought professional advice, did not defend. By taking this course she disarmed herself completely, for a wife found to have committed adultery forfeited her right to any maintenance from her husband; a compassionate allowance—enough to keep her off the parish—could, in theory, be granted, but it was done very sparingly. The probability is that her account is true, for Mercer would not have found it easy to establish his charge on the evidence available to him.

There was much to-ing and fro-ing during the last months of 1932 and the first of 1933, with Mercer going to London to confer with his solicitors, and to Oxford in order that Richard might be kept abreast of events. He kept up a regular correspondence with Thérèse in his schoolboy French, much of it fussy details about things to be done in the house or small jobs for Ramon to carry out on the car. On no account, she was

162

told, was anybody to be given any information about Madame save for the fact that she was in America.

Early in March 1933 the case came into the Warned List. Mercer moved into a London hotel, bringing Thérèse with him as his essential witness. He was worried not only about the outcome but also over any possible publicity. Few people could identify the Mercer, C. W. of the List with the famous Dornford Yates, but there was always some risk and the press would certainly make the most of it. Personal publicity was always distasteful; publicity of this kind might be very damaging to the repute of White Ladies and the champion of aristocratic manners and behaviour. Divorce suits have to be held in public; there are restrictions upon what may be published, but anybody has the right to be present and note what is said. There were, however, ways and means of mitigating the danger, known to clerks as well as their own mystery was known to the frequenters of The Wet Flag. With a little nudging it was usually possible to have a case called on at a time when nobody was likely to be about the place, and it may easily have been that Mercer was well served. On 13 March 1933 the case was called on, before Langton, J. Par for the course in an ordinary undefended was about twelve minutes. The Registry declines to release the transcript of evidence, but a fair guess can be made at what happened. Mercer, presumably, gave formal evidence, Thérèse told her surreptitious-visit-and-rumpled-bed story. The Judge, having no other version before him, granted the decree nisi. Six months later, on 20 September 1933, du Parcq, J., made it absolute at a formal hearing in the Vacation Court. Mercer was free: to all appearances his conscience was not over-burdened. Nor was it a matter of putting on what Mr Gladstone had called a front of seven-fold brass. He was entirely persuaded that his conduct merited no reproach.

Richard, still at his preparatory school, seems to have accepted it stoically. Years later, in a contribution to a centenary symposium at Summer Fields, he told of remembering his father as 'a rather aloof and wrathful figure, smelling of bay rum, surrounded by books'. Bettine, however, took it hard. In all probability she was guiltless of the charge laid against her, and the last forty years of her life were exemplary. Whether she is right in her assertion that Mercer bilked her by reducing the promised £500 by half, and cutting it down to £120 during the war, is unprovable and no expression of opinion can be of any value. All the same, she is hardly likely to have invented a story that would be of no use to her and of interest to few. For years she seems to have made her living by employing her talent for languages and when, in 1973, she died at Lugano she was by no means destitute. A visitor who saw her when she was past eighty described her as beautiful still and very chic; her estate in England amounted to just under £1,800. As she passed out of Mercer's life, so did Richard pass out of hers. It was a heavy price to pay for marrying the wrong man.

Mercer went back to Maryland and turned his mind to the next book. *Storm Music*, published in 1934 and dedicated simply 'To My Son', was another variation on the old theme. A castle in Austria, the fifth so far, inhabited by a beautiful and haughty countess, daughter to an American mother. Inside is a great treasure; without are dogs, murderers and two footloose Englishmen. Chandos was still being rested but his alter ego, John Spencer, was an acceptable substitute. He ends the tale with a score of three—one stabbed, one shot, and one with his spine snapped across a table. Despite this promising start he was never employed again. The faithful knew what they were buying without bothering to look at it. The critics approved once again and three more printings appeared before the year was out.

Storm Music was not the only event of 1934. On 10 February, at Chertsey Register Office, Cecil William Mercer, forty-eight, writer, of Dormy House Club, Sunningdale, married Doreen Elizabeth Lucy Bowie, twenty-eight, spinster, of Orminston, Sunningdale. It was the best day's work he ever did for himself.

Elizabeth Mercer, because of her disability, had led a sheltered life but she understood her new husband better than anybody had done before, and he in his turn adored her. It is a measure of wifely affection that Elizabeth suffered herself to be called Jill and did her best to conform with the idea of her new incarnation. The Jill of the books is innocent almost to the point of being simple-minded whereas Elizabeth Mercer was nothing of the kind. An intelligent, educated Englishwoman with few interests outside their home and equipped with a robust turn of phrase was exactly the complement Mercer needed; this time husband and wife suited each other admirably.

Early in 1935 there appeared his first *Windsor* story for a long time, a White Ladies frolic obviously set in the distant past. The Knave, an Alsatian, was a real dog and Mercer's letters to Thérèse had been larded with directions for his care during his master's absences. 'Enter The Knave' promoted him to the rank of a Berry Character. The story is set in an hotel called Cock Feathers—'old Amersham's place, now an hotel'. It does contain one lapse of memory. 'Jill has never grown up. Though she is more than twenty she has the look and the way of a beautiful child. Her great grey eyes and her golden hair are those of the fairy tales. Who runs may read her nature—a lovely document.' William Mercer was certainly in love; readers of *The Courts Of Idleness* would have remembered Jill as having been twenty-two as long ago as 1918. But no matter. The story is a good one, with Boy sad-dogging away in the old style. A year later came another Berry, the last to appear in the *Windsor*. It is called 'Lady Friends' and tells of the intrusion upon the family of a preposterous and enormous woman called Theresa Weigh. Apart from two unconnected stories that were to be published just before the Second War, the collaboration between Mercer and the magazine, begun in 1911, was over. He had grown out of such things and had become a novelist of the first rank. 'Enter The Knave' and 'Lady Friends', however, were not wasted. The next Berry book found a use for them, explaining for the benefit of the captious that it had all happened in the summer of 1920.

Life at Villa Maryland was better now. Thérèse, on her best behaviour, lady's-maided Elizabeth whilst her husband Joseph doubled as butler and chauffeur. The kitchens were in the charge of Edouard, who remained there until 1940; Mercer had previously had trouble with a female cook 'who brought an action against me which was heard at Lescar, and which I won hands down'. He had firm ideas about servants; a man who wanted to create anything needed to have his own requirements properly attended to. The Mercers were always excellently served and his exhibitions of temper became rarer under the new dispensation.

As always, he worked like a beaver and he had it firmly in his mind that he wanted to write a book for his new wife. Not just another *réchauffé* of castles and treasures, but something better. He began it soon after their marriage and in 1935 the bookshops put it on sale. *She Fell Among Thieves* is dedicated simply 'To Jill' and it marked a new departure. First, there was the matter of Chandos, whom he wanted back. Some books ago he had married a wife and therefore he could not come. Mercer would see about that. Imperial Airways had an admirable safety record, but they must be allowed an occasional lapse. They took it, and thus disposed of Leonie, Grand Duchess of Riechtenburg, Mrs Richard Chandos. It seemed a good idea and would be employed again when his pay-roll became over-crowded. Chandos, 'grey-haired at thirty', Mercer's alter ego—or one of them—became available for further exploits. This time they did not take him so far afield. It seemed un-necessary to visit Austria when the Pyrenees, on the very doorstep, offered everything. *She Fell Among Thieves* tells of a wicked old lady who drugs a girl—it is not entirely clear in what relationship to herself—and reduces her to the mental age of a small child. Chandos frees her and entrusts her to the care of Jill, to whom the experience of coping with a mental inferior must have been as gratifying as it was unexpected. There is, of course, much more to the story than that. Mansel, for example, is back, purged of guilty passion and at one point apparently on the way to taking on a beautiful idiot. And a subsidiary character, Virginia, finally marries a Scotsman and accompanies him to Rhodesia. Mercer was well pleased with it but it was not received with the rapture that had attended the others. Chandos adds one more to his bag which stands at the end with a score of four. Casemate, knifed; Major Grieg and Jean the chauffeur, both dejected; Luis the Spaniard, battered to death with a pair of field-glasses. As with *Safe Custody* (or *Anthony and Cleopatra*), it concludes with a mass poisoning. In spite of that the book sold well only in England. The American *Saturday Evening Post* had run *Safe Custody* and *Storm Music* as serials, but this one was not in accord with American taste, female villains being abhorred. Mercer's agent in the States was firm about this, but the author could now afford to disregard the such whinings and write as he pleased. Captain Mercer was, indeed, becoming rather rich. The ladies of England were made of sterner stuff and *Woman's Journal* was glad to publish the work in the form of a serial.

Elizabeth settled in happily enough and ran the household to perfection. Thérèse, who accorded her far more respect than she had ever shown Bettine, tells that she was kept hard at work during the day and sometimes had even to deal with evening parties. Possibly the fact that Elizabeth had nothing like Bettine's command of colloquial French put more of a barrier between them, but there were certainly no servant problems. Naturally enough she wanted her own family and friends to see her in her new home and Mercer, though his attitude to Pau society remained unchanged, did not discourage the idea. Amongst the first of the house guests were Elizabeth's sister, Mrs Humphreys, accompanied by her husband and their twelve-year-old son Colin. Mr Humphreys had had a far rougher war than had Mercer and still walked on crutches by reason of wounds received on the Somme. Mercer's behaviour to them was everything that could be expected from a good host. One cannot avoid the impression that with the departure of Bettine he was becoming a more amiable man. This was certainly due to the influence of Elizabeth, probably the only person apart from his mother who ever understood the workings of his mind. Elizabeth would have fitted in perfectly at White Ladies; Bettine, never. Mercer's change in attitude, however, was not spectacular. The Conan Doyle character who put a board at the end of his drive with the legend 'General and Mrs Heatherstone have no wish to increase the circle of their acquaintances' would have merited unstinting approval.

Far from being stricken with premature senility, Mercer at fifty was working harder than ever. Almost simultaneously with the appearance of *She Fell Among Thieves* from Hodder & Stoughton, Ward Lock brought out *And Berry Came Too*, again with a fulsome dedication to Jill. It was reviewed in *Punch* on 29 January 1936 between heavy black borders, for this was the Memorial Number to King George V. The review was an entirely fair one, and it confirms the suspicion that the middle-aged Mercer, with two marriage certificates and a divorce decree in his desk drawer, was still essentially the Mercer of 1911.

The absence of Berry, perhaps most silver-tongued of all the great masters of inactivity, from the fiction-lists since 1931 has been a grief to me and to many. A loud and general cheer is likely to greet the publication of . . . eight stories in which Mr. Dornford Yates describes as well as ever the hair-raising adventures and idiotic situations in which the Pleydell family are embroiled . . and so long as the Pleydells are in danger or Berry in oratorical mood I could go on reading about them for a very long time. I tire a little of the unrelenting opulence in which Mr. Yates rather revels . . . but though I can forgive this I cannot so easily pardon the lush sentimentality which engulfs Mr. Yates whenever he contemplates his women-characters. This is a curious blind spot in a writer whose sense of humour is beyond question . . . In six out of the eight stories, and eleven times altogether, Boy, the narrator, likens his girl-friend with enthusiasm to a child (never explaining why, for her mental and physical development seem perfectly satisfactory); and when he gets going on the beauty, sweetness and virtue of the others I must admit that I shudder, for such glucose goes ill with Berry's magnificent asperity.

All this had been pointed out to Mercer long ago and with some regularity. He remained quite unrepentant, but one has to admit that Mr Punch had the right of it. 'Sapper' could be nearly as bad; his heroes regularly address young women as 'Kid', or even 'Kiddie'. The following year saw *She Painted Her Face*, a pot-boiler that appeared in serial form within the covers of his new friend *Woman's Journal*. We go back once more to a Countess, a castle in Carinthia, and a well. The book is dedicated to the memory of The Knave, soon to be succeeded by the terrier Tumble, and the doggy beginning is kept up with the introduction of a Duchess of Whelp—a title long known to the Almanach de Gotha. A secret chamber containing a desiccated corpse had been used five years before by Buchan in *The Blanket of The Dark*, but it was still serviceable. The plot is Mercer Mark II; the characters bear unfamiliar names, but come straight out of his stock; only one old friend appears, a passing reference to Porus Bureau—late of *The Stolen March*—'a rich, French Jew . . . entirely and utterly leprous, body and soul . . . no woman-servant would enter his room'. M. Ollivier, too, has his memorial. Having said all that, it is necessary to admit that the yarn is an excellent one, tautly written and as exciting as ever. The fight in the dark around and finally down the well is admirably done; the theme of inclination plus opportunity, sternly resisted, comes back again. Few writers possessed such a gift for turning old material into acceptable wear. The Duchess of Whelp, an entirely original character, bears the name of Mercer's much-loved grand-mother, Harriet. It can hardly have come about by accident. She was due for an apology after Aunt Harriet in 'Ann', and the Duchess shares common characteristics with Lady Harriet

Touchstone. Nor was it chance that named the heroine Elizabeth.

A few weeks after the book appeared came the break-up of a triumvirate that had dominated the English thriller market for so long. Cyril McNeile, Sapper, died on 14 August at the age of forty-nine; his friend Gerard Fairlie continued the work, but it was not to be quite the same again. Mercer, never a man to let up, put himself to work on the strangest book in his list.

This Publican was written in 1936, the year in which the Spanish Civil War began and Pau was haunted by sinister gentlemen resembling those in the advertisements for Sandeman's Port. It tells of a dreadful woman, Rowena, who is married to a serious-minded young barrister named David Bohun, and it is dedicated to 'That great ring-master Satire who plays so big a part in the circus of Life'. It also, for the first time, observes that 'The characters of this book are entirely imaginary and have no relation to any living person'. Rowena leads her husband the kind of life that no dog would have tolerated. Towards the end unmasking takes place. Rowena is not what she seems to be. She is an impostor, a murderess, and the mistress of 'a Whitechapel Jew of the filthiest kind', a dress designer by trade and O. Leta by name. Forsyth is recalled to help bring her down and consequently all ends well.

There is a school of thought that holds *This Publican* to be Mercer's revenge upon Bettine, a fictional account of their marriage. The case for this rests upon a letter from Mercer's secretary in Rhodesia who appears to have said that Mercer once remarked to her that Rowena was a similar character to his first wife. Mercer, however, employed two secretaries; the other of them, Phyllis Beeching, has told this writer that when the assertion appeared in print Mrs Barbara Cripps, the first secretary and the one in question, 'wrote refuting the article' in which this attribution appeared. Apart from the fact that there is no possible resemblance to fact in the story or to Bettine's known character in the villainess, it is hard to credit either that Mercer, happily married, would want to open an old wound or that he should wait years to do it. O. Leta, admittedly, sounds like Ollivier and to that extent he may have drawn from memory. Olite is also a castle in nearby Navarra and *letame* is a rude Spanish word, which in French becomes *merde*. Proponents of the theory point out that the initials E. B.— Rowena's true name was Elsie Baumer—may be what Heralds

call a 'canted' version of the initials of Bettine Edwards. This I
find far-fetched. Mercer commonly used the same initials in
order to disguise a real name—such as Weston Gale for William
Grantham—but he made no effort to obfuscate them beyond
recognition. His own explanation appears in *As Berry And I
Were Saying*. In reply to a question from Jill, Boy asserts that
although Rowena was true to life he had never known a woman
like that. 'But she combined the worst characteristics of three
women that I did know.' Mrs Pankhurst? Mrs Seddon? Ethel le
Neve?

There is another inexplicable point about *This Publican*.
Boy, having denied receiving a lot of rude letters about it, later
says this.

> *This Publican* appeared in serial form in *Woman's Journal*
> and the Lady Editor begged me to change the last few words.
> 'They're absolutely true to life, but they're too savage.' So I
> laughed and re-wrote the last few sentences—only for the
> serial, of course. The book stayed as it was.

The closing words of the book are 'Rowena had had a good
year. Juliot's letters alone had brought her five thousand
pounds.' The present Lady Editor tells me that *This Publican*
never appeared in her paper at all. To be just, Mercer was
writing this in his old age and may well have been muddled, as
he was over the Seddon case. He calls the book 'The best thing I
ever did', but the readers did not go along with this. Later
editions, indeed, were prefaced by a kind of apology. If
customers complained that they asked a fish (Berry) and were
given a serpent (Rowena) he was for the moment out of fishes
but was expecting more shortly.

I have set out the proposition, although it does not persuade
me. Before leaving it, there are two points which I suggest
deserve consideration. If Rowena was Bettine then inevitably
Mercer pictures himself as Bohun; and he would hardly have
held himself out in a character so feeble and flaccid. The man
who had thrashed M. Ollivier would have put Rowena across
his knee and reached for a hairbrush.

The suggestion of another and more credible explanation
stems from *B-Berry And I Look Back*, published in 1958 when
Mercer was nearing the end of his life. It soon becomes clear
that he is running short of autobiographical material, for everything is brought into it, from the sinking of the *Titanic* to the

Tichborne Case. If you have forgotten it, all that you need to know is this. Roger Tichborne was lost at sea on his way to Australia; a dozen years later arrives Arthur Orton from that continent with a claim that he is the missing man. It took a three-month hearing in a civil Court followed by an even longer one before a judge and jury before he was shown to be a liar. He had been defended by a barrister named Coleridge who, in the fulness of time, would sentence James Barber Edwards. Every law student was brought up on Tichborne. Orton, a Wapping butcher, very nearly got away with the role of the Old Etonian Roger Tichborne: Elsie Baumer very nearly got away with the role of the Roedean or Cheltenham—or somewhere such—Rowena Howard. Of the real case Mercer wrote that 'It was probably the boldest and most determined attempt to steal away another man's birthright that ever was made, and but for the tireless efforts made by Sir Henry Tichborne's advisers it would undoubtedly have succeeded.' It was excellent material for a novelist. Arthur Conan Doyle had used something like it in 'The Gloria Scott'. Put Rowena into breeches and you have a passable imitation of Arthur Orton upon which to build an improved story. Bad wives were no novelty to Mercer. Peregrine, in *As Other Men Are*, had fled from one and set up house with a mistress long ago.

Richard had gone on to Harrow in 1934, but he did not take kindly to the place. Bettine, far away, was writing in her diary that her ex-husband was 'crushing him and driving him and shutting him up if he says anything he does not want to hear', but she was no longer in touch with things and could make no allowance for the influence of her successor; this was wholly to the good, but stepmothers do not have an easy task. Father and son, so very different in characters and intellectual powers always seem to have been rather at arm's length and Mercer, as he told Mr Kennard, was not over-pleased by his son's perform-ance. The world outside Pau had also turned uglier. When Adolf Hitler first came to power in 1933, as Hindenburg's protégé, he had been regarded by most of the expatriates with suspicion, but not despair. The man had been a soldier of sorts; the Germans, whatever they might be saying now, had been squarely beaten in the field but they were deserving of better things than their politicians inflicted on them. Perhaps this was the man to raise their heads for them. By 1936 it was clear that he was raising them too high for comfort: the Hun was still preferable to the Bolshie, but only just. Nearer to Pau the Spanish republican government doubtless was doing its best according to its distorted lights, but its followers included much that was worst in Spain. General Franco was a man who had held the commission of King Alfonso and was, therefore, a decent fellow, a gentleman with whom it would be an honour to dine. This pleasing simplicity was confounded when the bad Hitler became the ally of the good Franco. Nobody bothered much about Mussolini; as soldiers, his Italians were reckoned not quite as good as the Portuguese. It was possible, however, to remain an interested bystander. The French Army was still the Army of Foch, and no upstart would care to take on the Royal Navy. The air? That was certainly a weak point, but Mr Baldwin would see to it. The bridges at Hendaye and Behobie, scenes of so much careless fun, were clogged by human debris getting out of Spain whilst the going was still tolerable. The smugglers of the Pyrenees did nicely, conducting refugees through little-known passes at handsome fees. As the war dragged on it was possible to drive to a high place and see the woolly clouds that told of shell-fire. Very animating, but not Pau's business.

Mercer's work went on. The *Windsor* story published in April 1937, 'The Real Thing', was a tour-de-force of its kind, though it appears in none of the books. It consists of nothing, but a court scene, based upon the trial of Brown and Kennedy for the murder of P C Gutteridge, and goes relentlessly on, line by line, to show how an expert liar can be destroyed by skilful cross-examination. It is a very competent piece of work, demonstrating plainly that Mercer had forgotten nothing of his days at the criminal Bar, and it ends with the discovery of certain keys in the prisoner's possession which indicate that counsel for the prosecution was next on his list to be burgled.

Though they could not help seeing something of the driftwood of the Spanish war, the Mercers were unaffected by it. Elizabeth, may have been hampered in walking by ill-health, but she was an excellent driver and together they proved the western Pyrenees pretty thoroughly. It can be an eerie place, especially after dark. More than one of the Peninsular diarists has written of its effect on veteran soldiers during the winter campaign of 1813/14 and has told how sentries of proved courage would quit their posts at night and seek human company for no reason that they could explain. An ancient and a haunted land, ideal for dirty deeds.

The Pyrenees, and the long roads between them and England, were to serve as an admirable substitute for German-occupied Austria when Mercer sat down to plan the shape of his next two books, *Gale Warning* and *Shoal Water*, which came out in 1939 and 1940 respectively. Each bears a similar dedication, the first 'To Jill, to whom I owe so much' and the second 'To Jill, who does all things well'. They run to a pattern, but it is so cunningly woven that one is hardly aware of its existence.

Jonathan Mansel, rising fifty though you would never know it, at last reveals what he has been doing for all these years. He is head of a small private organization dedicated to the suppression of serious crime by methods sadly unavailable to the regular police with whom, nevertheless, he remains upon terms of the greatest cordiality. Very early on he shoots a villain, of importance so slight that he does not merit a name; his employer, one Barabbas, promptly murders a member of Mansel's team, an Earl no less, in order to balance the score. Barabbas, who bears some resemblance to Cammy Grizard of putrid memory, has a familiar called the Reverend Bellamy Plato; this is a mild joke, for there is little of Plato but much of Bel-Ami about him and, being one of those rare characters, a clergyman affected by satyriasis, he calls to mind a better-known cleric of the time, the late Rector of Stiffkey.

Mansel acquires new friends. Chandos is amongst those present but George Hanbury is sunk without trace, unless trace it be that Rowley is introduced in *Gale Warning* as having been 'in the service of a very great friend of ours'. At the very end of the book comes mention of 'Maintenance, Chandos's Wiltshire home'; possibly his joint tenant and his ex-Countess have, like others, met with misfortune in the air and the subject is too painful to be mentioned. The new characters are John Bagot—a favourite Mercer name, ranking just below Bohun but above Plantagenet—who is at pains to announce himself an orphan. The other is the Lady Audrey Nuneham, affianced wife of the murdered Earl but a donna outstandingly *mobile*. By means into which it is needless to go, Bagot discovers Plato to live at Virginia Water—by an odd coincidence the same place as Elizabeth Mercer's family—and Barabbas to dwell somewhere in France. The avengers of blood set out in pursuit. Their trail comprehends a lot of violence and a measure of sublimated sex. Bagot and the lady are constrained to share a suite, a villa, and finally a bedroom; with complete opportunity and considerable inclination on tap any divorce judge would have drawn a certain conclusion without calling on counsel. We, however, know our man better; at all material times there is a drawn sword between them, even when Bagot strips and towels the frozen heroine. He might mutter, that 'If I liked to ask you to-night, I know you'd deny me nothing', but ask he does not. It could have been otherwise had he been sure that the lady loved him but, after all, it had only been a few weeks back that she had been betrothed to his best friend. Orphan though he was, John Bagot had come from a good home. Besides, you never knew quite where you stood with the Lady Audrey; she might easily have said 'Certainly not'.

Those who remember the roads of Normandy before, during or soon after the Second War can have little difficulty in following the chase. The punishing hill by Pont de l'Arche, an old friend, is still there but the rest of the first part is buried beneath motorways and fleets of huge, stinking *camions*; Dreux and Evreux, once pleasant little towns enough, now sprawl hideously, showing what French town planners can do when they really try. The N514 and N10 no longer lend themselves to adventure and are best avoided. Mercer obviously knew every furlong of them, for the account of the chase across France is one of his best efforts; it is easy to picture Elizabeth at the wheel of the Delage with her husband beside her making notes of likely spots for ambushes.

The chase takes them to the Castle of Midian, successor to Gath and Jezreel, and all business is satisfactorily concluded. Bagot breaks his duck by slaying Plato with one of those heavy glass objects made to hold matches that you seldom see nowadays outside clubs; Mansel adds one more, killing Barabbas with a single blow of his fist. Chandos has much hard work but no score. There is no treasure and the hire of all those houses, taxis and vans must have cost a lot of money but, like their creator, Mansel and Chandos could now afford some extravagance for the sake of the game itself.

Shoal Water came hard on its heels. Jeremy Solon is only inferentially an orphan but since, at twenty-two, he is still being brought up by uncles it seems fair to afford him the preferred status. He too begins his tale with a drive from Dieppe to Rouen and onwards to the South. Before that, at Newhaven, he falls in with a Miss Scrope, a name worthy to stand alongside the Bohuns and Bagots. Miss Scrope, however, is not what she seems, as a chance encounter in that agreeable pot-house The Wet Flag—whether the flag is a *drapeau* or a *carreau* I have never been quite sure—demonstrates. After their hurried departure in Solon's car with villains in hot pursuit, she explains all. In order to support her blind father in his castle in, apparently, the Massif Central or the southern end of the Cévennes, she has allowed herself to be blackmailed into doing duty as a courier for jewel thieves. Once again the hill by Pont de l'Arche and the rest of the N10 earn their keep as a private race-track. Soon after arrival at Cardinal, Miss Scrope, professionally known as Formosa, is kidnapped by the ungentle Shepherd; Solon, along with his friend George—the con ventional name for the hero's number two man—sets off to find her. At Rouen once more, improbably disguised, they meet by chance with Mansel, himself travelling incognito. From him they learn the truth. Miss Scrope, a marketable commodity, is being purveyed to the disorderly houses of Buenos Aires. Mercer knew something of the white slave traffic of an earlier day for it had been the specialité de la maison of Stinie Morrison and the drill was probably not all that different. The release of Miss Scrope, from a coaster moored near Caudebec, is accomplished and Mansel adds one more to his total, this time by drowning. Both books are swift-moving, plausible—just—and still bear re-reading after all these years. You cannot say that of many thrillers written in the 1930s.

The dust-jacket of *Shoal Water* bears these words on the back: 'The making of this book enabled me to forget the gathering clouds: it is my great hope that the reading of it will enable others to forget the storm.' The storm was coming right enough, but Pau was not excessively worried. Mercer and his wife returned to England from time to time, partly to see Richard and partly for reasons connected with publishing. The last *Windsor* story came out in April 1939, an odd little yarn set upon a cruise ship called the *Harvest Moon*—a near-miss for *Arandora Star*—on a voyage to Madeira. The author's remarks upon how it had changed since his last visit suggest that Mercer had, in fact, been there some time before 1914. It is needless to dwell upon the doings of two precocious little girls in bringing about a suitable romance. It is neither magnificent nor is it Mercer (Richmal Crompton seems nearer the mark), but it may have amused Elizabeth. During one of the visits Geoffrey

175

Stedall was bidden to dine and to bring his wife with him; they travelled 'to a place at the end of a long tube journey, called Cockfosters' and Mrs Stedall met the Mercers for the first time. She did not instantly warm to them. Mercer did all the talking, mostly about himself; his wife was hardly given a chance to utter.

It was not only the prospect of another war that was occupying Mercer's mind. Richard had not done as well at Harrow as his father could wish, and he was sufficiently disappointed in him to tell Mr Kennard that he was thinking of putting the boy to work in a furniture factory at Nay, not far from Pau. Then came the matter of housing. Maryland had served well enough, but it had memories and it was time for a change. For some while past the idea of building a house on the side of a hill, remote from the society of Pau and suited to an anchorite, had been in his mind. As Elizabeth had no objection, they prospected and eventually found the place of Mercer's dreams, a little way out of the town of Eaux Bonnes and about twenty miles from Pau in the direction of the Spanish frontier. This in itself posed no difficulty, for the Spanish War was nearing its end. A Fascist Spain was something less than perfect, but to the Mercers, it was a more wholesome neighbour than a Bolshevik Spain.

How the house came into existence is accurately told in *The House That Berry Built*, even down to the soap-niche, which is still shown to the curious. It is, of course, necessary to discard the gift-wrapping, but the description of each stage in the building can be relied upon as truth. Cockade was its real name, so called because it projected from its hill as does a hackle from a hat. Gracedieu comes from the convent in *The Forest Lovers*, the place in which Isoult la Desirous found her sanctuary. It was a fair analogy. Mercer was to write, many years later, to Mr Carter in Pau of the effect the view of the mountains could have.

When the house was little more than half built, I took a London friend of mine to see it. He was a rich man and a bachelor and had lived in London all his life. The foreman wanted me for something and I left my friend standing at one of the windows of my bedroom. I was away longer than I had expected and looked for him everywhere on my return. Eventually I found him standing exactly as I had left him quite twenty minutes before. I came up to him to apologize, but he didn't seem to hear what I said. He just turned and looked at me. Then he said, 'Mercer, if I were to live here, I should never go away.' This was in the winter. I sometimes think that that is the highest compliment the place has ever had.

His own word for it was 'incomparable'.

Cockade, when it was finished, contained six bedrooms, three bathrooms and three of the rooms called by house-agents 'reception'. The grounds extended to something over three acres and the view from the terrace was stupendous. Inevitably there was a price to be paid for such elevation, a long, long flight of ninety-three steps up from the road. Wits of a certain kind in Pau were fond of saying that Mercer was going to a lot of trouble in order to make sure that his second wife did not decamp as the first had done. There can be no denying that the steps were a great trial to Elizabeth, but she readily agreed to her husband's plan and bore the difficulty philosophically. Like Mercer's friend, she seldom wanted to go away and the two of them were well content with their handiwork. No expense was grudged; the pillars from old Waterloo Bridge were there to be seen and were no flight of fancy. The total cost of the work exceeded £12,000, a sum of which the significance is told in *Gale Warning*. It was the exact amount that the murdered Earl had left to his friend John Bagot and it was sufficient, so the tale says, to merit the newspaper headline 'Fortune for Hunting Crony'. A fortune it was indeed in 1938, but Captain Mercer could afford such an investment now. Only one worrying thought lurked at the back of his mind. Long ago the famous Cheiro had told him that 'something that was anything but pleasant was going to happen to me when I was fifty-five'. And he was nearing his fifty-fifth year.

9

Wife's Eye View

Cockade was finished by the summer of 1939, whilst Mercer was still in the throes of writing *The House That Berry Built*. Being a man of orderly habit he took the opportunity of tidying up certain matters. After twenty seven years White Ladies had to go; at the time of 'The Busy Beers' it had been a substantial country house, but no more than that. By 1939 Berry is able to tell an awed French workman that 'There were fireplaces there which would have accepted a car. And the Royal Chamber was twenty-two metres long.' As it was costing the family nearly £8,000 a year to run they were well rid of it as a gift to Mr Chamberlain's Government. There was also a family matter demanding attention. Mercer liked to run his dream life as nearly as might be in tandem with reality. Now that he had found his Jill and disposed of Adèle there were certain characters who had become surplus to establishment. Mercer dealt with them summarily, in the modern and convenient fashion. 'It was awful, you know, when Piers and my babies were killed. They went down in a plane together.' Thus were his feet cleared.

In the world of tiresome fact, there were some difficulties. Bettine, for one thing, refused to disappear completely. Her worries, centred entirely around her son, were wholly creditable. Elizabeth Mercer was doing her best with Richard and had some correspondence of a friendly kind with his mother about him, but Richard was not settling down. After Harrow, he continued studies of one kind and another in France and went to London to learn shorthand and typing with journalism in mind, but he was not a regular resident at Cockade. When Majorie Hare, one of Elizabeth's oldest friends, visited her at Pau on the way home from Egypt she noticed that Richard,

whom she calls 'a nice lad', appeared to be kept down by his
father although his stepmother did her best for him. Bettine
avers that her late husband threatened to cut off even the
meagre sum he was paying her should she come anywhere near
Pau. What exactly passed between them on this subject is
unlikely ever to be known and one can only guess about
motives. On Mercer's side they probably amounted to a fear
that the irruption of the boy's mother into a newly-settled
household could do no good but positive harm; the use of
money as a weapon is always undelicious but it was his only
one against a determined *revenante*. One cannot but have
sympathy for Bettine, though a little might be spared for
Mercer. There is so much that we do not know, nor have any
business to know, about their intimate affairs. On the bald
facts Mercer does not show up well; but he is dead, and his case
is gone by default. He left no diary nor any statement to be
compared with those made by Bettine.

Majorie Hare was taken to see the house, still half built, and
her feelings about it were mixed. The beauty of its situation
was beyond argument but equally so were the steps. Elizabeth
would never be able to manage them unaided. The second Mrs
Mercer was admirably loyal and no word of complaint was
heard; to an old friend, however, speech was not needed.
Elizabeth liked congenial society as much as did any other
woman; she had been very lonely in Pau, 'though there were
plenty of nice people living there whom she could have known
. . . She loved meeting people but this place looked as if she
would spend her life shut away. He was twenty years older
than she was and, as far as I could see, spent most of his time in
his very fine library writing his books and shut away from her
also.' Elizabeth accepted it all without complaint, for she had
gone into the marriage with open eyes and knew her husband's
measure. Mercer was a compulsive writer, with more than
twenty books behind him and with a near-certainty of more to
come. Their later departure from Cockade may not have been
an unmitigated disaster; year after year of immurement might
not have proved all that agreeable.

The author was at the peak of his form with *The House That
Berry Built*, in which he tells with obvious relish of the building
of the house of his heart's desire, and Berry was never in better
voice. He speaks of the furniture available locally. 'Did you
ever see a dog get up in a French chair? He's not such a fool.' To

an intrusive pleb, 'I present my wife's brother—also, alas, my cousin. He has spent many years in prison, but is reformed. He will very shortly take orders.' When he observes to M. Caratib that he would be improved by death he is quoting directly from 'Saki', who had said the same of Waldo in *The Feast of Nemesis*; his address to a pensive Boy is all his own: 'And may we, poor scum, be permitted to foul the luscious meads of philosophy on which you stroll?' His encounter with the bear you must read for yourself. It deserves better than a paraphrase.

Whether Mercer buried his time-capsule in the foundations I have not been able to find out, but it is not difficult to identify the subject in his mind when he wrote of it. 'She was all things to one man—her husband. Gentle in fair weather, gallant in foul; gay, resolute; honest, wise and kind, she was for all time a model of excellence.' As yet he did not know the half of it.

Events were happening far from the Pyrenees that were soon to change their lives and to show the stuff of which they were made. They were also responsible for putting back completion of the book for a long time. At Cockade, on a September day, they heard of Mr Chamberlain's visit to Munich and drew the only possible conclusion. Britain and France, at the price of public humiliation, had bought a little time. War with Germany was coming again, as sure as a gun, but no action by them could be even remotely useful. Mercer had resigned his Yeomanry commission in 1924 and his only military credential was as President of the Pau Branch of the British Legion. The years of living in a decent climate had made his rheumatism no more than a memory; he was not yet senile and had no mind to be left out. With his knowledge of France and the French he might be serviceable in some sort of liaison job. A letter went to the War Office, but nothing seemed likely to come of it.

Like everybody else Mercer completely misjudged the temper of the France of 1939. The German Army and the German Air Force were, without doubt, immensely strong and had learned much from the rehearsal in Spain. The French Army, however, was not so far behind, if at all. The Somua 50-ton tank was the most powerful in the world, the Maginot Line could keep out anything that might attempt it and the men were the sons of *ceux de Verdun*. The British Army was, as usual, small and still equipped with the worn-out weapons of 1918. For a while it would be of little value, but, as before, it would soon build itself up to something formidable, so long as the French could stand the first shock. There would be plenty of time, although the civil population would have to put up with being knocked about by Hitler's bombers. It would not be pleasant, but the prospect was not too discouraging. Mercer, at a loose end, went back to his desk and wrote some more short stories of the old kind which he called *Period Stuff*. It accurately reflected his mood.

The splendid summer of 1939 was coming to its end when the placards went up. General mobilization, announced by the ringing of church bells, thinned out many of the younger English, along with some others who would have been pleased with the adjective. Though war was declared it seemed otherwise to make little difference, and the Mercers carried on planting Virginia creeper to cover their great wall. Mercer noticed, as did many of the BEF, one strange phenomenon. The Frenchmen in uniform seemed for the most part to be men of middle-age, while great numbers of those whom one might have expected to be in the line still picnicked and rode around on bicycles singing 'Boum', the chirpy little song to which the Third Republic died. The sentiment was widely expressed that this was not France's war; she had been dragged into it on the coat-tails of the miserable English. It was bad enough to hear such talk from civilians, but it was no less common amongst the troops and many senior men were beginning to wonder what had got into their old ally. Not everybody quite realized that the Maginot Line ended far from the sea and that only very makeshift defences covered the wide Belgian flank. Nor did they know that the fine Chars B—capable of killing any German tank—were scattered piecemeal and that the French commanders had no idea of fighting a battle of armour against armour. Or, some of them, of fighting at all.

In April there came a moment of personal sadness. Mercer had always been a little undecided about Mrs Patrick Campbell. On the one hand she had been close to the unspeakable George Bernard Shaw but against that she was in some fashion related to Winston Churchill by virtue of being second wife to Winston's mother's second husband. When she died at Pau on the 9th, fortified to the end by the presence of the pug Moonbeam, he decided to forget Mr Shaw and mourned her genuinely.

Mercer was told by the War Office that, at his time of life, he could serve no military purpose but might be useful doing propaganda work on the spot. The winter of 1939 and the spring of 1940 were passed in attempts to arouse the *furia francese* by showing the folk of the Basses Pyrénées motion pictures of the visit to Paris by the King and Queen; the effects were not obvious. Departing reservists, with the honourable exception of Henri, foreman of the work at Cockade, left sullenly. Henri at least survived, coming back eventually from a prison camp in Poland with a snapshot of Mercer still concealed in his sock. Joseph the butler went unenthusiastically for a soldier; the big Delage was laid up and a less thirsty Citroën took its place.

The Mercers were not without company, for out of the past came Matheson Lang and his wife, Brittie. Lang was still suffering from the effects of a stroke and said that the altitude of Cockade was too much for his heart; they lived at an hotel in Pau and the families met up with every excursion to the market there. Still nobody could perceive the obvious; even in the Zone des Armées it was puzzling. The Maginot Line was well enough, but what the British troops saw of their old allies inspired little confidence. Even allowing for all that, the events of 10 May 1940 came as a thunderbolt. Very soon the roads of the north were crammed with refugees, the distinguishing mark being the mattress on the car roof; and British units, half trained and quarter armed, were hurried into the gaps where the French Army ought to have been. With some, but not many, honourable exceptions, the French Army was running for home, the Devil with the Charlie Chaplin moustache taking the hindmost. It was not long before the first mattresses reached Pau.

Sudden calamity can bring benefits. The Lang's hotel having been commandeered, there was nothing for it but for them to risk the mountain air. Elizabeth Mercer drove them the twenty-three miles to Eaux Bonnes, very slowly because of Lang's heart; on arrival he went up the ninety-three steps like a young ram. This pace could not be maintained and it was agreed that the Langs must depart at once for Spain; Lang, however, had left his passport with the Consul in Pau for renewal. The Mercers drove back to get it. Apparently a photograph was needed and they had none. Mercer left Elizabeth outside a café in the Place-Royale while he went in search of Lang's laundry. Elizabeth had never been fluent in French and the message coming over the wireless meant very little although everybody in the square who could hear it burst into tears and lamentations. On Mercer's return she told him that something awful had happened; he went into the café and, unbelieving, learned it for himself. France had surrendered to Germany. And the Boche was nearing Bordeaux.

As they were on the point of driving away they happened to see their lawyer in uniform. Mercer went across and spoke to him, saying that he was leaving and adding in a loud voice for the benefit of all within earshot that his countrymen would go on fighting. Back to Cockade for Lang's photographs, back to Pau again with them, just in time to catch the British Consul before he left. Mercer sought out his Vice Consul and persuaded him to obtain the official seals before his chief departed. There was much trouble over the papers, for the French authorities had turned awkward and posed every possible difficulty. They began by refusing exit permits, adding helpfully that the Portuguese Consul, from whom visas must be obtained, was in Bordeaux and so were 'les Allemands'; nobody used the customary 'Boche' any more. The courtyard of the Prefecture was jam-packed with cars of the departing English; Elizabeth sat in the Citroën for hours while her husband battled with officialdom. For the moment he wore the coat of Jonathan Mansel and knew exactly what he must do. Mercer got his papers.

They tried vainly to buy a car for the Langs; many other people, including Mr Kennard, were after anything with wheels and an engine and had got in first. The Kennard family eventually reached Bordeaux—the Germans were not as near as all that—in a furniture pantechnicon containing, amongst other things, all the portable assets of Lloyd's Bank, Pau. Mercer managed to get a taxi, from a place thirty miles away, and it took up residence at Cockade. That night was spent in packing, hurriedly and haphazardly. The Langs left in the taxi at about 10.30 a.m., the Mercers in the Citroën at noon. The house and all it contained was left, with Thérèse—'a Medusa in tears'—being entrusted with everything until further notice. It was she who insisted that they must be over the frontier that night. Apparently Dornford Yates was on the list; the Germans have long memories and the description of a Berlin flat of 1913 in *As Berry and I were Saying*, with the lavatory in splendour forming part of the kitchen furnishings, must have rankled. The Herren Stunkenblotch, Splodgenblunk (of *Berry and Co.*)

and the rest were on his trail, probably sicked on by Beach-comber's military commentators Konrad von Spurius and Kurt Durt.

At this point in the tale one sees a new Elizabeth Mercer. Up to 1940 she had appeared as a deutero-Jill, the grey-eyed goddess with the attributes of a child and all that. Her hardest task had been to remember to tell casual visitors never to speak the name of George Bernard Shaw unless they wished her husband an apoplexy. All of a sudden she emerged as not merely a congenial figure about the house but as a woman with whom to ride the ford, and the narrative which follows is hers. It was Elizabeth who did the driving that day and it was no longer a party of pleasure. Rumours, of course, came in thick and fast and it was impossible even to make an intelligent guess at the truth. There is no motor road to Spain through the mountains and it was necessary to get to Irun; this meant joining the main Bordeaux road just short of Bayonne, and it was entirely possible that German motor-cycle troops might have beaten them to it. Mercer sat in the passenger's seat with an automatic pistol on his knee. Whether he intended to use it had they encountered the enemy is uncertain, but Mansel and his friends had driven through danger in this fashion on many occasions and it was obviously the right thing to do. One cannot but suspect that he rather enjoyed it all. Or, at any rate, some of it.

By mid-afternoon they were at Hendaye, with only about thirty cars in front of them. During the wait a red-headed Englishwoman, in great distress, formed up to ask help in getting her husband across the bridge. She could go by herself, she explained, but for him there was flat refusal. It turned out that he was Alexander Kerensky, and the first revolutionary Prime Minister of Russia was unwelcome in Fascist Spain. There was nothing that the Mercers could do for her; they learned later that the Kerenskys had reached America by sea. At the risk of breaking the story for a moment, it seems only right to mention that Britain owes much to General Franco. Spain, her own war hardly over, was bankrupt and starving. When Hitler demanded right of passage to Gibraltar he was refused. Spain was in no position to oppose his will, but even Adolf Hitler knew the reputation of the guerrillero and had no appetite for adding new Empecinados and Minas to his enemies. The loss of Gibraltar would have meant, possibly, loss of the Battle of the Atlantic; it would certainly have made Malta untenable and have rendered the Tunisian campaign out of the question. Franco acted for the good of his own country, but he also rendered a great service to the British and their friends.

Mercer once again attended to the endless paperwork whilst his wife remained in the car in company with 'our little saint of a dog, Tumble—wire-haired terrier'. There was plenty for her to see, as the number grew from about thirty to nearly 3,000. There was the hillside which they had seen torn by shells during the war, now surmounted by a great white cross; there were several Rolls-Royces whose French chauffeurs had handed them over to the owners, and the owners had little idea of driving. Horns blew by accident, engines stalled and the chauffeurs laughed themselves sick as their late employers lurched across the bridge. Less amusing was her first sight of the black and silver uniform of the Gestapo. Mercer emerged at last with all the pieces of paper needed, Elizabeth started the engine and they drove slowly over the bridge that had seen so much of Berry and the others. By midnight they were at the Maria Christina in San Sebastian. The Langs were already in the crowd; so were the Gestapo, though they did nothing worse than peer over Elizabeth's shoulder as she registered them in.

At San Sebastian it was Lang's turn to become the prime mover. With all Lloyd's money bouncing about in Mr Kennard's pantechnicon, it had been impossible to draw any large sum before leaving, but Lang, being a Scot, was awash with the stuff. The Mercers relieved him of half of it and immediately split that with chance acquaintances called Ivan and Muriel who had an enormous Buick. The bargain was that they should keep together and thus halve the risk of being marooned. Ivan 'drove like a scalded cat', but Elizabeth, much practised on mountain roads, was better.

They had no sort of a plan, but only to get on as fast and as far as possible with Portugal as the immediate goal. Each drove in turn, becoming sleepier and sleepier as they went; this was not surprising for, as they later found out, the tops of the reserve petrol cans had not been tightened and, the car being closed, they were gently asphyxiating. Whilst they were putting this to rights Ivan swept past in the Buick; Mercer endured his erratic driving for a time but after miles of it he had had enough, as Jonah would have done. With the horn blaring and going at some seventy-five miles an hour, the Citroën moved out to pass. The Buick, affronted, kicked up a stone through the windscreen. Neither of them knew how Mercer managed to keep the car on the road, but he fought with it and won. They reached a crowded Salamanca on a Saturday evening. The scene would have made the Great Duke rotate under his tomb. To drive slowly through silent, black-dressed crowds to an over-full hotel was bad enough. To find it apparently under Gestapo supervision was worse. Mercer insisted that his wife and Tumble dined in their room. Later, he explained why. He had come up against the Gestapo, who were going through all the passports. 'Your wife's passport is incorrect.' You can guess for yourself the tone in which he replied 'No, it is not.'

'You have a transit visa, why are you still here?'

'I dined with the Spanish Consul, a personal friend, in San Sebastian last night, and he gave me this visa.'

'When do you go?'

'Tomorrow morning.'

'See that you do.'

Humphrey Bogart could have learned something from William Mercer, late of the OUDS.

Citroën and Buick set off together the next morning in pouring rain with a steady deluge coming through the hole in the shattered windscreen through which the driver was constrained to peer. At the Portuguese frontier Ivan drove straight past the line of waiting cars with Mercer on his tail and noisy expostulations further behind. Ivan claimed to have a diplomatic visa and it was reasonable to suppose that formalities would not be protracted. Five hours later Muriel went in to find out the state of play, insisting that Mercer accompany her. Once inside, she turned her anger upon the unfortunate Spanish officials with all the aplomb of a gentlewoman affronted. 'Why am I kept here? We have diplomatic visas and I demand to go at once.' The Spaniard wilted, only adding faintly, 'And who is this gentleman?'—'He is a member of my suite.' Muriel must have been well up in *Jonah and Co.*, for the cars were at once permitted to move with a *guardia civil* on the running-board of each. When Mercer inquired about Ivan's diplomatic status he was told, apologetically enough, that it was minimal; he had some job at the Embassy in Oslo. Elizabeth observed that she could have kissed the first Portuguese policeman she saw.

Inevitably the station yard was crowded with refugees and the prospect of food seemed remote. Once again the unexpected happened. 'A nice young man with a brown hat raised it and, of all things, asked if Bill was Dornford Yates.' Acknowledgement was followed by an excellent meal in 'a most marvellous sort of canteen that had been set up by volunteers from the British Embassy at Lisbon and the British Consulate at Porto'. It did not, however, run to any sort of accommodation. 'The Buicks had got a room in the only hotel, so Bill and I had the back of the Buick to sleep in, which was palatial compared to the Citroën;' though the wind was bitter enough to compel Elizabeth to wrap herself in a fur coat with the collar pulled over her head. Mercer hated the cold, but got some comfort when 'The Buicks' showed up early in the morning, bitten all over by assorted vermin. Berry would have dealt memorably with the situation, but his maker's comments are lost. A pity.

They had neighbours in the station yard. On one side were three cars full of American pilots who had been ferrying aircraft to France. Possibly they had heard that the French had refused to take off in them and that they might have saved their trouble, for they were noisily drunk. On the other side was Lady Mendl and her companion, both in mink and lodging in an enormous Rolls, full of steamer-trunks and driven by a young American secretary. Lady Mendl was believed to be over eighty, but art had assisted nature in concealing this. At about 6 a.m., the pilots having left with much shouting and slamming of doors, she decided to follow their example. Then followed another scene that Berry would have relished. The Portuguese police furnished her with a driver. The Rolls, unaccustomed to such, declined to have anything to do with him and refused to start. The secretary had been diverting himself with his countrymen and was disguised in wine to the extent of making his services valueless. When somebody suggested that the Rolls be pushed he attempted to butt it; his employer fell off the seat. Several times they repeated this to no good end. The Mercers missed her departure—though they heard her to observe loudly that she would not be driven through an arid waste by someone who . . . for they were taking turns to stand in a queue for papers. Such an occupation is hard on anybody's feet; for Elizabeth it was torment and Mercer suffered her to do it only when absolutely necessary to spell Ivan or himself. She—and possibly even he—had a brief conversion to socialism when six enormous green cars 'footmen and chauffeurs complete rushed by—much too fast and unnecessarily so'. Even the Grand Duchess of Luxembourg could not expect praise for such an exhibition. Re-conversion followed swiftly; by tea time their papers were in their hands and they had learned of an hotel, run by an Englishman, not in Lisbon but away to the north. Late that night Buick and Citroën were garaged at the Urgerieca at Cannas, and a chalet called Mimosa gave them refuge.

Refugees seldom show up to advantage and those of 1940 were no different from the ordinary run. First to arrive, says Elizabeth, was 'our English dentist from Pau, in complete dithers, having lost his wife and children who "were in another car"—he, presumably, having driven damned fast'. Next came

An American b—— from Pau (who I must say had apparently driven down alone), 'Oh, I can't sit down, for I have no maid to press my frocks, isn't it awful?'—she was right, she had no maid . . . Ivan and Muriel having had a valet and maid to pack were too, too lovely! Ivan was best, all in green—shirt, trousers, socks and suede shoes (the first time I'd actually seen it on a man)—he went through all the shades—blue, violet, tan etc., all to match—it was a bit hard to be polite at that time.

When Charles, the hotel owner, agreed to cash Mercer a cheque for £10 Ivan asked whether the same office might be performed for him. Charles said, 'Of course, how much?' Ivan answered, '£2,000,' without turning a hair. Mercer and Charles 'came to me with a mixture of tottering from the shock and laughter'.

Ivan was a man of parts. By sending a number of telegrams he collected a great deal of money, went to Lisbon and shipped his Buick to America. Several of the Rolls parties met at the frontier—including, inevitably, that of Lady Mendl which was accompanied by another, belonging to Lady Granville Barker, once Mrs Archer M. Huntington of New York City. The horrors of war, indeed. The Langs, who had travelled by train, turned up and took the next chalet.

The Portuguese were kindness itself, for the descendants of Wellington's Fighting Cocks had not forgotten the great days. Elizabeth was particularly touched when a notice went up saying 'No Tips'. Poor though they were, the hotel staff had realized that many of the refugees were now poorer still and they did their best to spare nearly empty pockets. Not many other people would have done half as much. Both the Mercers acquired and retained a great affection for the country and for those who lived in it. Portugal might have been a dictatorship, but it did not show any signs of bearing down on its subjects. It charmed Elizabeth, with the village fêtes complete with fireworks, 'men who really did seem to love their neighbours and also accept strangers', and the animals. There was a mule in 'a very dressy straw hat' and 'he had trousers on his legs, fore and aft! I mean properly made trousers, suspended round his body, and very contented he looked, poor old man.'

It was a long way from the war, and Mercer was determined not to be left entirely out of things. The War Office wanted none of him but a possibility remained. Ellis Robins had long settled down in Rhodesia and was now commanding the Royal Rhodesia Regiment. In all probability he would be willing and able to find a billet for an old brother Yeoman and, with the seat of battle moving to the Middle East, it might be a step on the way towards getting back to Egypt. Elizabeth, naturally enough, would have liked to share in England's trials, but she accepted the sense of this. After an enjoyable visit to Oporto, taking in the Factory and the rest, they moved on to Lisbon, where a passage to somewhere in the southern half of Africa might be arranged. They did not see the capital at its happiest, for the Gestapo was much in evidence, and people distasteful to it were disappearing in an unaccountable way. 'One day we were going out to our faithful Citroën and we heard marching feet, and there were about twenty Boches of all sorts, who had automatically fallen into step, coming to the Hotel, having just arrived by Luftwaffe. Nice.'

They were having tea with the Langs at the Palace, Estoril, when

a man came in and sat at a table and he was immediately surrounded by pretty ladies . . . Brittie Lang told me that he was head of the Gestapo—had been in Norway and Belgium before they were over-run. As I watched, a barman came through the curtained doorway and the Boche followed him out after a few words. I then became conscious that he was standing in the doorway, curtain in hand, watching Bill, who was half turned to him and didn't know anything about it. Finally I decided I must catch his eye and stare him out;

this I did successfully, but it made me feel sick. I believe he was one of those who went to Russia in the end. I afterwards read that the Palace barman was the chief liaison and informer to the Gestapo heads.

The passages were eventually arranged. Mrs Mercer is economical with dates, but it appears to have been early in 1941 that she, Richard, her husband, the Langs and about half a dozen other English people, all of them over fifty, embarked in a Portuguese steamer bound for Lourenço Marques. Richard, as always, is an elusive figure. He does not appear in Elizabeth's narrative until after their arrival at Charles' hotel, when she mentions that 'Richard was unwell and Bill thought he ought to stay with him'. Then he vanishes again.

On arrival in Lourenço Marques, they saw little enough of the place and were only permitted to remain for a fortnight. The landing of animals in Africa has always been tricky and Portuguese East was not prepared to take on Tumble. There was nothing for it but to go back to Durban, where he could be regularly quarantined. Half a dozen other people were in the same predicament. Durban was famous for its hospitality towards the convoys of British troops that were now its most regular visitors; many of them still remember Mrs Perle Seidle, the Lady in White, who never failed to turn up and sing them on their way. But Captain Mercer was no longer part of an army. Great liners, dressed in grey and crammed with men, reassuring-looking cruisers, their White Ensigns grimy from work, passed regularly around the Bluff, a constant reminder that the Empire was getting into its stride. All Mercer could do was to watch, and to cling to the hope that some part of the Imperial Armies might still find a place for him, no matter how lowly.

Elizabeth found the climate different from anything she had known before and was taken badly ill. For three weeks she lay abed, while Mercer bent himself to arrangements for the extension of their journey to Rhodesia.

It is possible to put a date to this, thanks to Mr Gary Rymer, formerly of the Royal Air Force. Mr Rymer was serving in Durban at the end of 1941 and had the good fortune to have acquired a girl friend who worked in a book shop there. When she told him of Mercer's presence Mr Rymer, a right-minded man, decided to seek him out. 'He was most charming and hospitable . . . He didn't resent my mild criticisms that he had made life a little easier for himself in his stories by making his heroes financially free of worries by presenting them as wealthy, or at least well to do people.' Mercer's parting letter is interesting.

> You belong to a Service for which I have always had the greatest admiration. When you return to duty please remember that I am one of those who wish you exceptionally well. I resisted the considerable temptation to stage the exposure of Rowena in Court for two reasons. In the first place, it would not have been true to life, for exposure in Court only belongs to the realms of imagination: secondly, Rowena's public exposure would have cleared Bohun in everyone's eyes. You see the bitter moral of the tale is that Bohun (This Publican), who was the better man, was written off as their inferior by his fellows (The Pharisees).

A last note, also from the Caister Hotel Durban and dated 29 November 1941 says simply 'Your friend shall have her book.' Both are signed, as were all his letters to readers, 'Dornford Yates'.

In Durban he bought a Chevrolet van, which lasted them for the rest of his life, and loaded it with the heavy baggage. He was 'big news' and as soon as Elizabeth was on her feet again there were invitations that had to be accepted. He opened a bazaar for the Red Cross and patronized a roulette party; no hardship this, for he adored the game. They met Seymour Hicks—'a perfect pet'—and Simon Elwes—'most dashing and very handsome, and [we had] a whale of a time, he did me a lot of good,' says Elizabeth. 'Actually he had gone through Lisbon just before we left . . . and here he was, a full Captain of Hussars. He was, I think, arrested at Marine Hotel, as he had been staying there when he should have been in Transit Camp. He was certainly CB for a couple of weeks, much to everyone's amusement. There's a lot more to it, all of which is most reprehensible, but was very funny.' Elizabeth writes that 'We are both interested in people—Bill naturally, to him the best remains.' The man whom Bettine once described as preferring to send people away with a flea in their ear had mellowed a lot. 'One night (looking from their balcony down to the swimming pool) a most attractive six arrived, all went in but one most beautiful and beautifully gowned girl—she was all in white—the others all went in, and they were baiting her in merriment. All of a sudden she cried "All right" and did the most perfect dive. I don't know why that stuck in my mind—perhaps I'd like to have done it myself.' There was much more to Elizabeth Mercer than the grey eyed child of nature.

From Durban they moved on to Johannesburg, Elizabeth at the wheel of the Citroën while Mercer followed behind in the van. After a stop there, they continued on their way through the kind of rain seldom seen outside Africa, passing a mosquito-ridden night at the Zimbabwe ruins and on to Salisbury. There they arrived on 23 December 1941, to be greeted by Mercer's old Oxford and Yeomanry friend, now Lord Robins. They rented a house called Bentree, which Elizabeth thought 'awful' until she learned that it was a sight better than most of its kind. At a dinner party they were introduced to Sir Godfrey Huggins, whom Mercer immediately buttonholed. There had been some suggestion of his taking an emergency commission in the RAF, but that was not what he was after. The Governor gave his blessing and Captain Mercer was soon re-commissioned as Second Lieutenant in the Royal Rhodesian Regiment. Though he was happy at his translation, Elizabeth was not. The General's lady took to issuing quasi-royal commands that they lunch or dine with her; 'I couldn't do anything. But many are the times that I have driven to the corner below their house, with Tumble beside me, stopped, lit a cigarette and used all the language I knew, taken a deep breath, had a heart-to-heart talk with Tumble, and driven on to lunch.'

His military duties were not exacting. Dick Hobson, then an eighteen-year-old recruit in the Southern Rhodesia Light Battery at King George VI Barracks in Salisbury, encountered him in 1943. 'Mercer was given the task of delivering current affairs lectures to us during the hot afternoons after a morning pushing field guns around a barrack square. The result was that many of us lost the battle against sleep and I really cannot recall much of the lectures except one at which most, if not all, the time was taken up by Captain Mercer reading to us one of Churchill's speeches. He lacked the delivery of the author, and his audience was less than rapt.' There have been sneers about his appearing in battle dress far from any battle, but he was an officer, on duty, and it would be instructive to learn how the critic feels he should have presented himself.

During this war he did not need to neglect his ordinary work entirely, and Elizabeth tells how she did his typing with one finger. 'There was also a Jew doctor who had written a highly technical book, but couldn't write good English and this too Bill did for him. It is now a standard work, but few knew, or know, of Bill's part. I caused raised eyebrows by always wearing trousers in town when shopping, which, to my amusement, was very soon copied.' It was not all fun. 'Bill was never really well in Salisbury, and the doctor and I were getting worried about his over-working, and he was getting towards a breakdown when he was told he was to be sent down to Jo'burg on a job to do with a propaganda film.'

Before he attended to this Captain Mercer, as he now was again, had the satisfaction of learning that the battered islanders had a chance to escape for a little while. *Period Stuff* came out a few weeks before Alamein was fought and it was eagerly snapped up. At the end of 1943 followed *An Eye For A Tooth*. The author explained disarmingly that it had followed immediately upon *Blind Corner* but, for compelling reasons, it was only now that its secrets might be revealed. On the way home with Axel the Red's treasure, Mansel had nearly run over a dead man in the road but deemed it inexpedient to waken the slumbering Chandos and Hanbury. The corpse was that of a Major Bowshot, an English gentleman foully murdered by foreigners. Such crime demanded vengeance and got it. Another castle, another lady of high degree blessed with an American mother, more beastly solicitors and an evil Duke of Teutonic antecedents. The dénouement this time seems to have been suggested by Christopher Marlowe's in *The Jew of Malta*, which ends with most of the characters precipitated by a pivoted floor into a vat of boiling oil. Mercer dispensed with the oil, but the principle was the same. It may have been an eighth carbon copy of the earlier books but the fact remained that the faithful lapped it up gratefully and demanded more. It was reprinted six times within a twelvemonth. There was still plenty to come.

Should you ever be in Grantham, walk along Castlegate and you will find the photographic studio of Chris Windows. In 1943 Sergeant Windows, a cameraman with the Eighth Army Film & Photographic Unit, was ordered to take himself to Rhodesia and make a film about the country's war effort. It was not easy, for Rhodesia was the last place on earth where Rhodesia's war effort was obvious. The aircrews of the RAF, the Rhodesian Anti-Tank Battery at Alamein, and the commissioned ranks of the black battalions of the King's African Rifles and the RWAFF now at sea and bound for Burma owned most of the young men. The film could hardly include them. Windows and Sergeant Grayson, late of Warner Bros., acted as director and cameraman, Mercer wrote the script for the civilian part of the show and Wing Commander Fletcher of the RAF provided the commentary for the military end of it. The film, which ran for half an hour, was completed in Johannesburg and had its première there at the Colosseum. A distinguished audience attended but it was no *Gone With The Wind*. 'Veracious' wrote to the editor of the *Bulawayo Chronicle* that he 'left the cinema utterly depressed and disappointed. It is devoutly to be hoped that this film will never be shown beyond our borders.' The newspapers were kinder, but they could hardly have been otherwise. ' "This has been an entirely new and tremendously interesting experience for me," Major Mercer told an interviewer, "I have not yet heard my voice and am awaiting the audition with considerable curiosity." ' Later, ' "It has been a tiring day for those who had to give me my cues," he smiled.' 'Major Mercer will broadcast to-morrow at 8 p.m.,' said the *Rhodesia Herald*. Mr Windows, however, is clear about one thing. Mercer was 'a very nice man'. It was not an isolated opinion.

Mr Faktor of Keswick Road in London tells me that he served under Mercer at much the same time and 'he went out of his way to befriend me, and I spent a few harmonious evenings at his house where I also met his wife. I feel it is high time that tribute was paid to this outstanding gentleman.' No signs of fleas in the ear now. On the other hand I am told by a former Naval Officer, Mr Boyle of Walberswick, that when he arrived in Durban in 1943, 'I was surprised to find how intensely he had been disliked.' Presumably some toes must have been trodden on; few of us avoid ever doing something of the kind once in a while.

By 1944 he had been promoted to field rank, and Major Mercer he ever afterwards remained. He had not been at all well during the making of the film and the cold of Johannesburg after the heat of Salisbury made him really ill. Even worse was the sudden death, following an operation, of the much-loved Tumble. 'We were broken-hearted . . . but he came back to *me*, several times . . . usually when I was sewing or ironing in my work room, and much too preoccupied to be thinking of him—but he passed the door DEFINITELY—I *saw* him, bless his faithful and trusting heart,' wrote Elizabeth.

Mercer had been mightily taken by Rhodesia, particularly by the part around Umtali, and it was during the making of the film that he surreptitiously bought two stands of land there. Only when the matter of their return to France became imminent did he confess what he had done; he 'didn't know what we'd find on our return to France'. Elizabeth had firm views also. 'Don't let anyone criticize this country to me now—even though I may not be happy here—grouses, grumbles, what have you, they are wonderful people, as long as they are not swamped by the "immigrant" . . . One should come out in one's twenties, or be born here,' she wrote many years afterwards. In 1944, however, with D-Day long past, their one idea was to get home to Cockade.

Mercer was released by the Rhodesian Forces, they railed the Citroën and the van to Beira and waited three weeks for a ship. Eventually one arrived and they sailed under the Portuguese flag, touching at Capetown and Luanda (waters charted a century earlier by Admiral Mercer), where they picked up a sufficiency of Portuguese travellers to cram the ship almost to bursting. At Madeira they took on another 350 passengers destined for Gibraltar. As the ship had been constructed to carry no more than 300 all told, and blue sky could be seen between the strakes of the lifeboats, it was not a prosperous voyage. When they reached Lisbon in October 1944, 'Bill and I were near to a breakdown—both of us this time.' They had very little money, for currency restrictions were tight, and although the shops made their mouths water they could only run to a set of Trollope from the library. Trollops of another kind formed the clientèle of the hairdressing salon where 'I was treated like a Duchess . . . The best and quickest perm. etc. and the best attention and manicure.' It was marred, however, by Elizabeth falling out of a lift. 'Quite honestly, I've never been quite the same since. I got up and went out but I have never been as mobile since that moment.'

There were interesting visitors in Lisbon as 'the tide began to turn against the Boche, who became fewer and fewer in number and greener and greener of face'. One was Herr von Papen, 'complete with four or more attendant thugs who kept their hands in bulging coat pockets'. They were not all evil; the top 'contact', a Portuguese, 'had a dachshund which had adorable puppies and I, of course, fell for the puppies to Bill's horror'. The remark demonstrates the superiority of Mrs Mercer's discernment to that of her husband. Eventually they got their permits through 'a Cabinet Minister who had been at Oxford with Bill and who we met shortly before leaving S. R. at a dinner-party', sold the Citroën to a member of the Embassy staff at more than the price they had paid for it ten years earlier, and set off for France in the Chevrolet van. In February 1945, with the war in Europe nearing its end, they drove back once more across the International bridge to Hendaye.

Spain had shown a picture of increasing prosperity, but the condition of France was pitiable. Mrs Lauchlan, whom you will remember as Joan Tassell, went back to Pau many years later, 'to learn what had happened to my Basque caddie and many other brave French people who had kept their loyalties to the English and in many cases paid the penalty with their lives. The people that I met, and the stories they had to tell, showed a very different set of values from the lush life of the 1930s. When I emerged from the station I suddenly recognized a frail, down-at-heel old man. He had been chauffeur to one of the richest Americans in Pau. The shining Rolls-Royce that had taken us to play golf at Chiberta . . . and all the other good memories of a lost world which Dornford Yates had made a vivid reality to so many.'

The Mercers had received by clandestine methods a certain amount of news about the fate of Cockade. It had been occupied by a German Oberst but the servants, apprised by telegram of the imminent return, had assured them that no damage had been done. The changes in the country began to show themselves from the moment when a Filipino major in the American Army greeted them at the Bridge and when, a little later on, they were held up by ferocious-looking members of the Resistance, armed to the teeth though there seemed little enough to be resisted.

The account of the return to Cockade is given by Elizabeth Mercer. It is right to say that a very different one is presented by Mme Capdevielle, Thérèse of the old days. I see no need to conduct an inquest and any possible reader of this book must make up his own mind whether or not Mrs Mercer is to be believed. This is what she tells of finding.

So, through a very shabby and uneasy country to our house and the servants. The latter had *completely* changed. Were RED, and we were to find were apparently heading the local black market, though we didn't get anything, and it was a bitter blow and disillusionment to Bill. The house was not aired or warmed, and Bill promptly went down with congestion and near pneumonia.

The doctor from Pau could not come for lack of petrol but recommended a young man nearby who coped adequately. M & B could only be bought from one of the barmen, who presumably had got it from the Americans. There was no food. 'We always say that our tummies shrank so much in those few months that we've never been able to eat a proper meal since.' To add to their misery, Mrs Mercer learned there of the death in action of her brother, Jeff. 'That day we started off down to Pau and suddenly, for some unknown reason, I started to feel deadly ill, and continued, though I did the chores until *suddenly* I was all right. That, I found afterwards, was *exactly* the time between when he was hit and when he died.' The French authorities, openly hostile now, refused her an exit permit to visit her mother.

Thérèse, to comfort her, produced a young poodle, christened 'Aesop' by Mercer; as soon as he had been deloused and accepted she demanded 3,500 francs for the 'present'. 'He served his turn, poor pet, as he certainly gave me something to think about.' He was eventually stolen. Elizabeth had a shrewd idea by whom. Joseph, Thérèse's husband 'would do nothing for Bill, though he had formerly valeted him.'

Thérèse would do nothing for me, though she had been my personal maid—and certainly the *confidential* of the family— but Joseph would serve me and Thérèse would serve Bill, and how you work that one out with Communism I still don't know. And Bill walked round and round the little fountain and up and down the terrace, and the decision was made to return to Southern Rhodesia—I didn't want to go back and I said couldn't we look at Kenya (was he right when he said *no*?) or Jamaica before deciding. His decision was most likely right, but if we did *I* thought we would come back to England either every 18 months, or anyway about every three years . . . and this attitude of Bill's that he would *not* go back to England, wanted to remember it as it used to be, nearly broke my heart.

It was especially poignant that *The House That Berry Built* was published during their last visit to the place. The loving account of how the intended new home had come into existence, the kindly people and devoted servants who played their parts in it, now seemed to belong to ancient history. The dream world had been overtaken by reality, and reality had won. Never again could life be quite the same.

Mercer's own heart had been damaged by what they had found, and he had fallen in hate as his characters had fallen in love, hard and for ever. Unaccustomed rudeness on all sides, the jacquerie within the gates and the general beastliness of life under the new dispensation were too much for him and, at sixty, he was too old to put down fresh roots in an unknown place. The only enjoyable moment was the sacking of Thérèse and Joseph. 'We leaned idly on the parapet of the terrace watching them staggering down the steps with *tons* of stuff, wondering how much was our property and how much black-market meat, and knowing it was quite useless to try and do anything about it. And so ended the last of the good servants, who had at one time served us so well and of whom we had been fond and had considered our friends.'

The state of England after the German surrender seemed no more promising; a country that could dismiss Winston Churchill at this of all moments was capable of anything. The new Government inspired no sort of confidence, a state of mind not peculiar to the Mercers. The fact that those who led it, or some of them, were gentlemen who ought to have known better made it almost worse than red revolution. Mr Attlee— he had been Major Attlee until the war—was a University College man who had gone down as Mercer had come up; he had been a good soldier in the Kaiser's War but now he seemed to have much in common with the Kerensky they had met by the bridge in 1940. Some of his coadjutors did not bear thinking about. Particularly noteworthy was a Mr Bevan, recently described by Winston Churchill as 'a squalid nuisance,' whose contribution to victory had been two-fold: a suggestion that the British Army, of which he knew nothing, be placed under foreign generals, and a threat to stump the coalfields and bring the miners out on strike if a wage claim was not met. The miners, those not fighting with the 50th (Northumbrian), the 9th (Scottish) and the 53rd (Welsh) Divisions, were better men than their self-appointed spokesman. Yet some day he might easily become Foreign Secretary and thus have the freedom of White Ladies.

While things were still fresh in his memory, and while they waited for the French authorities to grant them exit permits, Mercer sat down to make a record of it all. It is all there for the reading, in *As Berry And I Were Saying*, the bitter record of a hatred, malice and uncharitableness all the worse for having been so unexpected. Thérèse's comment is 'Bien sur nous avons été un peu surpris de tout ces mensonges.' Diplomatic relations were ended, and for years to come Mercer, in correspondence with his friend Mr Carter who acted as a kind of agent, preferred to leave the house empty rather than let it to anybody who might be associated with the former curators. When he hated, he hated very cordially.

One exception to the studied freezing indifference meted out by the French authorities came from the District Commandant at Pau, a man who had done his soldiering under Foch and Mangin. Mercer met him at the Club and he undertook to do all he could to procure the necessary pieces of paper. Even with the help of a man so senior everything had to be done by the back-stairs. 'We had to go thirty miles in a most peculiar direction—I mean nowhere near a frontier post, and there seemed absolutely no reason to have the office there at all, even in war, except to make things more difficult—to once more get our exit permits. Then, when we eventually left Cockade— refugee caretaker in charge complete with Pyrenean dog—we followed the M.C.'s instructions, we first drove into the foot-hills, were filled up with petrol. When we got near to the frontier post intact, with the necessary official to pass us through the French side—'Ye Gods and little fishes'! The Spanish side were correct and helpful.'

With Elizabeth once more doing most of the driving, they reached Lisbon in the middle of October 1945 and 'went to a new hotel opposite our old Tivoli where we had spent so many revolting months'. The harlots' hairdresser once more unrolled his red carpet. At the end of November, 'we got on the ship, complete with Chev. van, which was crowded and I got worse and the Portuguese ship's doctor came and gave me what had every appearance of a *horse* injection, and I just passed out and remember little more until just before we got to Lourenço Marques . . . Bill nursed me *most beautifully* all those weeks, alone.'

199

10

The Last Decade

Exactly when Mercer found time to write *Red In The Morning* nobody is ever likely to know for certain (he says he wrote it very quickly), but it came out in 1946, a matter of weeks before he and Elizabeth had settled upon the place where they intended to lay their bones. The dedication is understandable. 'To Jill, for her great heart'. By now Mrs Mercer had risen above an understandable confusion over her name. For the first twenty-eight years of her life she had been Elizabeth and by that name I always take the liberty to call her. To her husband, however, and to friends made since their marriage, she was Jill. A change of surname is commonplace; a complete change of identity is rarer and no doubt attended by difficulties. The name given at her baptism seems less likely to confuse.

Although Mercer regarded the title as 'Not one of my best, my darling', the book ranks well up his now formidable list. It begins in Biarritz and treats of the country he knew best of all. As he wrote to an admirer in 1950, 'I am afraid that to identify any of the houses or villages I mention in my tales of England is impossible. Most of them are really composite photographs. If, on the other hand, you visit the South of France and make Pau your headquarters; and if you drive south from Pau into the mountains, you may recognize some of the places I have described. One day you could drive from Pau, by Gan, Rebenacq, Sevignac, Laruns, Eaux Bonnes, over the pass to Argeles and so back to Pau. On another day you might repeat that drive, which will bear repetition, as far as Laruns and, shortly after that townlet, turn right to Eaux Chaudes and so on to Gabas and beyond. If you take those ways, I think you will recognize some of the places I have written about.' They, and places not far distant, are the scene of *Red In The Morning*, a story that brings back old friends. Not merely Mansel, Chandos and their suite but Audrey and John Bagot, late of *Gale Warning* and now respectably married, and the bad Auntie Emma, last seen at The Wet Flag in *Adèle and Co*. Mercer had two aunts so named; possibly one or other had incurred his displeasure. A new villain, a lapsed gentleman named Brevet, is an admirable creation. As he has been unwise enough to lay hands on Jenny, Chandos and Mansel very properly asphyxiate him with his own car exhaust. This I count as a half for Chandos, but he has one bird of his own for the bag. He strangles Auntie Emma. Add them to Casemate, (knifed), Major Grieg, (dejected), Jean the chauffeur, (the like), Luis the Spaniard, (battered to death) and perhaps a half share in the Shepherd (drowned) and he is amassing quite a score. Chandos, though usually armed, never shoots anybody; probably, like most British officers, he was a poor hand with a pistol. Once again he behaves so immaculately towards a girl that he goes almost into priggishness. Mona Lelong, the Stoat, whose father 'commanded his Regiment and died by Ypres', is extracted from the waters under the earth in a state of nature, or as near such as no matter. Having thus become acquainted and after further excitements, she has to kiss him '—and slipped away'. Like the girls Lelia and Virgina Brooch. Sunset, in *The Stolen March* had put the question more directly. 'Won't your mouth work?' This was not the *Windsor Magazine*, nor was it a romantic story. Solemnity was more suited to Richard Chandos, who denies Mona so much as a cousinly peck. The dust-jacket tells of 'the great love of a lady for a husband that is not hers'; and a very one-sided business it was. Temptation nobly resisted was a regular Yates theme; Bagot seemed to find it harder than did the lofty Chandos.

It is not necessary to look far in order to find the reason why *Red In The Morning* was finished in unusually quick time. A substantial part of Mercer's private fortune was tied up in Cockade, and it was beginning to look uncomfortably likely that he might find post-war life there unendurable. Though still more than comfortably off he had to consider his financial future and it was a high necessity that he should not lose his place amongst the big-selling authors. He was rising sixty, an age at which men have to ask themselves how much work they have left in them, and Cheiro had given him no further guidance. Most important, for he would certainly have returned a reassuring answer to the last question, was the need to find out where he would stand amongst readers in an age very different from that which had formed him. The Old Guard was contemplating stirrup-pumps and gas-masks, wondering to what useful purposes they might be turned; the Middle Guard was waiting to take the surrenders of the King's enemies; the Young Guard, even its youngest members, had grown up amidst wholesale violence and bloodshed. A new story, of a kind likely to be acceptable to all of them, was urgently needed, before the coming authors still in khaki or one of the shades of blue might thrust their noses ahead of his. It would have to contain elements of the old successes, romantic and exciting, but nobody was much in the mood for funny dialogue.

The first line made it clear to the reader exactly where he came in. 'It was, I remember, in the summer of 193—', a formula which avoided any need for future tinkering with dates. All Mercer's stories are summer stories; a man cannot lie out night after night in the snow. It had been common knowledge for centuries that the Pyrenees are riddled with pot-holes, but the subject had only attracted much general interest with the discovery of the Lascaux Caves in September 1940. This proved useful, for the subterraneous breaking into the château by Chandos, and his withdrawal by the same means encumbered by a reformed but under-dressed Stoat, makes exciting reading. That accomplished, Mercer shifts his scene to another well-known sector of France, between Dieppe in the north and the Vendôme in the south. Near-misses, near-murders and two killings by Chandos and his friends that Marshall Hall himself would have been hard put to it to justify before a jury. The Stoat, surplus to establishment, is made to end up as a columnist with something like the *Sporting & Dramatic*. Chandos assures us that in this harmless occupation she found happiness.

The book shows no trace of scamping and is reckoned by many of the cognoscenti to be Mercer at his best. Wartime restrictions forbade production in the old quantities but, for its time, it was highly successful. Any worry that he might have been left behind as a museum piece was dissipated.

The Mercers trained the Chevrolet to Umtali and looked around for somewhere to live. As the law permitted hotels to accept guests for no more than a few days at a stretch, they searched for a furnished house, and found one. It had been subjected to recent additions and was out of the ordinary. 'One room had been built round entirely, and had two doors and no windows at all, though it was furnished as a bedroom.' It was 'very old, half furnished, and thoroughly revolting'. A month later 'we were rescued and went into a funny little house on the edge of the golf course, and we were there about eight months'.

By the end of 1946, after yet another move, it became obvious that, if they intended to stay in Umtali, a new house would have to be built. Mercer already owned his two parcels of land, but they stood on the side of a mountain and great quantities of Africa would have to be displaced in order to provide a shelf on which the house could stand. This discouraged him not at all, for Mercer knew just what he wanted. Cockade had been as near perfection as any home could be and he intended to create as accurate a reproduction of it as local conditions allowed. He was over sixty now, but his vigour seemed undiminished. The land, whether by accident or design, was much the same in area as that at Eaux Bonnes, three and a half acres as against three and a quarter. Once again he designed the house himself, and a very good job he made of it. Elizabeth, who had not been at all well, had misgivings. 'I often wish we had bought that cottage and added to it, it was a smaller property than this . . . and it is not so easy as you get older.' Her husband, though twenty years her senior, seemed quite unperturbed. Not only did he draw out the plans and supervise the work; he wrote another book. *The Berry Scene*.

Berry had vanished from sight since he had written to Boy from Oporto at the end of June 1940. By common consent his resurrection was overdue. The book is dedicated 'to those who have done me the honour to ask me to write [it]'. It is not a connected whole but throws back right beyond *The Brother of Daphne*, beginning with some improbable verbal exchanges between the central figure and, presumably, Mr Stephen of Harrow School. Immediately we move on to the summer of 1907 to find Berry, already married to Daphne and lately appointed a Justice of the Peace, awaiting the arrival of Jonah with the first Rolls of them all. An unanswerable case can be made for pointing out that Jonah was sixteen at the time, but Mercer had reached a point where such things could not be helped. The next elegant extract, 'Berry Calls The Tune', seems to owe something to memories of that other Elizabeth who had written *The Caravaners*. The bad Lord Withyham not only designs to block up an ancient right of way but harbours as his guest a comically dreadful Prussian *Graf* while he attempts his ill-doing. When Berry engages Hoby's Steam Roundabouts to play the 'Washington Post' and 'Daisy Bell', crescendo and accellerando, under the dining room windows, assisting personally in the guise of a clown, some admirable fooling follows. A village cricket match of July 1914 is described, with Berry accidentally catching a German spy for good measure. In the next offering, 'Ten years had gone by', Mercer, rather surprisingly, tells a story centring on his own most loved possession, the picture-clock. If this is to be taken at its face value, he had bought it in 1924 for £21.

The canvas was very dirty, but the painting had been well done. It was an English scene—the skirt of a little hamlet, whose decent inn was commanding a pleasant green: cows stood knee-deep in a horse pond, with rising woods beyond: comfortable clouds rode in a pale blue heaven, and, peering between the trees, was the tower of the village church. And in the tower was a dial—a little silver dial, the size of a two-shilling piece. Behind the canvas was the clock-case; and, when you lifted the frame, the face of the clock left the picture to stay with the works, for a hole had been cut in the painting, to fit the dial. The picture was not dated; nor was it signed. The clock was dated 1754. This had three gongs—two for the chimes and one for the stroke of the hour.

Berry called it Bughaven. 'They'll fairly swarm in that casing. We'd better hang it in the garage.' Reprehended by Daphne, he continues. 'How do you know there aren't any now? They only come out by night. There they are in the cracks, listening to all we're saying . . . It's the chimes. Bugs are mad about music.' He stooped, to set an ear to the picture-clock. ' "Down in the crevice something jeered".' It was Mercer, mocking this time his own love for the inanimate.

The stories would have suited the *Windsor*, but the *Windsor* was no more. They include one mention of Jill in her married state—'Cousin Jill had been at White Ladies for nearly three weeks and now was to join her babies, who were at Pau.' Eighty-odd pages on, we are given a reminder. 'We had all flown for ages. Piers, Jill's attractive husband, had introduced us to the air. We found the element glorious and used it whenever we could . . . And then Fate stretched out an arm. What happened will never be known. Enough that an aeroplane crashed and that passengers, pilot and crew were instantly killed.' Amongst those present had been Piers and the children. The date is early 1935—Berry kept a diary, recording all that happened when the survivors took Jill to Portugal as a form of therapy. Her babies would have been about to sit for their Common Entrance, but no matter. The last date given in the book comes at the head of a letter from Berry—'Brooks's Club, 25th June 1936'. It has a PS. 'Must Adèle sail so soon?' Indeed she must, for, a few lines further on, and in brackets: 'Adèle had sent me a letter, to say she was not coming back.' You can, if so minded, tie this in with the penultimate page of *The House That Berry Built*. Boy and the widowed Jill 'were married very quietly in Pau, on New Years' Eve (1940). Jonah was my best man and Berry gave Jill away.' Five days later Boy went off to war and, in July, 'I was lying in Hertfordshire with a splintered knee'. Boy had always been unlucky with his knees; first the cab-horse in Boulogne, then something of the same kind in *Perishable Goods*, and now this. The Epilogue leaves them all living in Portugal and obviously feeling themselves at last to be stricken in years. The hairdressing establishment gets a mention.

William Mercer, however, was a very spry sixty-two, in far better shape than his monarch. During the Royal visit of 1947 the command came that they present themselves at Government House for an evening reception. 'We were shattered by the appearance of the King,' wrote Elizabeth, 'who was obviously "made up" to look bronzed and sunburned, as the Press was always saying at that time, and he also looked doped, and I suppose he was, poor man.' Seven years of war had taken heavier toll of His Majesty than most of his subjects realized. '[Princess] Elizabeth I found enchanting and too lovely, and though she was so beautiful I remember saying, "There's another Queen Victoria".' Bill 'was entirely taken up with the building, which was done by a Yugoslav of great dignity'. Their conversation was mostly about bricklaying, something always near to Mercer's heart, and he came away owning a large pair of gates that were about to be demolished.

While he supervised the work, Elizabeth flew home for a month, partly in order to see her family but also purchase such furniture as could be had in a coupon-ridden England. She got little, save for a bath, and what she saw of the new England was disenchanting. 'It was so cheap and sordid, which wasn't like England, and all the b—— foreigners, "I'm as good as you". But if I smiled at people they always smiled back—people found this surprising.'

The house was coming on famously, the furniture—or some of it—arrived from France in huge packing cases—'three the size you could crate a Rolls in'—brought by lorry up the one-in-four road to the house and then slid off the tailboard. The first 'slid all right, but on reaching the ground it tipped on its edge and damn nearly went over and over down the hill'. Nothing was properly packed, nothing was labelled and much had been damaged by sea water. The sofa—'given to Bill by his mother when he went to Oxford'—and the armchairs had to be re-upholstered, the gilt picture frames were knocked about, but it was there, even to the pieces of Waterloo Bridge whose alignment at Cockade, described in *The House That Berry Built*, had nearly broken Mercer's heart.

The Mercers' new home, into which they moved early in 1948, was quite something. With its hilltop position it was a very fair imitation of Cockade; it lacked the ninety-three steps but it was still very difficult of ingress and egress to its châtelaine. The black marble staircase, in particular, was a showpiece. The great pedestal writing table, the family portraits, the library, Josiah Dornford's telescope and the pastel of Admiral Sam as a midshipman all found their allotted places. The house was named, Elizabeth says, out of a nursery rhyme: 'To and fro, and up and down, that's the way to Sacradown'. After having lived in, by Mercer's calculation, thirty-six hotels since leaving Cockade for the first time, it was pleasant to come to anchor.

The Mercers became an accepted feature of the landscape, but it was in many ways like the old Pau state of affairs. The passage of time had not made Mercer more clubbable, and he was still working as hard as ever at his writing. At some time he had acquired 'a splendid fur coat—a truly magnificent Martin Harvey type of garment, quite in keeping with his histrionic manner'. Thus attired during the cold season, it became his habit to pay a visit on most days to Mr Woodward, the jeweller. 'He was received always with grave dignity,' Mr Woodward's nephew tells me. 'The purpose of the call was to have his petrol cigarette lighter topped up.'

Dick Hobson, the sometime gunner, had left the Army and joined the staff on the *Umtali Advertiser* as a reporter. In that capacity he visited

the important personage living in the best suburb. Here, he told me, he had built a replica of his house in France, and it was certainly a charming villa filled with expensive furniture and important-looking old pictures of large dimensions. Mercer was deeply conscious of his own importance and was a snob of both the social and intellectual kinds. Socially he might at that time have met a few new settlers of the upper middle classes and even a few associates of the landed gentry, since Rhodesia represented at that time (and the Eastern Districts perhaps in particular) a haven for wealthy people driven out of England by the war, or out of India by partition. Intellectually there can have been little to attract him, and for this reason he seems to have led rather a reclusive life. His wife—a most charming lady who suffered from some disability and walked with a stick—appeared in the shops, but Mercer himself was rarely seen.

There was, however, one semi-public appearance of which Mr Hobson tells.

Before I left Umtali in 1949, he had been persuaded to address the Rotary Club . . . He not only demanded that his talk be printed verbatim or not at all, and that he should see a proof of it, but he also insisted that we print at the end a copyright notice. I need hardly add that in view of the speaker's eminence we did not hesitate to meet these unusual demands.

The old magic of which reviewers speak from time to time had not deserted him, as Hobson tells.

An acquaintance of mine at that time who was better read in the lighter literature of the 1930s than myself claimed that he had joined a cocktail party at Meikle's Hotel in Salisbury that included Mercer, whom he did not recognize by that name. He said that as conversation with Mercer continued he formed the odd sensation that he had been physically transported into a Dornford Yates novel, and found himself expecting Carson to appear and announce that the Rolls was waiting outside.

Dick Hobson at twenty-two, was exactly the usual age for a Yates hero at the beginning of his adventures and the gap between twenty-two and sixty-two had become suddenly apparent. To him, very understandably, Mercer was an old buffer of mildly comic aspect and behaviour. The older people seem to have appreciated him more highly, whether or not they had been brought up on his work. Mrs Lucy Day, who was as nearly as possible their next door neighbour, made friends with both of them though in the nature of things it was with Elizabeth that she had the more to do. Colonel Wyrley-Birch, now over ninety, has been kind enough to tell me that he liked the man. Several others of the seniors have said the same. Mercer, to the outside view, was at least inoffensive in his stronghold and could be amusing company when the mood was on him. It is Dick Hobson who gives a glimpse of the almost phantom figure of Richard, now a grown man. 'I have some recollection of a son who came once or twice, and of some rumoured story that he had been more or less "cut off with a shilling", but that may well be idle and ill-remembered gossip.' It was more than most people could tell. As a subject for conversation Richard ranked below George Bernard Shaw or Modern Art.

Between exhorting bricklayers and hanging gates Mercer had regularly gone back to the study and more proof of his diligence was on the way. In 1949 there came *Cost Price*, with the Old Guard back on parade again. Mercer was very clever in the way he mustered his characters. If you count in all those who made up the cast of the short stories and add them to the regulars and the one-off heroes, they amount to a formidable number. As they are all of the same totem he builds up an impression of one big family, for nearly all of them are familiar friends to each other and thus become friends to the constant reader. One feels, indeed, that once Mercer has awarded you your Colours you are almost an honorary member yourself. In *The Berry Scene* he brought back for a moment Derry Bagot, Cousin Vandy, Forsyth, 'the Fairies at Charing', Patricia and Simon Beaulieu, Toby Rage and Mrs Medallion, the Duke of Culloden and his Susan, Lettice and William Red Spenser, Sir Andrew Plague, Coker Falk—a much improved character now—Mr Baal and Mr Lemonbaum, and even Elizabeth's Portuguese friend, the mule in trousers. *Cost Price* gives us Mansel, Chandos, the indestructible but relatively harmless villain Punter, Andrew Palin and the Ferrers (last heard of in 1932 in *Safe Custody*) and new villains to replace those previously expended.

It was a labour-saving kind of story, picking up where *Safe Custody* had left off. You will recall that the Borgia treasure, soused in poison, had been walled up in the bowels of Hohenhems along with certain corpses. It was now, by inference, about 1937 and the Boche was about to take over Austria; thus it became expedient to get the stuff out and, if possible, to smarten up a Boche or two in the process. Mercer was going to teach the Gestapo, or what was left of that defunct organization, not to put his name on their list again. They had cut loose in Pau in 1943; the place had been one of the centres for smuggling baled-out aircrew over the Pyrenees and when Unoccupied France had ceased to be, the Gestapo had had a field day. Pau had suffered much at its hands and this was the best Mercer could do in the way of vengeance. Other villains were also after the jewels, thus creating an interesting little problem.

Mansel makes his own comment on the business as it nears its end. 'The fact remains that, though we have brought it off, it has been an untidy business from first to last. I mean, not one to be proud of. Nothing clean-cut about it. Up to the last, it was on the knees of the gods.' Apart from encompassing the downfall of some villains of the second rank, Chandos adds two and a half to the score. Friar, skull fractured; Orris, cast into a waterfall to make a third of his kind along with Jean the chauffeur and Major Grieg. The half was more satisfactory, being a Gestapo man, and Mercer seems to have licked his lips over it: 'And then I saw the pier-glass. This was a heavy sheet, applied to the stout, stone wall. I forced the brute to the mirror, and let him gaze. When he saw who it was that held him, the light of burning hatred flared in his starting eyes. "Look on your own face," I said, "for, by God, when you see it next, it won't look the same." Then, as a man puts the weight, I put his face to the wall beside the pier-glass—with all my might.' The result was entirely satisfactory. Very probably there had been a pier-glass in the hotel at San Sebastian that had set Mercer thinking.

The asportation of the gems is accompanied by another of the unrequitable-love stories. For reasons it is unnecessary to examine, Chandos seeks sanctuary with a travelling circus. To such work he was accustomed, having done it before in *Fire Below*, but this time he is to be a professional strong man. This again was not entirely strange to him, for Richard Chandos had quite often thrown young women about in earlier times. It did not take long to master the technique. The girl Colette was 'slight but well-made'; when, at the end of the performance 'she sat down on a mushroom—really a stool—and I lifted the mushroom up and, finally, held it high with one of my hands', it was as much as he could manage until he found that it was 'a matter of balance and that, taking the strain as I should, I could have easily lifted a heavier girl'. The exercise, apart from its agreeableness, stood Chandos in good stead when swinging on ropes over torrents, usually carrying Colette, a sackful of gems, or both, and thus encumbered fighting off and drowning the beastly though loyal Orris.

It was the nobility in Chandos that had given his final victim some last hours of life. Only a little while before, in this nameless place amongst mountains and with night falling, Colette had murmured, 'We are alone now, and so we can do as we please. There is no one to watch or whisper, because I have lost my heart.' Colette deceived herself. Lurking in the undergrowth was Orris, faint but pursuing, meditating homicide and only awaiting an opportunity to catch Chandos in an unguarded position. The chance was never really there. 'Do you want to distress me?' begins the customary allocution, and virtue is rewarded. As he has for some time past been carrying the girl around like a suitcase, Chandos feels under some obligation to her. She is suffered to kiss him, and he returns the compliment though his heart was not in it. Though she never knew it, Colette was more privileged than Lelia, in *Fire Below*, had been. Not only does she get her grudging kiss but Chandos even finds her a suitable husband in Andrew Palin, a man sharing many attributes with Pomfret Tudor who had espoused the equally surplus Eulalie. Lelia just got shot.

All this time Mercer had been greatly worried about the future of Cockade. His correspondence with Mr Carter speaks for itself. 'I should think perhaps it is a good idea that Madame Mahieu should stay on until September,' he wrote on 23 June 1949, 'because I certainly don't want the house empty. I am afraid I cannot have Julie Emanualie as concierge. We both liked Julie when she came to us as a housemaid on the outbreak of war, but she had deteriorated very much when I saw her in

1945. What is more to the point, she was well in with the Capdevielles and I should not be in the least surprised if they put her up to asking for the job. I am quite sure that, despite any assurances she were to give you, Joseph and Thérèse Capdevielles would be visiting Cockade the whole time if Julie were in charge. I never liked Strub and can't see that he had any right to start work upon the refrigerator without instructions.' He goes on to say that the refrigerator had better be sold. 'We ought to get a good price, for they are very expensive everywhere to-day and the old ones are very much better than the new'. Speaking of the taking of an inventory, he adds 'As you know, I can get along in French, but I do not know a great many French words and . . . the French describe things differently to the way in which an Englishman would . . . I am inclined to think that we might as well have out the copper pans from the kitchen, for they are rapidly becoming antiques and could be used here for flowers.' His anxiety about the place increased with the passage of time. In September 1949 he wrote, 'The projet de bail submitted by M. Laveau is, I agree, grotesque. I should not be surprised to learn that the Capdevielles were behind the whole thing . . . It is most provoking, for I think we both hoped that here was a solution of all difficulties. I quite agree that, essential as it is that a tenant be found, one cannot let oneself in for God knows what . . . After all, we are prepared to accept a purely nominal rent.' A few days later Carter was told that a Mr Godfrey-Faussett had offered the sum of £300 a year, out of which the landlord would have to pay £100 to the caretaker and, 'as he seems a very nice man and wrote very pleasantly', Mercer had accepted. A month later came a telegram saying that the proposed tenant had had to drop out. 'It is really most annoying and I am sure you are as upset as I am.' Carter held his power of attorney, was an old friend and a valuable agent. All the same the formalities were kept up. 'My dear Carter' begins each letter, Elizabeth is always 'Mrs Mercer' and 'yours very sincerely, C. W. Mercer' is the standard ending.

By this time old age was creeping up and Mercer was beginning to show his years. The thick dark hair and moustache were now very grey though his eyebrows remained strikingly black, and his old enemy, rheumatism, was troubling him again. Mrs Semple, a physiotherapist, became a regular visitor at Sacradown. 'I always enjoyed going there,' she tells me. The owners seemed very happy together. 'Major Mercer spent a good deal of his time in his study, writing. This was his main form of relaxation as he once told me that he was in a completely different world when he was writing. Mrs Mercer spent a good deal of her time crotcheting, sewing and knitting. She had a little Maltese poodle to keep her company.'

The work was still sufficient to keep two secretaries fairly busy. Mercer, in his capacity of Dornford Yates, was punctilious about answering letters from his admirers, and they seemed as thick on the ground as ever. Demands for more books still came in but he was now becoming doubtful about his ability to keep the flow going. 'About the writing of another Berry book I am uncertain. One of the arts of life is to know when to stop,' he wrote to one of the followers on 1 December 1950. He underrated his own powers.

As long ago as March 1946 he had written to Colonel Alexander, that 'I am receiving many letters from high and low, all begging me to write of the old days and to leave the new order alone: but, before they began to come in, I knew that I could never write happily of a world in which all that I set store by had gone by the board. So I am setting out to write *The Berry Scene* and then to do my best to bid yesterday return.'

This he did with *Lower Than Vermin*, but it came about more by accident than design. The title came from one of the more winning speeches of Mr Bevan, the 'squalid nuisance' of Mr Churchill's great days. It may not be out of place to quote from a book written by Sapper in 1917, before he was famous and when he was still a fighting soldier. In *No Man's Land*, he ends his trench stories thus.

Winnowed by the fan of suffering and death, the wheat of the harvest will shed its tares of discord and suspicion. The duke and the labourer will have stood side by side, and will have found one another—men. No longer self the only thing; no longer a ceaseless grouse against everybody and everything; no longer an instinctive suspicion of the man one rung higher up the ladder. But more self-reliant and cheery; stronger in character and bigger in outlook; with a newly acquired sense of self-control and understanding; in short, grown a little nearer to its maximum development, the manhood of the nation will be ripe for the moulder's hand. It has tasted of discipline; it has realised that only by discipline can there be true freedom for the community; and that without that discipline, chaos is inevitable. Pray heavens there be a moulder—a moulder worthy of the task.

None had appeared after 1918. Class hatred, rather of a one-way kind—and very largely kept going by interested professionals— came back more rancorous than ever. Even after Hitler had given the nation a second chance, it threw it away. Mr Bevan had shared none of the experiences of Sapper or of the millions like him. In his view all men save registered trade unionists were vile and his assertions of this went largely uncontradicted.

Mercer began his book out of a sense of duty; not of duty to any class or classes, but of duty to England, a country that he saw to be drowning in the sewage brought up by wicked men. He may have over-egged his pudding, but the idea was sound enough and it was written with complete sincerity. Nobody much under eighty can know how true to life were the characters he created, their actions or their speech. Mercer always asserted firmly that what he had written was the truth and that he spoke of what he had seen and heard about him. The book treats of the history of a noble family from about the Diamond Jubilee until after the Second War, much of it being related by the governess, Miss Carson, a highly respected name in Yates circles. There are people in it who certainly had some parallel in real life: Major de Guesclin who is found in a bed where he has no business to be but purges his fault by dying like a hero; Virgil Coleton, middle-aged gentleman of inde- pendent means, who vanishes from sight into a recruiting office in 1914, turns up again in 1918 and, on his death-bed, hands over a letter to 'Dear Sarge' and the DCM. It was the last saga of the landed gentry, dedicated to 'The Gentlemen of the Old School who, whether they were peers or ploughmen, masters or servants, shop-assistants or statesmen—whatever walk of life they adorned—justly commanded the respect of their fellow men'. 'Respect' was the word of power: not 'affection'. There was always something of *oderint, dum metuant* about William Mercer.

The book was not all that of a success.

'*Lower than Vermin*,' said Jill, 'was one of your best.'
I shook my head.
'Thousands didn't get it,' I said.

213

The trouble was that to most of the then generation of readers, brought up on different fare, it seemed a caricature completely divorced from reality. Mercer was depressed, and it made him feel old. When one admirer wrote to congratulate him on the book—and many people did—he replied sadly, 'It was very kind of you to write. I am so glad my people do seem real to you. At the same time I am not sure that I have not written enough. I am afraid my people have outlived their day—as I have.' A few months later, however, he was writing much more cheerfully to Mr Carter.

I am very glad you have read *Lower Than Vermin* and I am delighted to know that you appreciated and, indeed, enjoyed it so much. What we used to call the nobility and gentry of England have been so monstrously maligned and misrepresented for so long that I felt it was only right that some author of standing should present a true picture of them and their habits and manners before it was too late. Throughout the book I have exaggerated nothing. People exactly like my characters did live and move and have their being exactly as I have set down. And we must only pity those people who to-day deny the truth of this. They did not know the great days of England as you and I did, and you and I know how contemptible it is for anyone to pretend that to-day compares with yesterday . . . . I agree with all you say about Cockade. The place is incomparable and I decline to give up hope that one day somebody who is prepared to afford it will feel that it is the only place at which they could live.

There can be no doubt about Mercer's mild obsession with the kind of people whom he ranked only a little lower than the angels. The nobility comprised an order capable of strict definition and, on the whole, its members could truthfully lay claim to ancient family and broad acres. His acquaintance with authentic Peers of the Realm was slight. No doubt at Harrow and at Oxford he had come into contact with sprigs of great houses but, apart from promoted lawyers, his only belted friend appears to have been the Earl of Cork, a man twenty-four years his senior and the owner of a house in Pau. The gentry were another matter. Though none of his own ancestors, save for Admiral Sam, had been able to make much of a claim to gentility Mercer had passed all the necessary examinations. As a matter of law the man who had held a Commission, was a graduate of Oxford University and a member of the Bar, had a three-fold right so to style himself, and by this Mercer set much store.

His ideas had, of course, been formed well before 1914 and they were never mitigated. During the war years many a man had found himself suddenly to be an officer and also a gentleman even if he was demonstrably nothing of the kind. More often than not the circumstances did not prevent him from becoming a good leader of men. It was not, however, with such as these that Mercer concerned himself. In his eyes the gentry were the modern, or fairly modern, equivalent of mediaeval knights. A knight might have come up from almost any background, but once dubbed and spurred, the meanest of them, owning no more than horse and weapons, was socially equal to the master of a score of castles. On top of that, a poor knight followed the same code of manners and conduct as did a royal prince; nobody expected that from a rich merchant. Most of Mercer's heroes take the opportunity one way or another of showing themselves to be armigerous. He did not lack for fuglemen; the Officers' Mess of the 3rd County of London Yeomanry had everything. Should Mercer, against all probability, ever have entertained doubts about the value of good blood, then Dandy Beatty, the trainer of race-horses, could have put him right. Should he desire to learn how the rich lived in a hunting county he had only to listen to Squire Burnaby of Baggrave Hall; and did he want to find out how a young man of means and spirit occupied his time there was Geoffrey Stedall available for study. One may suspect that there was no great affection between Lieutenant Mercer and his Commanding Officer. Berry is made to say—truly—that Sir Horace Smith-Dorrien was 'the greatest general of his day', but has to add a dig at Haig as being 'not in the same street'. Smith-Dorrien's work finished in early 1915: Haig still had most of his before him. It looks as if Mercer's rather catty streak took the chance of unkindness to Oliver Haig as well as his famous uncle. By the end of his thirtieth year Bill Mercer had seen a good cross-section of the gentry of England and, wittingly or not, he preserved it like a fly in amber.

Meantime he cultivated his African garden, took Elizabeth regularly for Sunday luncheon at an hotel called Peplow, some fifteen miles away, and contemplated further books. The money had long ceased to matter. It was the writing itself that

was the thing, intellectual exercise that may be kept up long
after polo players and hunting men are thinking of buying
tricycles. Richard appeared now and again. Mrs Semple relates
that 'he did visit Umtali once and worked in Salisbury for a
while. His stepmother certainly did not like him as she told
me.' Mrs Semple, incidentally, tells me that 'The estate agent
that I mentioned earlier told me that he has in his possession
several manuscripts that were left to Richard, who apparently
is not interested in claiming them.' Is there an unpublished
Chandos story still buried in Umtali? It would be well worth
somebody's trouble to find out, for Chandos was finished. 'It
is kind of you to ask me to write another Chandos book,'
wrote Mercer in 1956, 'I am afraid this is rather unlikely for I
am not as young as I was.'

In the last years he wrote rather for his own pleasure than for
that of his readers. As the Biblical threescore years and ten
crept up on him he attended more closely to family matters.
Almost the last of his blood relations, apart from Richard, was
a cousin in Hampshire, Mrs Sharp, with whom he kept up a
regular correspondence, but there were other cousins on the
Munro side in Northern Ireland for whom he plainly felt a
sense of kinship. When Charles Munro died in 1952 Mercer
wrote a charming letter to his widow, whom he addressed as
'My dearest Muriel':

I am so very grieved. Though it is many years since I saw you
both, time has drawn us together. It is very kind of you to
tell me that he was glad of my letters, it gave me great
pleasure to write them, and I shall certainly write to you if
you would like to hear from me. From the day he wanted me
to be his best man—I was really too young—I have always
felt that I was your cousin too. I was looking forward to
sending him a copy of my address to the local Rotarians, on
'Humour in English Literature' which I have promised to
give in ten days' time; for I have, of course, included Hector,
and I hoped that my reference to him would give Charlie
pleasure. . . . Surroundings make such a difference in these
hard times. Jill is fairly well, but I fear she will never adapt
herself to life here, as I have contrived to do. Of course, she
is twenty years younger, and so possesses neither the experience nor the rude philosophy which experience brings.
To lose my home in France was a terrible blow, but I am

used to hard knocks and have come to count myself fortunate to be in this land and to be able to live quietly in a pleasant home, with nice grounds and really beautiful country views. England was ruled out for us both; for me because of my health; for her because she is not strong enough to wait upon herself, let alone me. I am still very active and people say I don't look my age, but then I do a lot and work hard—but I am able to go quietly and am well fed and served. And if that is not good fortune to-day, I do not know what is . . . I always regard death as a promotion. It hits very hard those that are left, but I know you are proud to think that, as he came to the River, the trumpets sounded for the passing of a gallant gentleman. That is how I shall always remember him. So unassuming, too, but then great gentlemen always are.

It ends: 'Always your affectionate cousin, BILL. PS 'Willie' is a survival, which I have long deplored.'

A few months later, in August 1952, he wrote to Muriel's younger daughter. 'We are either second cousins or first cousins once removed—I don't know and I don't care which. Anyway our relationship entitles me to call you Juniper and, as I have none of the dignity of age, I hope you will think of me as Bill. I am very happy to know that you are to be married, and I am sure that, as your Father's and Mother's daughter, you will make a splendid wife.' This very proper expression of feeling was fortified by a handsome cheque. Being a girl of excellent judgement the recipient spent it on a honeymoon in Paris, a course that the donor would have wholeheartedly approved.

As men grow old and watch the newspaper to learn of the death of friends, they tend to think more about mortality. Dornford Yates had been a known and respected name for a very long time now. It was back in 1935 that Cyril Connolly had written his famous piece in the *New Statesman*. Mercer would not have warmed instinctively either to that periodical or to a man who described, in *Who's Who*, his recreation as being 'the Mediterranean', but the sentiment was admirable. 'Sometimes, at great garden parties, literary luncheons, or in the quiet of an exclusive gunroom, a laugh rings out. The sad, formal faces for a moment relax and a smaller group is formed within the larger. They are admirers of Dornford Yates who have found out each other. We are badly organized, we know little about ourselves and next to nothing about our hero, but we appreciate fine writing when we come across it, and a wit that is ageless united to a courtesy that is extinct.' If those of whom Connolly spoke were to learn something about their hero, there was no time for him to lose in putting this right, Mercer set to work on *As Berry and I Were Saying*.

The book 'is really my own memoir put into the mouths of Berry and Boy and so related in a fictional setting. I like to think that has made the book more palatable and less dull than an ordinary volume of reminiscences', Mercer wrote to an admirer. As far as it goes, that is true but it does not go very far. The world of White Ladies was known to tens of thousands; it was admired, and people of a simpler class looked up to its inhabitants as beings of a superior kind. To bring them down to earth by relating the bald facts of Mercer's own life would have been not merely a literary disaster but a stroke of great unkindness. And Mercer was a kind man. He begins, once again, by poking fun at himself.

> Berry leaned back, fixed his eyes upon the ceiling and fingered his chin.
> 'None but the great,' he said, 'should write their reminiscences. For a lesser man to do so, it is a gross impertinence. Who cares where he was born or went to school? Or what his nurses smelt like, or why he fell off his pony in 1894?'

Having thus reproved himself, Mercer got on with the job. The book can by no stretch of imagination be called an autobiography; rather it is a scrap-book of the Edwardian age as it was seen by the upper-middle or lower-upper classes. It is none the worse for that, provided that you are content to learn no more of Dornford Yates than that he was at Harrow, moved on to an unspecified college at Oxford where he was a pillar of the OUDS and was later called to the Bar. His experiences there, in his own right, were not remarkable but he was on the fringes of great things. Those with some knowledge of the legal profession before 1914 can pick out many gobbets of information that you will not find anywhere else. Real characters, and some thinly disguised, abound; but in reading it one is hard put to distinguish between the experiences of William Mercer and those of Boy Pleydell. It could hardly have been otherwise. In a Note, the author insists that 'I have, in some cases, no right to tell "the whole truth". But I can honestly say that I have told "nothing but the truth".' There is no reason why he should not be believed.

As Berry and I Were Saying sold well enough, going to four printings in three months, but a change had come over the world and it did not command the sales that Chandos had done. Though the faithful were fewer in numbers and greyer of hair there still remained enough of them to call for more, and many of them possessed children who had been brought up on Dornford Yates. Mercer did not immediately gratify them. His next books bear the signs of being the work of an elderly and not over-robust man, for they are short on action and concentrate rather on states of mind. *Ne'er Do Well*, of 1954, is a story of murder, but not of the common kind; it is set in a convent and all the characters, including the killer, are high-minded and high-class. Two years later came another oddity. It was originally named *Lady In Waiting*; a note explains what happened next: 'Not until this book and its dust-jacket had been printed was it discovered that another novel was shortly to appear bearing the title, *Lady In Waiting*, which I had chosen. In these days of expensive paper and high production costs, to "scrap" one whole edition was unthinkable. So we have done the best we can . . .' The best we could do was to over-stamp the dust-jacket with a new name, and whilst 'Lady In Waiting' remains in white there appears, printed above it in red, the words '*Wife Apparent*'.

Mercer set much store by the book, but it is not amongst his best. The demobilized officer with the head wound that from time to time renders him amnesiac had done good service in the past, from Anthony Lyveden to Captain Boleyn in *Maiden Stakes* but he was overdue for retirement. The wood-magic in a favourite elm tree—possibly old days at Elm Tree Road were in his mind—had been seen before and jactitation of marriage by a respectable young woman for excellent reasons had done duty twice. The female domestic, Florence, somehow never seems to be other than a contrived figure, though many people take a more appreciative view of her than this. Mercer's imagination was beginning to flag, and there was cause for it. By 1958 it was becoming more and more plain that he had a worse enemy than rheumatism with which to contend. Cancer of the lung had set in, even though it was still controllable.

The comparative failure of *Lower Than Vermin*, *Ne'er Do Well* and *Wife Apparent* did not seem to deject him, but he was set upon responding to the demands for more Berry so long as he had the strength to do it. *B-Berry and I Look Back* was the last effort to fill in gaps in the forty-odd-year White Ladies saga. The beginning is Yates at his funniest. Berry has at last succumbed to the necessity for false teeth. At his bedside in the nursing-home,

'Mhat mife hmeebig mogs now?' he demanded.

'Darling,' said Daphne, 'for heaven's sake don't try to talk.'

Her husband seized his pad and wrote some words violently down. . . . 'I abhor my vacuum. How soon can it be filled?'

Later, the teeth having been furnished and food suggested, Berry demurs; they might tarnish.

'They'll recover,' said Jonah. 'A little paraffin in the water and no one will know they've been used. Carson'll do them for you: he's got to wash the Rolls.'

[That night] kneeling beside his bed, leaning over a face-towel, Berry was man-handling his jaws.

'But why the posture?' said Jonah.

'In case I drop them,' snarled Berry, 'Then they'll fall on the bed and come to no harm.'

. . . 'I'll get a torch,' said Jonah, 'I expect there's a spring you press.'

'What do you mean—a torch?' asked Berry.

'Well, I don't want to fumble,' said Jonah . . .

After some frightful contortions, he laid the towel carefully down and looked about him. 'Mell, matph map,' he mouthed. 'Mope a mam ptmep mem mack.'

Could a pompous man have written that, do you think?

This, the last book, was Mercer's leave-taking. It is again a patch-work, including short visits to the Bar, the stage and the amusements of a London now rapidly vanishing into history. He treats of the future of publishing:

'Before the first war the price of a new novel, whether it was written by Kipling or written by me, was four-and-six. Between the wars the price was seven-and-six. To-day it is fifteen shillings. . . . Well, people can't afford to pay such prices for fiction. That's why my books will shortly be published in paper-back form.'

'No,' cried everyone.

'It's a fact, I never thought I should see it, but it's a fact. . . .
But here is a prophecy. It's my belief that within a very few
years even new novels will cease to be published in cloth.'

All his own books, he assured them, were still in print. ' "Owing
to a shortage of paper, I think one or two ran out, just after the
war. But only for two or three months".'

The story ends with an epilogue in the shape of a letter
written by one of the servants to her brother. The family are
all living in Portugal, their old age unencumbered by children
or grandchildren. 'The Major and Madam seem exactly the
same—so gentle and kind and natural, just as they always were
. . . But I'm worried about the Captain, for he is so very tired.
You know, Jack, he works like he used to twenty years ago;
and he's over seventy now, though he doesn't look his age.'

He might not look it, but he was feeling it, for William
Mercer's work was done. At the end of February 1960 he was
admitted to the Isolation Hospital at Umtali and there on
5 March he died quietly. Elizabeth was with him, and the
Reverend Mark Wells, the Parish Priest of St John's. The
causes of death were pneumonia and cancer of the lungs.

His will, recently made and the last of a series, was a long and
complicated document, for Mercer was an exact man where his
possessions were concerned. Any latent anti-semitism seems to
have disappeared over the years, for he chose as joint executor
with Elizabeth a well-known lawyer named Benjamin Disraeli
Goldberg. As Rhodesian law does not (or did not in 1960)
require the value of the estate to be shown on the Probate it is
not possible to quantify them with any accuracy. It is said that
over the years he had received royalties amounting to something
over £400,000 and this seems entirely credible; the number of
books sold exceeded two million and that does not include a
very substantial amount of American sales. Most of his estate
went to Elizabeth. Legacies to Richard in earlier wills had all
been revoked. Some items, however, deserve mention. Mr
Woodward, the jeweller, was desired to dismantle the picture-
clock and to destroy it in accordance with precise instructions.
As compensation for his trouble he was left the famous fur coat
which he in turn passed to his nephew, Donald Clark, in
England. Having little use for so regal a garment Mr Clark tried
to sell it but found no takers. In the end he persuaded his

London tailor to accept it in return for a small discount on a new suit. The coat was last seen doing duty as a rug in the fitting-room to which it was the new owner's custom to retire for his siesta. There was one clause even more affecting. Mercer's budgerigar was to be taken to a named veterinary surgeon, painlessly put down and interred in a specified place to a depth of not less than one foot. 'For the purpose of identification, my budgerigar has blue legs and blue feet.' His own ashes (his approval of cremation is described in *Wife Apparent*) remain in Umtali, immured in the north porch of St John's Church.

There is a line in his *Times* obituary to which Mercer would not have objected. 'There was something romantic and boyish in his make-up and he rejoiced to be called Victorian.' But there was more to William Mercer than just that.

EPILOGUE

Nearly all the characters have gone now. Elizabeth Mercer remained at Sacradown, helped by a succession of European women companions. Four years after the death of her husband, and at the age of fifty-nine, she in her turn went to join her ancestors. Her ashes lie with his in the churchyard of St John at Umtali. The greater part of Mercer's considerable estate had devolved upon her under the terms of his will and upon her death it was passed to a number of beneficiaries. Josiah Dornford's telescope and the pastel of Admiral Sam as a 'snotty', together with other heirlooms, found a new home with Mrs Bryan of Belfast—the 'Juniper' of the letters. The Cavalry Club, probably to its mild surprise, received two fine silver entrée dishes, the Inner Temple much of the crystal and the porcelain. The books passed to Peterhouse School in Southern Rhodesia and the Canaletto, which can be seen in some of the illustrations, were bequeathed to the Rhodes National Gallery, along with two great chairs of Spanish leather.

Richard had, by his father's earlier wills, been put down for legacies that progressively diminished in size. After his visit to Rhodesia, which does not seem to have been an unqualified success, he was cut out altogether. He had long since dropped out of the society of his family and has for some years past made his home in Denmark.

Bettine Mercer outlived both her husband and his second wife. After the divorce, by which she had been severely wounded, she remained for some time with her own family in America and poured out the bitterness of her heart into her diary. At some point of time she moved to London, supporting herself largely by her own efforts and turning her talent for languages to practical use. Eventually she settled in Switzerland and there on 12 March 1973 she died at her villa in the Via Cesare at Lugano. Even in her eighties she remained beautiful. No doubt she had had opportunities of marrying again, but

Bettine's Catholicism guided her life. Exactly what were the financial arrangements between her and Mercer will never be known with certainty, but Bettine never endured poverty. Apart from whatever she possessed in Switzerland, she left estate in England to the value of just over £1,700. Richard seems to have fallen out of her life as he had fallen from that of his father. He did not attend her funeral. One can only hope that her later years became reasonably happy, for Bettine was an ill-used woman. M. Ollivier, on the other hand, seems to have prospered. A few years ago he was still living in the South of France exhibiting all those things that the French tax laws call 'outward signs of wealth'. For all I know he is still doing so.

Cockade was put on the market soon after Mercer's death and the agents had difficulty in finding a purchaser. In the end it was sold for the equivalent of £4,000—less than a third of the pre-war building price—and is now an hotel. Thérèse and Joseph still live nearby. The Villa Maryland in Pau and Wellesley House in Walmer are—or were recently—nursing homes. The house in Elm Tree Road no longer exists.

The books, however are very much alive. Three Berry books are still in print; a Chandos story—*She Fell Among Thieves*—has appeared as a television play. It seems likely that more of the books will be back in the shops before very long. Quality, like blood, will always tell.

In his fashion of writing Mercer elected for a deliberate dignity; the English language, even its smallest coinage, was too sacred to be sweated or clipped and, up to 1944, his old Harrow master N. K. Stephen would be reading every word he wrote. The style has been tested by time and has emerged both triumphant and seemingly indestructible. Most of the books written by other hands either just before or just after the Great War proclaim their period; Mercer's do nothing of the kind. Though they may be a thought on the heavy side, it cannot be gainsaid that they leave a permanent impression upon the mind of the reader. These are not trifling things, to be read but the once and the then put aside for ever. The copies that turn up from time to time in second-hand book shops nearly always look well thumbed.

In the first years of this century, long before Mercer had thought of setting pen to paper, Sir Arthur Conan Doyle published in *Cassell's Magazine* a series of essays made permanent under the title 'Through The Magic Door'. They amounted to a kind of comradely exegesis of the styles of notable authors, beginning with the eighteenth-century trio of Fielding, Richardson and Smollett, and ending with the grandees of his own day. In their pages appear observations that might almost have been written with Mercer in mind. 'There is no reason why a writer should cease to be a gentleman, or that he should write for a woman's eye that which he would justly be knocked down for having said in a woman's ears.' This was a view that Mercer certainly shared. Doyle also laments that the heroes of Fielding and Richardson lacked 'any touch of distinction, of spirituality, of nobility'. Nobody can say that of Mercer's people. You may search in vain for any expression that could affront the most gently nurtured. His good men, for example, never demean themselves by the use of language that might be called either strong or foul. Even his bad men only swear in spondees: 'You —— ——'

The interesting thing is that nobody has ever attempted to follow his road to success. Amongst his contemporaries, Buchan stuck to matter-of-fact straightforward narrative prose, in the direct line from *Thraciam ex negotio petebam*. 'Sapper' added a touch of raciness and occasionally wrote at the top of his voice. Every so often a young man writes a fairly good adventure story and is hailed as 'the new John Buchan', though none seems to stay the course. You never read of 'a new Dornford Yates', nor is it now likely that you ever will. Austria, designed by Providence as a place for rattling good yarns, has become the fief of Helen MacInnes, but times there have changed. The Americans have taken over. The Wet Flag in Rouen was pretty certainly wiped away by bombing and is now municipal flats.

In the forming of a writer there are both general and special influences. The latter comprehend the sources from which his plots come, and it is virtually impossible for these to be entirely original. Some of Mercer's unwitting creditors have already been mentioned. Anthony Hope, who wrote *The Prisoner Of Zenda* in a month and saw it on sale sixteen weeks later, was a Balliol man; so was A. E. W. Mason, to whose 1935 book *They Wouldn't Be Chessmen* the second half of Mercer's *Shoal Water* bears considerable resemblance. His general influences determining the way in which he would write, were Harrow

225

and the University of Oxford, to which he always looked back in love. In 1943, far away from England, he added a new dedication to the coming edition of *Blood Royal*. 'To Oxford, as I remember it when I had the honour to wear a commoner's gown'. The past again, you will notice. Throughout the whole of his adult life William Mercer walked chin on shoulder. For all that, he was never Gilbert's 'idiot who praises in enthusiastic tone all centuries but this, one and all countries but his own'. It was simply that he possessed the ability to distinguish between good and bad, and could tell polished mahogany from varnished plywood.

A NOTE ON SOURCES

As this book does not qualify for heavy-weight status it seems unnecessary to burden it with a mass of authorities for everything. Births, marriages, deaths, wills and probates have all been extracted from registers of the usual kind and addresses from census returns and postal directories. All this has been done by Robert Atherton; the work sounds slight enough, but it was not. For events before 1836 every item had to be painstakingly disinterred from some parish register and the number of dead-ends passed belief. On East Kent in general I can draw on the accumulated recollections of a half-century spent there; part of this at Walmer, where my elder daughter was born at Wellesley House in 1948. Some evidence of the facts on which I rely must, however, be given and I set it out below.

Chapter One
The archives of the Dornfords come mostly from the registers of St Botolph's Church, Bishopsgate. Josiah's career at sea is set out in O'Byrne's *Naval Biographical Dictionary* (John Murray, 1849) and the records of the Naval Historical Society at Empress State Building. His Lieutenant's Passing Certificate is in the Public Record Office at Kew. Rear-Admiral Samuel Mercer was promoted to Flag rank in List H of the Captains promoted to Rear-Admirals (ret'd). He too has his record set out in the same places as that of Josiah. Ethel Munro's short biography of her brother appears at the end of the collected edition of Saki's works. William Mercer's story of his appearance at the wedding is contained in a letter from him to Mrs Juniper Bryan of Belfast dated 7 September 1952.

The suicide of George Mercer is reported fully in the *Solicitors' Journal* for 17 October 1891. Accounts of the Edwards trial appear in, amongst other places, the *Kentish Gazette* for

25 November 1893 and 27 February 1894. Details of the various partnerships were gathered from the archives of the Law Society. The *Calendar of Prisoners* for the Maidstone Assize, with Denman's note in the margin, is in the PRO under reference ASS31/43, vol. 16.

A Short History of St Clare School by John Aston, privately published in 1932 and in the possession of Miss Phyllis White of Hastings, a descendant of Alexander Elder Murray, contains all the information needed for this period of Mercer's life. I am most grateful to Miss White for making it available.

Chapter Two
Most of the details of Mercer at Harrow were given to me by Lieut.-Col. F. H. Farebrother of Letchworth, who was 'some months his junior'. The meeting with 'Saki' is set out by Lambert in *The Bodley Head Saki* published in 1963. On Oxford, apart from the King's letter quoted in Sir Charles Petrie's *Scenes of Edwardian Life*, (Eyre & Spottiswoode, 1965), I have been given my information by the College Secretary of University College and Miss Yvonne Coen, Archivist to the OUDS. It seems needless to identify quotations from Mercer's two quasi-autobiographies.

Chapter Three
P. C. Ryan's encounter with Miss Pankhurst is set out in Eric Bush's *Gallipoli*, (George Allen & Unwin, 1975). The Hon. Sir Gerald Thesiger—better remembered as Thesiger, J,. was good enough to identify the Gorse Hill murder for me, in addition to telling me of Mr Abrahams or Abinger. Inspector Wensley and the 'bloody foreign Jews' is recounted in Sir Travers Humphreys' book *Criminal Days* (Hodder & Stoughton, 1946).

Chapter Four
The unidentifiability of White Ladies is mentioned by Mercer in a letter, dated 1 December 1950, to Mr W. H. Hughes of Johannesburg. The Seddon case is described by Humphreys in his book and, more fully, by Edward Marjoribanks in *Famous Cases of Marshall Hall* (Gollancz, 1929). Mercer's mention of Madeira comes in a letter to his first wife; it is set out in full in Tom Sharpe's article in *The Times* Saturday Review for 17 July 1976.

Chapter Five

Most of this chapter derives from conversations with Major G. St G. Stedall. The references to 'Saki' are drawn from Ethel's biography. The stand of the 3rd County of London Yeomanry is described by the then Colonel A. P. Wavell in *The Palestine Campaign* (Constable, 1928). The letter regarding the identity of Boy is from Mercer to Mr J. Williams of Matson, Gloucestershire, and bears date 5 March 1957. Major Stedall is my informant about the Cavalry Club.

Chapter Six

'Le Melton Mowbray' occurs in Michael Alexander's book *The True Blue* (Rupert Hart-Davis, 1957). Descriptions of Pau in the 1920s come mostly from Mr Kennard, who was good enough to show me many brochures for the various English institutions there. Armand Praviel's *Biarritz and the Basque Country* was published in France in 1925 and, in translation, by the Medici Society the following year. Mrs Marjorie Hare of South Ascot tells me of Mercer's detestation of Bernard Shaw, a circumstance of which she had experience. The 'Sapper' quotation comes from Gerard Fairlie's *With Prejudice* (Hodder & Stoughton, 1952).

Chapter Seven

The observations of Stanley Weyman figure in his General Preface to the John Murray thin-paper edition of his works and bears date 1911. Mrs Lucy Day, formerly of Umtali, tells me of the 'brandy should burn the throat' remark. Josephine Edwards' letter is quoted in Tom Sharpe's *Times* article mentioned above.

Chapter Eight

Tom Sharpe has, with great kindness, allowed me to see copies of Thérèse's letters in his possession and has also shown me a statement she made to him on this subject. The letter about the cook is from Mercer to Mr Carter of Pau dated 10 October 1952. The description of the visit to Pau by Elizabeth Mercer's family was given to me by her nephew, Mr Colin Sharpe, CMG. Matters relating to *Woman's Journal* were provided by the Editor-in-Chief, Mrs Laurie Purden.

Chapter Nine

Practically everything in this chapter comes from an account written by Elizabeth Mercer in October 1959 for her friend Mr R. E. Croall of Edinburgh. I am greatly indebted to Mrs Croall for permission to use it. The contributions from Dick Hobson and Mrs Lauchlan are contained in letters to me.

Chapter Ten

The letter quoted is to Mr Hughes of Johannesburg and is dated 1 December 1950. The fur coat story was told to me by Mr Woodward's nephew, Donald Clark of Epsom. The letters to Mrs Munro were lent to me by Mrs Juniper Bryan and that on the subject of the autobiography, dated 17 November 1956, by Mr Philip Groves of Gloucester.

APPENDIX I

THE PUBLISHED WORKS OF DORNFORD YATES

1914   *The Brother Of Daphne*   Short Stories taken from the *Windsor Magazine*, 1911–14

1919   *Eastward Ho*   Musical comedy, written in conjunction with Oscar Asche

1920   *The Courts Of Idleness*   Short Stories

1920   *Berry and Co.*   Short Stories

1921   *Anthony Lyveden*   Full-length romantic novel

1922   *Jonah and Co.*   Short stories

1923   *Valerie French*   Full-length novel; sequel to *Anthony Lyveden*

1924   *And Five Were Foolish*   Short stories

1925   *As Other Men Are*   Short stories

1926   *The Stolen March*   Full-length novel

1927   *Blind Corner*   The first Chandos book

1928   *Perishable Goods*   Sequel to *Blind Corner*. Some later editions give the date, wrongly, as 1927

1928   *Maiden Stakes*   Short stories

1929   *Blood Royal*   Another Chandos book

1930   *Fire Below*   Sequel to *Blood Royal*

1931   *Adèle and Co.*   A full-length Berry novel

1932   *Safe Custody*   Adventure novel, without Chandos

1934   *Storm Music*   The same

1935   *She Fell Among Thieves*   The return of Chandos

1936   *And Berry Came Too*   Short stories

1937   *She Painted Her Face*   Another adventure story without Chandos

1938   *This Publican*   Full-length novel

1939   *Gale Warning*   Chandos returns again

1940   *Shoal Water*   Full-length adventure story. Mansel appears, but not Chandos

1942   *Period Stuff*   Short stories

1943   *An Eye For A Tooth*   More Chandos

1945   *The House That Berry Built*   The title explains itself

1946   *Red In The Morning*   Chandos once more
1947   *The Berry Scene*   Short stories
1949   *Cost Price*   The last bow of Richard Chandos
1950   *Lower Than Vermin*   Full-length novel with political
           overtones
1952   *As Berry And I Were Saying*   The first of the quasi-
           autobiographies
1954   *Ne'er Do Well*   Yates's only detective story
1956   *Wife Apparent*   His last romantic novel
1958   *B-Berry And I Look Back*   The second part of his
           memoirs

APPENDIX II

A DORNFORD YATES CONCORDANCE

Nearly all of Dornford Yates's contributions to the *Windsor Magazine* found their way into his books, but their sequence is not always consistent. Now and then he changes the name of a character; for example, Christopher John of *And Five Were Foolish* began life as Lucien John. Nor were the magazine stories copied slavishly, for the book versions are often considerably padded out. The differences are, however, immaterial and I doubt whether anybody would thank me for detailing them all. The entire output of the *Windsor Magazine*, from cradle to grave, can be found in half-yearly bound volumes embalmed in the British Library under shelf number P.P. 6004 glw.

This is the sequence in which Yates's stories appeared.

1910   'Temporary Insanity' *Punch*, May. The only appearance of this work.

The following appear as chapters in *The Brother of Daphne*, 1914 under the same title unless indicated

1911   'Busy Bees' Chapter 8, as 'The Busy Beers'
'Punch and Judy' Chapter 1
'A Drive in the Dark' Chapter 8, as 'When It Was Dark'

1912   No *Windsor* stories published.

1913   'A Private View' Chapter 14
'There is a Tide' Chapter 2
'A Point of Honour' Chapter 9
'A Lucid Interval' Chapter 13
'The Love Scene' Chapter 11

1914   'All Found' Chapter 15
'Fair Exchange' Chapter 4, as 'Adam and New Year's Eve'
'Pride Goeth Before' Chapter 10
'The Order of the Bath' Chapter 12
'Which to Adore' Chapter 6

The following appear as chapters in *The Courts of Idleness*, 1920
1914   'A Bébé in Arms'   Chapter 1, Book 2
          'And the Other Left'   Chapter 1, Interlude, Book 2
          'Contempt of Court'   Chapter 2, Book 2

The following are refugees from *The Brother of Daphne*
1915   'Every Picture Tells a Story'   Chapter 7
          'The Judgment of Paris'   Chapter 5

The following appear as chapters in *The Courts of Idleness*, 1920
1915   'What's in a Name?'   Chapter 1, Book 1
          'A Sister Ship'   Chapter 2, Book 1
          'To Seat Four'   Chapter 3, Book 1
          'Love Thirty'   Chapter 4, Book 1
1919   'For Better or for Worse'   Chapter 5, Book 1
          'Beauty Repeats Itself'   Chapter 3, Book 2
          'The Desert Air'   Chapter 4, Book 2
          'As Rome Does'   Chapter 5, Book 1
          'Nemesis'   Chapter 6, Book 2
          'Valerie'   October. Never published in book form

The following appear as chapters 1 to 11 in *Berry and Co*, 1920
1919   'A Blue Letter Day'
1920   'The Unknown Quality'
          'In This Connection'
          'The Accusative Case'
          'We Are Seven'
          'A Friend at Court'
          'Too Many Cooks'
          'A Trick of Memory'
          'A Bootless Enterprise'
          'A Lesson in Latin'
          'A Double Event'

The following became *Anthony Lyveden*, 1921
1921   'In the First Place'
          'In the Second Place'
          'In the Third Place'
          'Livery of Seisin'
          'A Month's Wages'
          'Gramarye'
          'Grey Matter'
          'Ex-Parte Motions'
          'The Return of the Spirit'

The following appear as chapters 1 to 12 in *Jonah and Co*, 1922

1921	'The Rule of the World'
	'A Run for Our Money'
	'By Order of the Trustees'
1922	'A Snare and a Delusion'
	'Nobility and Gentry'
	'Manners and Customs'
	'A Royal Progress'
	'Red Violets'
	'Zero'
	'No Thoroughfare'
	'A Tight Place'
	'Journey's End'

The following in *And Five Were Foolish*, 1924

'Fair Linen'   October. Became 'Madeleine' (in the story 'Aurelie')
'False Pretences'   As 'Sarah'

The ten instalments of *Valerie French*, 1923 appeared in the *Windsor* under that name alone between December 1922 and September 1923

The following appear in *And Five Were Foolish*

1923	'Three's Company' 'Katharine'
	'The Groom of the Chambers' 'Spring'
1924	'A Drink Divine' 'Elizabeth'
	'Private Papers' 'Jo'
	'A Fool's Errand' 'Athalia'
	'A Private Scandal' 'Eleanor'
	'Mesalliance' 'Ann'
	'Noblesse Oblige' 'Susan'

The following appear in *As Other Men Are*, 1925

1924	'Unto Caesar' 'Jeremy'
1925	'Shorn Lambs' 'Simon'
	'Without Prejudice' 'Toby'
	'Old Ale' 'Oliver'
	'The Lord of the Manor' 'Christopher'
	'Fallen Sparrows' 'Peregrine'
	'Contrary Winds' 'Hubert'
	'The Flat of the Sword' 'Derry'
	'Leading Strings' 'Ivan'
	'Ways and Means' 'Titus'

1926   Taken up by *The Stolen March*. Nothing else appeared that year.

1927   'Court Cards'   Never published in book form

'My Lady's Chamber'   Apparently put on one side and did not come out again until *Period Stuff*, 1942

The following appear in *Maiden Stakes*, 1928

1927   'St Jeames'

'Bricks Without Straw'

'Force Majeure'

'Vanity of Vanities'

'Childish Things'

'Aesop's Fable'

1929   'Letters Patent'   A 'Berry' story in splendid isolation

'In Evidence'

'Maiden Stakes'

'Service'

No further stories appeared in the *Windsor* for six years.

The following appear in *And Berry Came Too*, 1936

1935   'Enter the Knave'   Chapter 1

'Lady Friends'   Chapter 8

1937   'The Real Thing'   Never published in book form. A pity.

1939   'A Special Case' in *Period Stuff*, 1942

The Berry stories are these:

1914   *The Brother Of Daphne*

1920   Book 2 of *The Courts Of Idleness*

1920   *Berry and Co.*

1922   *Jonah and Co*

1924   Berry himself makes a brief appearance in 'Susan', a part of '*And Five Were Foolish*'

and in the *Maiden Stakes* short story called 'Letters Patent'. He also has a walking-on part in *Perishable Goods* of the same year.

The next true, full stories are:

1931   *Adèle and Co.*

1936   *And Berry Came Too*

1945   *The House That Berry Built*

1947   *The Berry Scene*

1952   *As Berry And I Were Saying*

1958   *B-Berry And I Look Back*.

INDEX

237